The Woodland Garden

PLANTING IN HARMONY WITH NATURE

REVISED EDITION

ROY FORSTER and ALEX DOWNIE

FIREFLY BOOKS

A Firefly Book

Published by Firefly Books Ltd. 2004

This book was created and originally published by Raincoast Books
9050 Shaughnessy Street, Vancouver, British Columbia, Canada, V6P 6E5
www.raincoast.com

First Printing

Publisher Cataloguing-in-Publication Data (U.S.)
(Library of Congress Standards)

Forster, R. Roy, 1932 -
   The woodland garden : planting in harmony with nature / Roy Forster and Alex
Downie._ Revised edition.
[192] p. : ill. (some col.) ; cm.
Includes bibliographical references and index.
Summary: A guide to all aspects of woodland gardening from design, plant selection and
planning, to maintenance.
ISBN 1-55297-898-2
ISBN 1-55297-744-7 (pbk.)
1. Woodland gardening. 2. Landscaping gardening. I. Downie, Alex M., 1958- II. Title.
635.9/67 21   SB439.6.F73 2004

Published in the United States in 2004 by
Firefly Books (U.S.) Inc.
P.O. Box 1338, Ellicott Station
Buffalo, New York 14205

Text design by Ingrid Paulson
Jacket design by Jacqueline Hope Raynor
Printed in Hong Kong, China

Contents

Zonal Maps

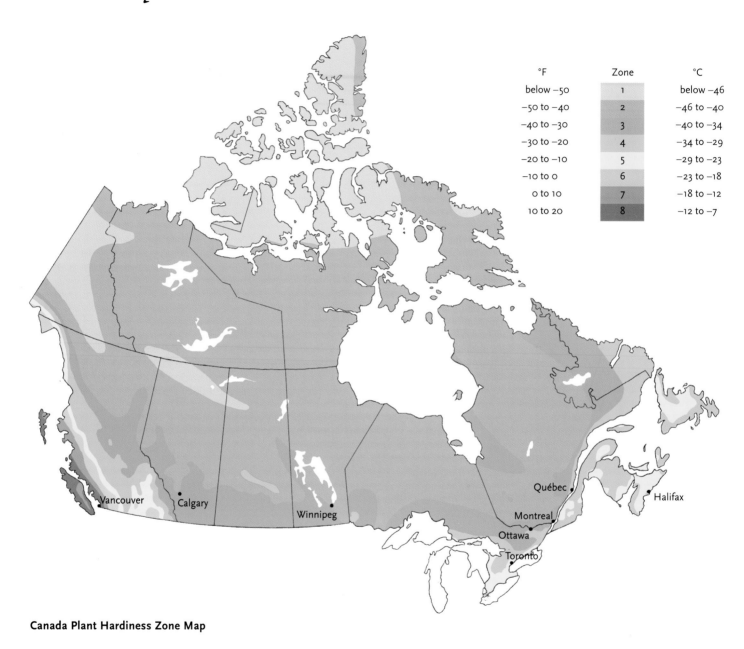

°F	Zone	°C
below −50	1	below −46
−50 to −40	2	−46 to −40
−40 to −30	3	−40 to −34
−30 to −20	4	−34 to −29
−20 to −10	5	−29 to −23
−10 to 0	6	−23 to −18
0 to 10	7	−18 to −12
10 to 20	8	−12 to −7

Vancouver

Calgary

Winnipeg

Québec

Halifax

Montreal

Ottawa

Toronto

Canada Plant Hardiness Zone Map

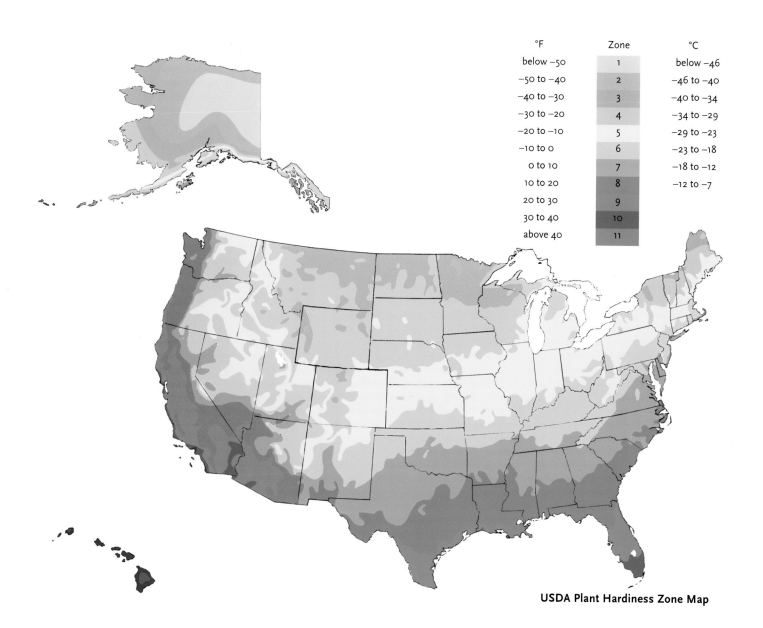

°F	Zone	°C
below −50	1	below −46
−50 to −40	2	−46 to −40
−40 to −30	3	−40 to −34
−30 to −20	4	−34 to −29
−20 to −10	5	−29 to −23
−10 to 0	6	−23 to −18
0 to 10	7	−18 to −12
10 to 20	8	−12 to −7
20 to 30	9	
30 to 40	10	
above 40	11	

USDA Plant Hardiness Zone Map

Introduction

ANTHROPOLOGISTS have linked humanity's biological ancestry to the woodland, and psychologists blame many modern urban ills on our alienation from this heritage. Perhaps in reaction, gardeners are turning increasingly to a natural style of landscape. They find deep satisfaction in the subtle play of dappled light on the varied textures of woodland plants or in the soft feel of moss underfoot.

The woodland garden style suits those gardeners whose bent is gentle trial and error, calm observation and a love of natural systems — those same qualities the frenetic conventional gardener would call laziness! However, in the early stages of site preparation, some hard work is always necessary. Undesirable plants must be grubbed out, weeds removed and trees pruned or thinned in a skillful way to enhance their naturalism — not neatly trimmed as in more formal gardens.

A woodland garden style is not easy to define, because woodlands, on which the idea is based, are found from the tropics to the far north, from sea level to timberline, and these woodlands vary vastly.

For the purpose of this book, the woodland garden can be defined as a relatively sheltered place where there is an upper *canopy* of large or small trees, beneath which there is a second layer of shrubs, the *understory*, and a third level of herbaceous plants and other low-growing species, the *woodland floor*. Because of the tree canopy, the lower levels receive a controlled amount of sunshine. This means the woodland garden is the ideal habitat for plants that need various degrees of protection given by shade. It also means that solar energy and the three-dimensional garden space are used to the fullest potential that nature can provide.

A woodland garden does not necessarily need large trees as the upper canopy. Quite small trees up to 25 feet (7.6 m) in height can provide the necessary shade in small urban or suburban gardens. The trees can be deciduous or evergreen, broadleaved or coniferous or any desired mixture of these, depending on the amount of shade required.

The woodland garden is inspired by a poetic vision of infinite balance and perfect harmony among all the forest components. The foliage canopy contains and defines the landscape, focusing attention on the immediate environment — fallen mossy trees, lichen-covered rocks and the living matrix of the forest floor itself take on a special significance. The woodland is all the more charming because it is a composition of form and texture without much reliance on color except for tonal variations of green. These impressions are the raw material of making woodland gardens.

The emotions stimulated by the woodland garden may be unwelcome to those whose perception of a garden is limited to structural orderliness. The wildness may intimidate those who feel that the outdoors is something to be tamed and ordered. But for those who appreciate and respond to the special ambience of the woodland garden, we hope that our knowledge of and experience in creating and maintaining woodland gardens will inspire and guide you.

Some woodland gardens are made with existing woodland, some are made on raw land and some on land reclaimed from conventional gardens. Owners of land partially or completely wooded will find information on thinning out unwanted vegetation while preserving what is valuable. Raw sites, small or large, are a special challenge, but help can be found in choosing the best trees to start the canopy. Adapting an older conventional garden to a woodland theme comes between these two extremes. This book will be useful to property owners gardening under many differing site conditions.

The richest North American woodland gardens are to be found in the temperate climate zones. This includes the forested coastal areas of the Pacific Northwest and the Carolinean zone of eastern North America, from the mountains of the southeastern United States to the southern and eastern parts of Canada. In most areas of North America, temperatures cover fairly extreme seasonal differences. Here the woodland garden is valuable for the softening effects of the microclimate created by suitable trees. Such a microclimate may make it possible to cultivate plants that are otherwise tender, either to summer heat or winter cold.

In this book we emphasize the more densely populated, temperate parts of the northern United States and Canada. Gardeners in the more climatically challenged continental interior or in the South, or those gardening on alkaline soils, will find sections of this book useful, if only to encourage further search for information. This book concentrates on those plant materials hardy from Zone 5 through Zone 9, according to the hardiness zone system devised by the United States Department of Agriculture. (See p. 159-60 for a further discussion of plant hardiness.)

The Origins of the Woodland Garden

Woodland gardens are a relatively recent development in garden history. They represent, in every way, a departure from conventional structured gardens. Through many centuries of horticulture, the modern flower garden has derived some of its essential elements from more formal forerunners, such as monastery gardens. The woodland garden, however, has as its precursors what were perhaps the earliest gardens of Europe and Asia: the woodland hunting reserves of ancient rulers. Before the systematic use of land for growing crops (or for the making of gardens), wooded land was more highly valued because it provided fuel and building material. Above all, it gave cover to the many kinds of game animals prized for the hunt and the table. Such a productive woodland required thinning, not with the cataclysmic methods of modern logging, but in the rather random fashion of taking what was needed for immediate purposes. The open woodland fostered by these methods was both productive and beautiful. In a more highly developed form, with areas of pasture between forest tracts, the landscape evolved into parkland.

Landscape of this sort became an integral part of the art and poetry of pastoral peoples and gave rise to the romantic, picturesque style of landscape gardening that changed the face of 18th-century England. Even today, it is an important influence in the design of large parks and gardens throughout the western world.

The wonderful botanical treasures of North America, such as American magnolias, halesias, witch hazels, rhododendrons and many other plants, provided the inspiration that gave rise to the "American," or wild garden, the 19th-century precursor of the modern woodland garden.

By the 1840s, the growing ranks of garden owners in the United States were demanding a wider range of plants and a more informal style of garden design. Nurserymen and landscape gardeners were there to meet the need with newly

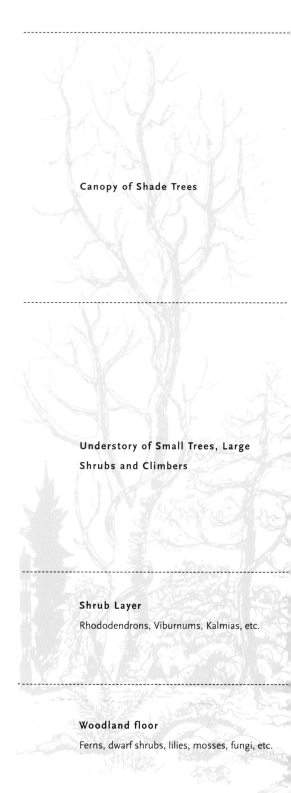

Canopy of Shade Trees

Understory of Small Trees, Large Shrubs and Climbers

Shrub Layer
Rhododendrons, Viburnums, Kalmias, etc.

Woodland floor
Ferns, dwarf shrubs, lilies, mosses, fungi, etc.

Figure 1 Structure of a woodland showing vegetation layers

introduced plants. Andrew Jackson Downing, a leading landscape gardener of the day, was influenced by the naturalism of the English landscape movement that had begun a century before. The so-called English park style, a forerunner of the woodland garden, became popular in the United States. Central Park in New York was the most ambitious example of this style. Designed by Frederick Law Olmsted and Calvert Vaux, the park stands as an important milestone in the development of landscape style in North America. The Olmsted firm later designed the Washington Park Arboretum in Seattle, which contains some fine woodland groves.

Plant-hunting and Woodland Gardens

Many gardeners are caught up in the enthusiasm for plant exploration and preservation. This enthusiasm is not limited to interest in the plant species themselves, but includes a concern for habitat, ecology and the plant associations and communities of which these species are a part. When these associations influence garden design and the arrangement of garden plants, it is possible to evoke nature.

It would be difficult to imagine the gardens of the southeastern United States without camellias and azaleas, or the gardens of the Northeast and Pacific Northwest with no Asian magnolias and rhododendrons. However, long before the botanical treasures of Asia were discovered, a wide array of American woodland plants was introduced to the gardens of Europe and America.

In prehistoric times, the Carolinean woods of the southern Appalachian Mountains were spared the destructive effects of the continental ice sheets that enveloped the northerly forest, and a rich heritage of plants survived in this protected habitat. As early as 1632, plant exploration had begun on an organized basis. John Tradescant the younger, English botanist and plant explorer, travelled in eastern North America in the years 1637, 1642 and 1654, and the flow of plants to England began. Tradescant's importations included spiderwort (*Tradescantia virginiana*), which is an excellent border plant suitable for planting in moist, sunny places on the woodland fringe. Mark Catesby, another Englishman, collected in the years between 1712 and 1725. His efforts yielded many important plants, including *Magnolia grandiflora*, *Nyssa sylvatica* (tupelo) and *Rhododendron maximum*, all of which are widely planted in gardens.

The greatest of the early American plant hunters was John Bartram. His contributions were recognized and further encouraged by wealthy British and American landowners and also by the botanist Linnaeus. Bartram began his botanic garden nursery in Philadelphia in 1728. He traveled widely in the eastern United States, collecting plants for his patrons, one of whom was King George III of England. His greatest find was the legendary *Franklinia alatamaha* (Franklin tree) in Georgia. *Franklinia* apparently became extinct in the wild and has not been seen since 1803. Happily, it is well established in woodland gardens in climatically hospitable parts of the world.

The British expedition of the 1790s under Captain George Vancouver brought the botanist Archibald Menzies to the Pacific Coast. His efforts are recognized in the genus *Menziesia*, a group of shrubs native to North America and Japan. Menzies found the coast redwood (*Sequoia sempervirens*) and the nootka cypress (*Chamaecyparis nootkatensis*). These and other western conifers, such as the giant sequoia (*Sequoiadendron giganteum*), became popular for planting the large estates then in vogue.

The Scottish botanist David Douglas explored western North America in the first quarter of the 19th century. In his short life he introduced many trees and shrubs that have since become of great economic importance in forestry and horticulture. Among these are Douglas fir (*Pseudotsuga menziesii*), grand fir (*Abies grandis*), Sitka spruce (*Picea sitchensis*), vine maple (*Acer circinatum*) and tassel bush (*Garrya elliptica*).

President Thomas Jefferson was an avid gardener who recognized the importance of plant collection in geographic exploration. As a result, the transcontinental Lewis and Clark Expedition of 1804–06 is remembered in the Western plants *Lewisia* and *Clarkia*.

Before the middle of the 19th century, the flow of new plants was mainly from America to Europe. One of the most significant was *Rhododendron catawbiense*, found by Andre Michaux in 1785. Hybrids derived from this species and others produced a new race of hardy rhododendrons. The nursery firm Waterers of England was the leader in this early hybridization, and the new plants were a sensation in the horticultural world.

Asia, with its temperate mixed mesophytic forest and large areas of varied habitat, offered plant explorers a treasure trove of new plants, many of similar character to their American relatives. In many cases, the same genera are represented, and their similarities have been frequently discussed by plant geographers and botanists.

Introductions from Asia peaked in the first half of the 20th century, thanks in large part to E. H. Wilson, the most famous of all plant explorers. In 1907 Wilson went to China under the aegis of the Arnold Arboretum of Harvard University. Founded in 1872, the arboretum, under the direction of Charles Sprague Sargent, led the field in plant exploration and introduction. Wilson's plants play a major part in woodland gardens in America.

In the early 1900s the U.S. Department of Agriculture became involved in plant exploration. The enigmatic Frank N. Meyer, one of the first government-sponsored plant explorers, led several expeditions between 1905 and 1916. He died in China under rather mysterious circumstances at the age of only 43 years. Meyer's major contribution was the introduction of many important crop plants, and he is remembered in a lilac (*Syringa meyeri*) and a juniper (*Juniperus squamata* 'Meyeri'). Joseph Rock, another illustrious name in the annals of American plant exploration, is remembered for the large number of fine rhododendron species he collected in China. One of these is *Rhododendron racemosum*.

Plant exploration continues at the present time, increasingly supported by private interests. Most modern expeditions retrace the steps of earlier plant explorers. The number of new species discovered is small, but there are good possibilities of finding new and perhaps better forms of species already in cultivation. If it were not for this vital activity, neither the economic nor the conservation and aesthetic sides of horticulture could make progress.

Growing species of plants that were collected in the wild is in many ways more meaningful to gardeners than the cultivation of hybrids or plants of unknown origin. In a shrinking natural world, we must use our garden space effectively to grow plants that may need protection because of habitat destruction. In cultivating the rare and beautiful, we can experience the excitement felt by plant explorers when they discovered these plants in their wild habitat. The woodland garden is the ideal setting for these endeavors.

The Woodland Garden Today

The woodland garden style was originally an adaptation of the deciduous hardwood forest of Canada and the eastern mountain states. But many other kinds of natural woodlands occur in America: the pine woods and cypress glades of the South; the coniferous North; the dry ponderosa pine forests of the West; the oak parklands and cathedral-like redwood forests of California; the somber rain forest of the Pacific Northwest. Each could be the basis for a woodland garden, using appropriate companion plants to build landscape associations that are ornamental and at the same time in harmony with the native vegetation.

The woodland garden is a response to the need for picturesque naturalism and romanticism, a revolt of the human spirit against rigid formalism. Since the woodland garden serves no utilitarian function, unlike the kitchen or vegetable garden, it comes close to being a work of art. Free of formal rules, such as those demanded by the Victorian-era carpet-bedding schemes, the woodland garden gives the landscape artist free rein to create naturalistic garden spaces that evoke a sense of harmony and freedom.

Today's woodland garden designer attempts to create an ecological balance among the various plant components by providing each plant or group of plants with a growing niche, taking into account a number of factors, including exposure, light, soil type, moisture and space. Each group of plants influences and is influenced by the plants either above or below it in the hierarchy of the woodland.

It would be naive to suppose that such a garden would be static and self-sustaining. Substantial intervention in the way of removing or pruning of plants is sometimes needed to maintain a balanced woodland. Some species are simply too aggressive to be left alone and others are too vulnerable. All the natural forces that lead toward the climax forest of the particular location will be at work. In a natural woodland, these conditions favor the survival of the fittest. In a woodland-style garden, some intervention is needed to help the desired plant associations become established.

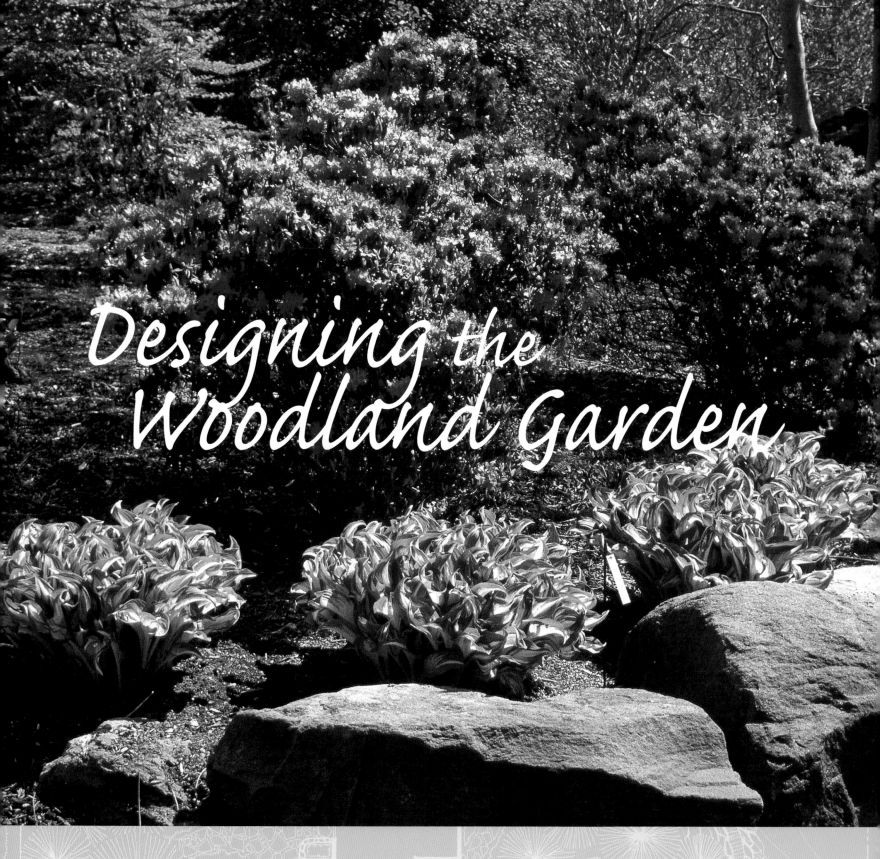

Designing the Woodland Garden

*I*T MAY SEEM that a woodland garden just grows beautifully by itself, but the success of a cultivated woodland garden depends on careful planning. Start by thinking of what sort of garden you want. A wildflower garden? A rhododendron garden? A garden of exotic plants from China or the high Himalayas? A garden of American native plants from the Appalachians or some other fascinating place in the vast North American woodland? Everyone has a personal vision of a garden, just as everyone has a special vision of paradise. With good planning and a thorough knowledge of your site, perhaps the two will coincide.

Next look at your site. Will it accommodate the garden you have envisioned? Be realistic. Tranquil meditative gardens may not fit a dramatic steep site with bold rock outcroppings. A very wet site may not suit a montane theme and could be better used for a bog garden of native plants. The important thing is to find the particular genius of the site and exploit it to the fullest, working with its natural attributes and not trying to impose a preconceived plan on it. If you are creating a naturalistic garden, it makes no sense to be fighting the forces of nature. This leads, naturally, to the next step — a thorough analysis of the site, however small.

Analyze the Site

Some gardeners think of the woodland garden as providing an opportunity to stuff as many plants as possible into a given space. This approach may create a botanical cornucopia, but the end result will be chaos and disappointment. When plants are crowded together they compete for light, nutrients and water. Some plants will die, and the survivors will show the scars of this battle by being drawn up and misshapen. Far better to resist the temptation and plan

PRECEDING PAGE: The hostas, plantain lilies, are bold companion plants in this composition defined by sandstone slabs.

for the future by anticipating the ultimate size of the plants and giving them the space they will need.

First look at the aspect — the lay of the land. A slope to the north will make it a colder place. An eastern exposure may give it protection from most winds, but it will be open to early morning sun that could damage frost-sensitive plants. A slope to the south or west gives additional warmth that is favorable for growing plants that originate from warmer climates. In the southern states, however, southern and western exposures may be too hot for most woodland plants unless well shaded from the heat of the midday sun.

Another important consideration is the soil type. This will limit the kinds of plants you can grow on the site. A deep, well-drained, slightly acid sandy loam will support the greatest range of fine garden plants, provided adequate water is available and the climate is not too severe. Most nutrient deficiencies on acid soils can be solved by making carefully staged, light applications of dolomitic limestone until the pH is raised to within the acceptable range. Simple devices for measuring approximate pH levels are available.

The range of plants that will successfully grow in a limy (alkaline) soil is quite different from those possible on an acid soil. Clay soils and loose, gravelly soils also place limitations on the plants you can grow. Soils can be amended to a certain degree, but the underlying nature of your area, determined by climate and subsoil, will continue to assert itself despite your best efforts.

It is always a good idea to have a soil test done by a qualified soil laboratory. It will determine if the soil is alkaline or acid, what the nutrient levels are, and if there is much difference in soil texture over the site. If the soil is not original, undisturbed soil and has been churned up with excavation equipment, it will be necessary to put more effort into site preparation.

Make notes on drainage. Wet spots may give a clue to where you might locate ponds, streams or bog gardens.

The amount of rainfall is an important design consideration. If your home is in an area where water-use restrictions are in effect, it may not be wise to design a garden with rhododendrons and other broad-leaved evergreen plants native to areas of higher rainfall, unless you are prepared to install an irrigation system and use a lot of expensive water. The most successful garden designs take local climatic conditions into account in the selection of plant material. The key is to select native and exotic plants that will thrive with a minimum of supplemental care.

Look at the condition of existing trees on your site. Will they need expensive pruning or even removal in a few years? If you are planting new trees, choose fast-growing species to give quick cover, but also plant longer-lived species for the long term. When the permanent trees are well established, the "nurse trees" can be eliminated well before they become so large that removing them creates a problem.

Next consider the topography of the site. Most building lots are flat, with few or no trees. This simplifies the design. Avoid attempting grandiose schemes on a small flat site, as the end result can look contrived and artificial. Often it is sufficient to plant beautiful trees and let them work their own kind of magic. Some of the best gardens are on small flat lots, and because they are not highly structured, they are inexpensive to build. The most important trees and shrubs are those around the perimeter because they create a sense of seclusion and focus the garden inward.

Sites that have many existing trees or have sloping ground with features such as rocks, running water, spectacular views, or other natural attributes are more complex to design but offer great possibilities. Keep the design simple. Most gardeners think of woodland gardens as places of tranquility rather than high drama, but sites that are naturally rugged, with valleys, rock outcroppings and other natural features, offer opportunities to make gardens that are dramatic yet close to nature. By working with the site instead of altering it, using the on-site materials, and blending structures with the flow of the land, a harmonious effect can be obtained. Visit public botanical gardens or well-designed woodland gardens to search for design ideas that apply to your site.

Draw a scale plan of the site

The next task is to draw a scale plan of the site, including underground and overhead features such as cables, pipes and hydro lines. This should be an accurate representation of what is actually there. The scale should be as large as possible so that every tree, shrub and plant can be seen on the drawing. Include any important features of neighboring properties that might affect your site now or in the future. Consider views, new construction, tree planting or removal, water drainage and excavation that could affect the water table, and thus the health of trees. It may not be possible to influence the course of

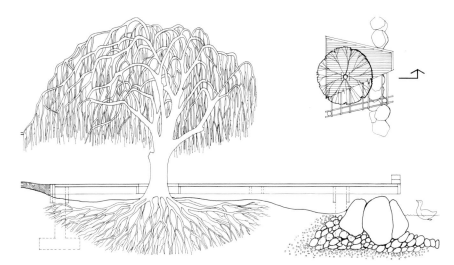

Figure 2
Low-lying waterfront landscape is often difficult to handle. The ground is wet or muddy, which limits year-round use. One way of solving the problem is to build a raised wood deck on pylons, in this example surrounding an existing weeping willow.

future events, but to be forewarned is to be ready to take remedial action. For example, planting around the perimeter will depend on what existing or potentially ugly views are to be screened, or what good views are to be enhanced by planting that will frame them.

If the site is not level, draw a contour map showing the slopes and a profile section that helps to visualize the slopes in relation to features such as existing trees. The contour lines should show elevation changes in 1-foot (0.3-m) intervals. (See Plan 1.)

Design the Garden

Designing a garden is like making a series of landscape pictures. The object is to create attractive views. Landscape design is also sculptural — the garden must look good from all viewpoints. There is usually one dominant viewpoint, such as a view from your favorite room in the house along the axis of the garden. The axis could be the main path, from which other minor paths radiate, but it could also be a natural feature, such as long pond or a ravine. Along the main path, try to visualize a series of landscape pictures using masses of foliage or specimen trees and shrubs.

Intimacy and texture are the keys to success in woodland gardening. Think of the woodland as a series of outdoor rooms. The tree canopy is the ceiling. Each room is separated from the others by masses of foliage. Pathways wind

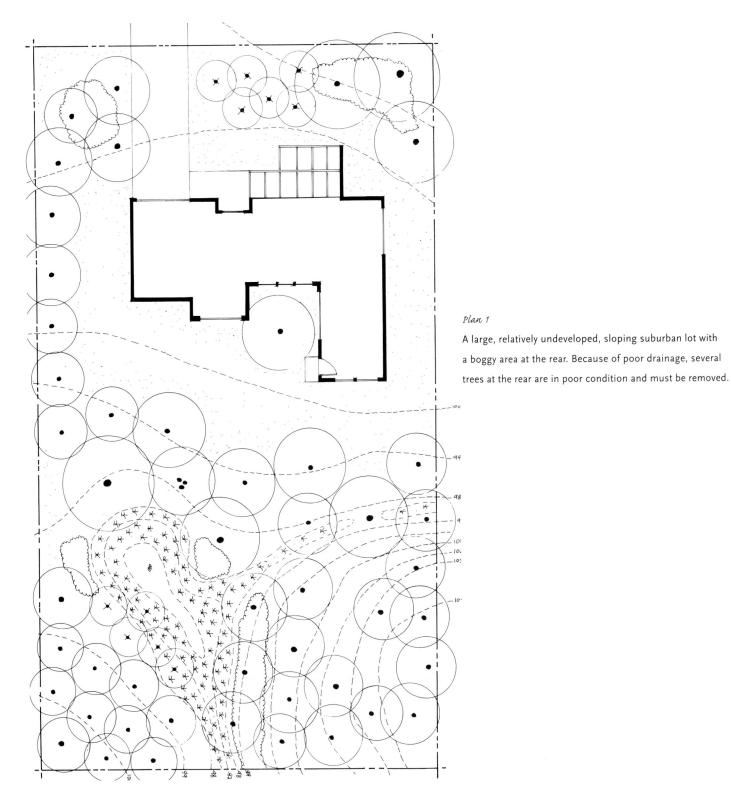

Plan 1

A large, relatively undeveloped, sloping suburban lot with a boggy area at the rear. Because of poor drainage, several trees at the rear are in poor condition and must be removed.

Plan 2

Best use of the site is made with meandering paths through the woodland. The lowest point is deepened and a pond added with a surrounding bog garden.

Plan features:

- crushed stone paths
- path ramped up to a mound (Serpentine paths increase perceived space.)
- existing low wet area turned into a pond
- plantings of water and marsh plants around pond
- coniferous trees planted at the lot periphery for year-round privacy
- decking around house providing substantial outdoor living space
- selective thinning of overcrowded, dead or diseased trees
- existing understory augmented with medium and large flowering shrubs
- herbaceous perennials planted around house

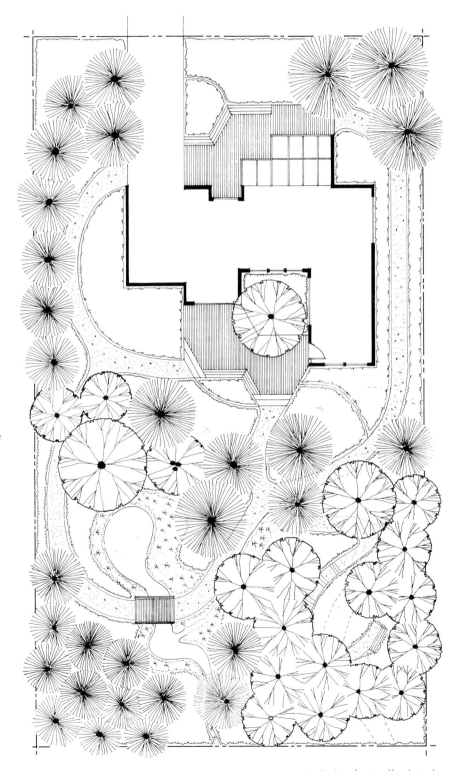

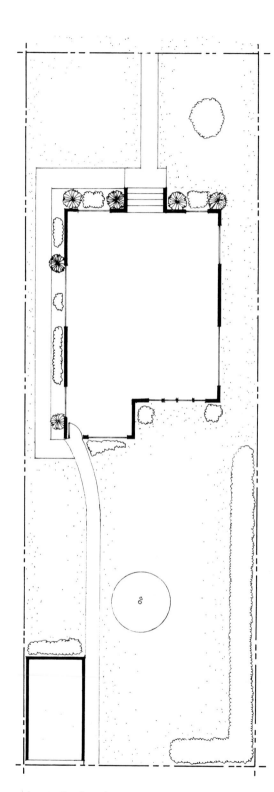

Plan 3

A challenge: typical narrow city lot with conventional landscaping consisting of a large lawn area with a few shrubs planted around the house and one solitary tree in the backyard.

Plan 4

In this transformation the best use is made of the site by means of economical use of space. An attractive small pond is flanked by a woodland of small- to medium-sized deciduous trees, and the front of the house is well screened by another grove of trees.

Plan features:

- low and native shrubs with accents of herbaceous perennials planted at the front
- grove of small trees planted at the front to buffer traffic noise and provide privacy
- fence planted with climbing plants
- large tile, cut stone or concrete patio at rear of house to provide usable open space
  (Low ground cover such as heather or grass provides a transition to woodland plantings.)
- small pond with carefully placed rocks — provides the illusion of greater space
- grove of medium-sized deciduous trees underplanted with shrubs and ferns — conceals garage from view, creates privacy and provides a habitat for urban wildlife

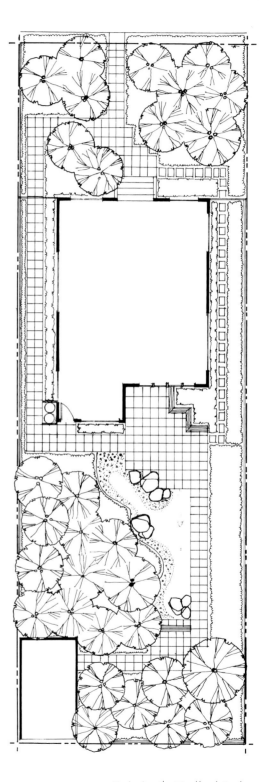

Plan 5

A wooded waterfront lot of great possibilities. The lot is irregular in shape and slopes up from the rocky shore.

Plan 6

Natural rock outcroppings are used to advantage in the design
and are enhanced by making new stone paths and planters using
similar rock. Most of the existing native trees, evergreen and
deciduous, are retained and a natural wood deck is placed on
a vantage point overlooking the water. Landscaping is done
entirely with shrubs and woodland plants native to the region,
which reduces watering and maintenance requirements.

Plan features:

- existing tree cover retained
- understory planted and extended with native shrubs, ground
  covers and ferns
- stone paths built around dwelling and leading to wood deck
  near the shore
- wooden pier or float built to provide water access

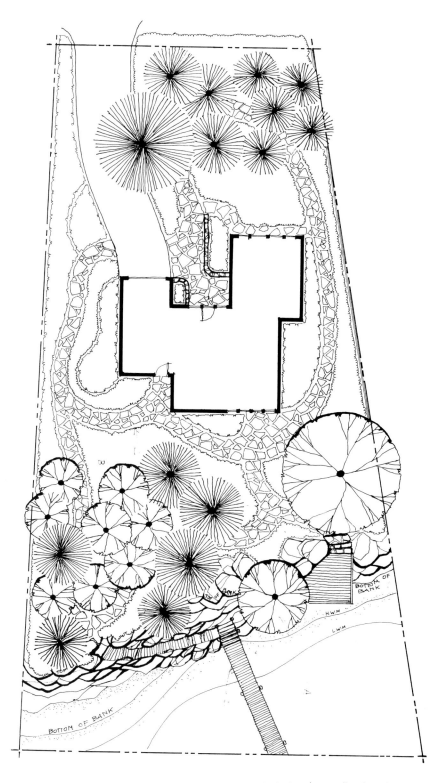

around and between these spaces so that the next landscape vignette is concealed until the viewer enters. The intimacy that gives such charm to the well-planted woodland garden is achieved by the use of ferns and other plants that have beauty of form whether in flower or not.

The layering of the woodland garden makes it multidimensional. The special quality of the light and the comfortable feeling of seclusion beneath the trees intensifies the enjoyment of the richly varied plants of woodland floor plantings. The great variety of habitats also allows a wide range of plants to be grown successfully.

SCALE

Scale is the relationship between the sizes of objects. In the landscape, the viewer's eye judges the suitability of these size relationships. When a landscape picture pleases the viewer, it is usually because there is not too great a difference in size between adjacent objects. In other words, they are in scale with each other. However, if the objects are too similar in size, the picture lacks contrast and the effect may be uninteresting and dull.

Scale also refers to the overall picture, that is, the width of paths measured against the width of planted beds, or the length of a pond in relation to the

Figure 3
Angular lines of functional architecture are softened by existing trees, which must be carefully saved from damage during the construction phase. House-building often changes the water table, and the moisture content of the soil must be monitored to avert irreversible damage caused by drought or waterlogging.

Asian Plants *in the* Woodland Garden

Asian plants fit well into a woodland tapestry. The large leaves of the empress tree (*Paulownia tomentosa*) and the Chinese tulip tree (*Liriodendron chinense*), the bold compound foliage of *Decaisnea fargesii*, the fine texture of the silk tree (*Albizia julibrissin*) or the filigree leaf detail of the Vilmorin mountain ash (*Sorbus vilmorinii*) all add great textural interest to the garden. Among conifers, the elegant, long-needled Himalayan white pine (*Pinus wallichiana*) and the graceful drape of Himalayan spruce (*Picea smithiana*) work well on high promontories or standing alone in a woodland clearing. Yunnan cypress (*Cupressus duclouxiana*) and Kashmir cypress (*C. himalaica var. darjeelingensis*; formerly known as *C. cashmeriana*) are trees of exquisite refinement for warmer regions.

depth of the garden. The height of a group of trees or shrubs in relationship to the distance from the viewing eye is another example.

Scale is related to mass — the solidity or the sculptural weight of landscape components. We speak of massing a group of shrubs to create one strong visual impact. Separately they would not have the same effect. A maple tree in full leaf has mass because it has width, height and depth and it occupies space. The same maple tree loses its mass in the winter because its leaves are gone. Evergreens, which have mass all year round, are valuable in giving a landscape structure. Too many conifers or broad-leaved evergreens, however, can make a landscape dark and somber. The empty space between the masses is what makes the masses stand out. The scale of the masses and spaces and their organization into interesting and workable relationships is what makes good landscape.

TEXTURE

The maple tree, when it loses its mass in the winter, gains texture because of its twiggy branchlets.

Texture has to do with the fineness or coarseness of the surface of objects. A large-leaved plant such as rhubarb is said to have a coarse texture; a small-leaved plant such as boxwood has fine texture. Putting together plants with different textures, alternating coarse and fine, or making harmonizing gradients of textures like pebbles on a beach, is all part of the landscape designer's palette.

Borrowing some of the principles of Oriental gardens helps to develop an eye for fine detail and harmonious relationships between all the parts of a garden. Direct imitations of this complex style do not rest easily in woodland because they are highly stylized and don't easily blend with romantic naturalism. But Japanese-style components, such as large boulders associated with drifts of fine-textured ground covers or moss, can be successfully used to enhance the woodland garden.

UNITY

Unity is another important principle of landscape art. Variety is what keeps the landscape from becoming boring, but unity is what holds it together. It may seem contradictory, but it is possible to have unity within variety and vice versa. For example, a number of plants may have widely different kinds and sizes of foliage but all have blue flowers. This feature may hold them together as a unit in the landscape. It would be more difficult to reverse this example, because color can be such a strong factor that it dominates any other unifying element. Unifying elements are many and varied. Examples are adaptation to the environment, such as succulent plants, or plants from similar habitats, such as desert or rain forest. A unifying element may be a harmonizing range of color, gray foliage or similar texture. One of the most interesting unifying elements, especially to plant collectors, is grouping plants that originate from the same habitat or biogeographic area.

On the other hand, some woodland gardens contain the widest possible mixture of exotic and native plants, a picturesque style without any geographic restrictions on choice of plants or theme. In favorable climatic areas, there are opportunities for making lush landscapes of bold-textured plants. In mild areas, landscapes can be built around exotics such as *Paulownia tomentosa* or the Chusan palm (*Trachycarpus fortunei*). Other large-leaved shrubs, such as evergreen *Fatsia japonica*, bamboo (*Sasa veitchii*) and Hercules' club (*Aralia spinosa*), help to create an exotic effect. Large-leaved rhododendrons, such as *Rhododendron calophytum* or *R. Fictolacteum*, are compatible in these groupings. For contrast, fine-textured trees such as *Metasequoia glyptostroboides* or the bald cypress (*Taxodium distichum*) provide a pleasant, soft contrast. On a smaller scale, heavenly bamboo (*Nandina domestica*) is appropriate, and the true bamboos can be massed under larger plants. Avoid bamboos that have a running habit, but clumping bamboos, such as *Sinarundinaria nitida*, are excellent plants for sunny clearings.

PATHWAYS

Guiding people through the garden in a meaningful way is important to their enjoyment of the garden experience. The natural tendency is to seek out the most interesting features, and this dictates the general location of the paths. Paths, therefore, are more than just access; they express the fundamental meaning of the garden arrangement.

Paths are usually best slightly depressed below the surrounding landscape, unless the drainage is bad, in which case they might have to be raised. Drains, irrigation pipes and other services are usually placed underneath paths as they are less likely to be disturbed there, and if maintenance is required, only the path need be excavated. Paths should be wide enough to give access for maintenance using a wheelbarrow or a small garden tractor, but do not make paths so wide that they spoil the scale of the design.

Visitors to your garden do not want to trek through muddy trails, so think of the paths as a cover for drains. An even grade is essential to avoid wet spots, and when the lowest point is reached, surplus water must be directed away from the path. On sites where drainage is bad, drain tile should be laid beneath the path and covered with a porous material such as gravel, bark mulch or wood chips. The latter eventually blends quite well with the woodland theme, but gravel is a better, more permanent surface. If the site is well drained, a woodland path may need no particular surface other than the natural earth, and would be defined by the plantings along its edge. Usually, no structured edge to the path is needed — a change in the texture of edging plants will be enough to define it. The path could also be surfaced with two or three inches (5–8 cm) of tamped gravel, wood chips or bark mulch. Chips and mulch have a pleasant spongy feel and walking on them is part of the woodland experience. The ultimate is walking on moss! This can be arranged in the less-travelled, shady corners of the garden. Path surfaces should be slightly convex to shed water.

Paths should be allowed to follow the line of least resistance in natural, curving shapes. They may be set slightly lower than the landscape, and the excavation material can be used to bolster the higher ground, perhaps forming a series of ridges and valleys. These must flow naturally toward lower ground, as they are part of the drainage system.

In larger gardens, a path may be made on the top of a slope or ridge. This gives another perspective to the landscape with the possibility of opening views and vistas to the outer fringes of the garden or beyond. These viewpoints may be defined with outcroppings of rock or simply indicated by low ground-cover plantings.

On a flat site arrange the paths in serpentine forms, using plants instead of landforms to define the space and conceal what lies beyond the next bend. The plants should increase in size as their distance from the path increases, giving the impression of a valley. The effect is more naturalistic if the plants are not rigidly ranked by size but somewhat randomly arranged, with larger trees providing vertical accents.

In small gardens, pathways may vary in width from 3 to 6 feet (1–2 m). Small, open areas (woodland clearings) should be made every 50 feet (15 m) or so, each concealed from the others. This allows small groups of people to assemble and facilitates the maintenance of the garden. Gardens of an acre (0.4 ha) or more need service corridors for trucks or other equipment. This facilitates moving bulky materials such as mulch and prunings and other debris. This kind of work can be done when the earth is frozen or in late summer when the plants are dormant and the earth dry.

ROCKWORK

You may remember exploring a woodlot or public park as a child. What fascination and mystery there was in finding a cleft in the rock. Is there a cave within? What mysterious creatures lurk there? Our landscaping predecessors capitalized on this by creating rocky grottoes and follies in the dark woods. These romantic rock structures are seldom made in today's gardens, and they may appear contrived to our more pragmatic modern taste. On the other hand, natural rock outcroppings do enhance the woodland garden, and some sensitively arranged rockwork adds a dimension that never fails to appeal to those latent romantic feelings. The avid plant collector will also welcome rockwork because it provides another range of habitats to increase the number of plants that can be grown. Woodland wildflowers and ferns fit into these sites very well.

The transportation and installation of rock is apt to be expensive, and unless artistically arranged by well-qualified personnel, the result can be disappointing. Anyone working with rock should wear reinforced footwear and headgear and possess a keen awareness of the dangers inherent in this kind of task. Much of the work can be done with levers and crowbars, but an experienced backhoe operator will speed the job considerably. Excavation contractors sometimes have rock to dispose of, but don't accept inferior material merely because it is cheap.

Sandstone is the favorite material of landscape designers because it usually has an unobtrusive mellow color and is soft and easily broken. Sandstone is relatively porous; that makes it friendly to plant roots. Granite is seldom a good choice as it is too hard and unyielding, and when quarried has sharp angular surfaces and edges. If limestone is water soluble it will enhance lime-loving plants, but most limestones are hard and will not have much effect on the soil pH. Limestone is sometimes found eroded into interesting forms, such as the Chinese Tai Hu, which literally means "rock from Lake Tai." In North America, as everywhere, this type of rock is rare and found only where limestone has been worn by water passing over it for many years. If it can be found or imitated, it is effective in making waterfalls or forming the banks of streams. Lava rock is common in western North America and is available

Figure 4
Rounded boulders and pebbles are used to line a waterway, which may serve as a surface drain and also suggest a natural streambed.

Figure 5
Vertical placement of rock in the oriental manner, contrasted with strong horizontal elements, suggests a sharply eroded landscape, yet the effect is highly stylized.

Figure 6
Horizontal rockwork suggests stratified outcroppings. It may be integrated with landscape features such as steps, paths and alpine plants. This kind of rock garden is best suited to the cultivation of the widest range of plants.

commercially. It may be composed of basalt or volcanic glass or conglomerate mixtures. Some kinds of volcanic rock are very light and easy to work with.

Don't mix different types of rock unless they are found together naturally in the area. Rounded boulders and pebbles may be used as dry or wet riverbeds at the base of outcroppings or to cover areas in the manner of glacial erratics and moraines. Boulders should not be used on steep banks where stratified outcroppings are appropriate. The most important functional use of rock is to hold the soil back in terraces, and stratified sedimentary rock is best for this purpose.

Rockwork should be placed on higher, relatively treeless ground where one would expect the natural elements to erode away the soil or at the valley bottom where under natural conditions the scouring effect of water would expose the rock. Looking closely at natural processes will usually produce a convincing landscape effect.

The placement of rock is an art, but there are some physical principles that must be followed. Sedimentary rock should be placed in restful planes, inter-locked to form terraces and reasonably level planting pockets. Position the rock so at least one-third of its volume is below ground, and place it at a backward-

Figure 7
An upland version on the same theme, but more of
an open space, at the edge of a woodland.

leaning angle to the slope so that moisture and soil are retained. An effective use of rockwork is steps. These can be made to suggest natural stratified out-croppings by blending them with adjacent parts of the landscape that also contain rock.

A well-conceived and planted section of rock garden is normally relatively easy to maintain but quite impossible if care is not taken to exclude perennial rhizomatous weeds such as horsetail (*Equisetum*) or quack grass (*Agropyron*). If the soil is infested with perennial weeds of any kind, it should be left fallow for a year before planting and all traces of weeds removed as they appear. During the fallow period, the soil between the rocks may be improved.

A fallow period of one year also allows the rocks to settle in thoroughly. When all the weeds have been eradicated, apply a preplant fertilizer of super-phosphate, two cupfuls to each square yard or meter. When the planting has finally been done, the surface may be covered with gravel or fine shale rock, or in the case of alkaphytes, limestone chips. This reduces the soil surface available for the germination of weed seeds.

Figure 8

A naturalistic arrangement of rock, suitable for a high
promontory or the summit of a woodland garden from which
to view the adjacent landscape. In this case the rock predominates over
the plants, and all shrubs and trees must be selected with this in mind.

Amending Soil in a Rock Garden

If clayey, add sand, lime (if required) and organic matter. Sandy soils should be amended with leaf mold and peat
moss for plants that need acidic soil. The soil amendment will depend on the kind of plants you wish to grow.
Acidophytes (plants liking acid soils) may need up to 50 percent of the soil mass as acid peat or leaf mold and
depending on the pH, even some iron sulphate. Remember that some sedge peats, unlike sphagnum peats, may
not be very acidic. Alkaphytes (plants that require alkaline soil) may also benefit from organic soil amendments (up
to about 10 percent) to stimulate vigorous root growth, and in these cases it is an easy matter to adjust the pH
with dolomite or limestone.

Figure 9

The entrance to a wet woodland, in which trees must be tolerant of having their roots submerged for at least part of the year. Willows (*Salix*), Swamp Cypress (*Taxodium*), Sweet Gum (*Liquidambar*) and Alders (*Alnus*) fall into this category. In more northern regions, the American Larch (*Larix laricina*) and the Black Spruce (*Picea mariana*) are suitable. Shrubs *Andromeda polifolia*, *Myrica gale* and *Cornus alba* are tolerant of high moisture. *Acorus calamus*, *Osmunda regalis* and *Lysichiton americanum* may be planted at the water's edge.

WATER

A water feature enhances any garden, particularly water in motion. A babbling stream has a pleasant sound, as well as a cooling effect in warm climates. A good counterpoint to the peaceful atmosphere of the woodland, a stream brings life, movement and sound to the landscape.

A property that has a natural pool or stream is endowed with a priceless resource, but like all natural resources, it does carry responsibilities. Care must be taken if you wish to make changes to a watercourse. In many jurisdictions it is an offence to tamper with natural drainage systems unless you have received permission. Before making any changes to water features, check with local, regional or federal water authorities.

In the absence of a natural water feature, it is possible to create one: a small pool, a fountain or even water seeping over a moss-covered rock are all appropriate. Plumbing must be well concealed, as any glimpse of it will destroy the most carefully contrived naturalism. Water conservation is an ever-increasing concern, and where possible water should be recirculated.

Pools are most effective in an open part of the woodland where there is a good supply of nutrients and a source of solar energy. If the sun strikes the surface of the pool for about half the daylight hours, it is possible to have some success with aquatic and bog plants. Still water is not often successful in shady places. Dark forest pools may be of interest to those with an affection for mysterious landscape, but they tend to be stagnant and lifeless.

The construction of a stream should not be undertaken lightly. There will be operating costs (recirculating pumps, power, metered water) to consider. Streams, however well made, have a habit of developing leaks, which are often frustratingly difficult to locate and expensive to repair. If well done, however, the effort is worthwhile because water enhances the landscape to such a high degree.

A stream should follow the line of least resistance between the landforms and need only be a few inches (several cm) wide in some places. Small, deep pools and overhanging rocks or logs hold an irresistible fascination for people of all ages. When the fall is less than one in 10, the stream will take a quiet, meandering course. The stream bottom and sides can be sealed with "puddled" clay, that is, clay mixed with water to form an impervious layer. Sealing with heavy-gauge plastic is acceptable, but it is difficult to conceal. If well done, the combined use of plastic, cement and rockwork can be very effective. Plastic deteriorates unless it is totally protected from sunlight, but this is easily done by covering the stream bottom with a protective layer of sand topped with rounded pebbles.

Steep streambeds with rapidly flowing water are best contained by concrete and rockwork. This usually calls for an experienced builder. The rocks should

Figure 10

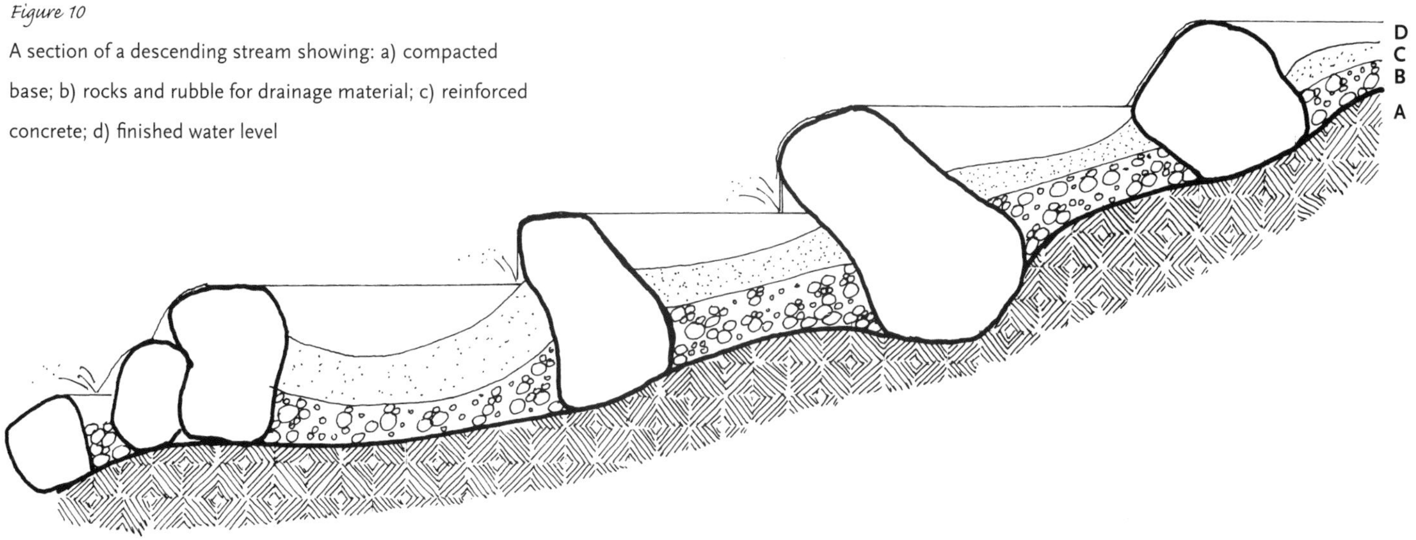

A section of a descending stream showing: a) compacted base; b) rocks and rubble for drainage material; c) reinforced concrete; d) finished water level

strengthen the stream bed at the critical points where water flow is greatest and also give the visual effect of strength and natural strata.

After the rock is placed and keyed together to prevent its sliding downhill, it should be allowed to settle for several months before the concrete grouting is laid. A layer of coarse sand or gravel under the concrete is helpful, as this may prevent damage in winter from the formation of ice. The concrete should be poured a minimum of 3 inches (7.5 cm) thick and agitated slightly to help fill all the voids. On large jobs, reinforcing wire mesh should be used to increase strength. The finished job should be a strong, integral structure of rocks and concrete. The concrete may be tinted if it differs greatly in tone from the rock, but this is usually unnecessary, as the natural earth and vegetable tannins in the water will soon tint the concrete. Iron sulphate tints finished hardened concrete a brown tone.

Concrete pools and streams must be built to withstand the destructive effect of freezing. In some cases a pool filled with water in winter can prevent frost from causing damage, but in very cold areas it may be necessary to drain the entire system and cover it with straw or other organic debris topped with a plastic membrane.

FRAGRANCE

When designing your woodland garden, be sure to plan for another sensory quality: scent. The shaded glades of the woodland are ideal for capturing the elusive fragrances of some of the most exquisitely perfumed plants known in gardens.

Smell is regarded as one of the most primitive of the senses, and the ability to detect fine nuances of odor is an important factor for survival in the animal world. In the plant kingdom, the fragrance of flowers attracts many kinds of insects that pollinate the flowers and ensure survival of the species. Some plants have fragrances that resemble the natural scents of moths and butterflies and are attractive to those insects. Night-blooming plants, such as spider lily (Crinum × powellii) and honeysuckle Lonicera caprifolium, have the most powerful fragrances because night-flying moths must find them in the dark. Magnolias and peonies have a fruity fragrance that attracts beetles, which crawl inside the unopened flower to feed on the stamens. Pollination follows. Richly fragrant flowers often have rather thick, fleshy petals or sepals; this is the source of the fragrance in magnolias. These and other very fragrant flowers are rarely highly colored, but more often white, cream or otherwise pale in color. On the other hand, red, orange and blue flowers are seldom highly fragrant. These flowers attract other kinds of pollinators, such as birds and bees, simply by visual means.

Woodland plants are more apt to use fragrance rather than color to attract pollinators because of the muted light and concealing masses of foliage. The calm atmosphere of the woodland allows fragrances to become concentrated, and thus more effective. The woodland also accentuates the elemental forces of growth and decay, both of which have their own sweet odor. These earthy scents are an integral part of nature's cycle, a change from the more predictable smells found in a conventional garden. Take, for example, the strange smell of ferns after a spring rain, evoking dark green recesses of the forest where these primitive non-flowering plants are often found. Those other primitives of the woodland floor — mosses, club mosses, lichens and liverworts — also have their own characteristic odors. But it is the fungi that possess the most pungent of the earthy scents, sometimes in such intensity that some people find them repellent. The rather bizarre appearance of some fungi, such as the poisonous *Amanita muscaria*, accentuates the sinister effect. Few people would deny that the odor of the stink-horn fungus (*Mutinus caninus*) or the skunk cabbage (*Symplocarpus foetidus*) are abhorrent, but the line between what is pleasant or unpleasant is not always so easily drawn. The sweet, heady perfume of *Narcissus odorus* can be cloyingly heavy, to the point of nausea, at close range. Some species of trumpet lilies have the same characteristic, but it is unlikely to be a problem out of doors. In fact, many scented woodland plants have quite inconspicuous flowers, and the source of a delicious fragrance may be invisible to the casual observer. This elusiveness is surely part of the woodland mystique.

The fragrance of some woodland plants often passes unnoticed because of their early flowering habit. Wintersweet (*Chimonanthus praecox*) blooms during the first three months of the year. The Chinese thought so highly of its fragrance that it is represented in Ming dynasty paintings, sometimes associated with *Narcissus tazetta var. orientalis*. This same association might well be used today with perhaps a hardier but no less fragrant narcissus, of which there are many. *Narcissus tazetta* 'Bridal Crown' and *N. odorus* 'Campernelle' are good examples.

Ancient gardens of fragrance, much loved by the Islamic peoples, were enclosed by hedges and walls. These served to exclude external influence, warm and becalm the air and instill moisture, all of which accentuate the fragrance of flowers. The walled classical Chinese garden has the same effect. In the woodland garden, small enclosed spaces may be made by planting conifers such as yew or hemlock or broad-leaved evergreens such as *Osmanthus × burkwoodii* or *Rhododendron auriculatum*, both of which are quite fragrant.

Fragrant shrubs and herbaceous plants are best placed where the warming rays of the sun can reach them. In winter and spring, however, it can be damaging to tender flowers when the morning sun strikes them with too great an intensity. Filigree shade provided by twiggy deciduous trees allows the correct amount of sunshine through.

An ideal place to plant is a warm yet shaded bank, or adjacent to overhanging rocks. Violets, for example, succeed well on moist, shady, mossy banks. A dark background, such as yew or hemlock, helps to bring out the pale and sometimes insignificant or sparse flowers of many scented woodland plants. Chinese witch hazel (*Hamamelis mollis* 'Pallida') or white forsythia (*Abeliophyllum distichum*) are good examples. So early and so muted in color are the flowers of wintersweet (*Chimonanthus praecox*) that, lacking a dark background of some sort, they may not be seen at all.

Fragrant-flowered evergreen shrubs such as laurestinus (*Viburnum tinus*), winter daphne (*Daphne odora*) and sweet box (*Sarcococca confusa*) are particularly effective in deciduous woodland because the flowers are accentuated by the foliage. They have the added qualities of solidity and mass that are so important in composing the landscape.

Plants noted for their scent are marked with ✿ in the plant lists in Chapters 3 to 6 and in the Authors' Favorite Plants.

Building the Woodland Garden

AFTER YOU HAVE analyzed your site and developed some design ideas, it is time to start building.

A well-made woodland garden may last many generations, but compared with the evolution of a truly wild woodland, this is a very brief life span. A natural plant community is a precisely balanced living system that may have taken hundreds, perhaps thousands, of years to develop. By comparison, our efforts at naturalistic landscaping seem crude. But if we remember that gardening is an art and not a science, then we will not be too discouraged when at first we do not succeed in achieving the harmony of a wild woodland in our designed landscape.

When choosing plants, keep in mind that native plants are better adapted to local conditions because they have evolved there, but using natives alone does limit the range of plant material to some extent. Exotic plants extend the range of color, texture and interest, making for a more spectacular, vivid landscape. Many plants from the temperate parts of South America and Asia blend well with native plants, but to avoid disappointment, check their hardiness rating. Some of them may require a little more care in terms of frost protection and watering until well established, but the effort is worthwhile, as the season of interest can be greatly extended. For example, in Pacific Northwest Zone 8 gardens it is possible to plant the Chilean brush-bush (*Euchryphia glutinosa*) to add flowering interest during August when few native shrubs are flowering.

Most successful woodland gardens use the widest possible range of plants, particularly in small gardens where space is limited. But avoid the more flamboyant garden plants usually associated with summer bedding schemes and flower borders. They do not blend well with the more subtle character of most woodland plants.

PRECEDING PAGE: Goldenrain tree (*Koelreuteria paniculata*) near water at a woodland edge. Sedges and rushes protect the bank from erosion.

Transforming a Conventional Garden to Woodland

If there are trees on a conventional garden site, nature will take care of transforming it into a woodland. As the trees grow and form a canopy, conditions begin to favor shade-loving plants. Think of the situation when a forest is clear-cut or burned. The first plants to appear are sun-tolerant meadow plants that now have an advantage over the weakened woodland natives. For a few years the open meadow is colorful with these bright flowers. Gradually, the shade-giving trees reassert themselves until sun-loving plants die out and shade plants can slowly regain their territory.

For various reasons the owner of a garden may tire of maintenance chores such as mowing lawns, planting annuals or raking leaves. None of these are necessary in a well-planned woodland garden. Imagine if a conventional garden were abandoned, and all maintenance were to stop. Quite soon the place would be overrun with annual and perennial weeds. This would undoubtedly cause great concern, but slowly, over the months and years, shrubs and trees would gain a foothold in a random way, softening the hard edges of masonry and flower beds. Order would give way to wildness, and eventually all would yield to the power of the entwining roots, like a lost civilization overtaken by the jungle. Imagine, again, if this process were directed intelligently, aided by a liberal dose of benign neglect. Instead of leaving it all to chance, the important trees and shrubs would be carefully chosen and under their shade, woodland wildflowers could be introduced.

There are good reasons other than reducing work for gradually transforming the conventional garden to woodland. The process is ecologically sound. The diverse mix of plants tends to discourage the periodic plagues of pests that affect ordinary gardens. The use of pesticides and other chemicals can be dispensed with. Water is used less extravagantly, provided that the correct choice of species is made. It is even possible to have a drought-resistant woodland garden (xeriscape) by choosing certain plants. (Plants that tolerate dry soil are marked in the plant lists with ✳) Some woodland wildflowers need moisture only during the period up to flowering and in the summer can withstand quite dry conditions. For example, the beautiful native cardinal flower (*Lobelia cardinalis*) grows in places that are moist in spring and often very dry after the flowering season is over.

The first step most people take when changing a conventional garden to woodland is to remove the lawn; the second is to plant trees and shrubs. This approach is fine, but remember that a lawn will eventually die due to shade if the process is left to the laws of natural succession. A lawn can also be disposed of by covering it with a deep layer of rotted leaves for a couple of months, and then turning it under with a Rototiller. This makes a rich, weed-free medium for woodland plants.

Conventional gardens often contain structures and furnishings that may not be appropriate to the aesthetic of the woodland garden. Masonry features such as linear walls or paths can sometimes be reworked in curved shapes that blend with the naturalism. A small gazebo or bench often fits well into the woodland, but generally formal structures look out of place or give a melancholy effect, as if the garden had been overcome by the forces of nature.

Existing underground irrigation systems are useful in establishing the new garden and can be modified if necessary. If you live in a low-rainfall area or where water restrictions are likely, do not fall into the trap of planting water-demanding plants. Root competition from trees will aggravate the water deficiency of plants beneath them.

Assuming there are no trees on a site, how many trees does it take to make a woodland garden? This is a reasonable question, since very few city lots are large enough to contain more than a few trees. Two trees — or even just one — may be all that can be accommodated on a small lot. It can be argued that small urban spaces should not be planted with forest tree species of any sort. Trees of more restrained growth, such as the golden rain tree (*Koelreuteria paniculata*), redbud (*Cercis canadensis*), paperbark maple (*Acer griseum*) or Oriental dogwood (*Cornus kousa*), all of which seldom exceed 30 feet (9 m) in height, are often more appropriate. These smaller trees then form the woodland canopy.

Working With a New Site

The most challenging aspect of woodland gardening is building a completely new garden on a site bare of trees, but this situation provides an opportunity to reproduce plant associations and geographical themes that reflect real plant communities found in nature.

Attempting to reproduce natural plant associations is a particularly difficult part of the art of gardening. The following simple example consists of four distinct but overlapping layers of vegetation. The dominant tree might be a red oak (*Quercus rubra*). Second is the understory tree, perhaps a flowering dogwood (*Cornus florida*). Third is a woodland shrub, *Rhododendron maximum*, and the fourth layer is the woodland carpet, which could be *Trillium grandiflorum*. This is a plausible natural plant association. A woodland has at least four layers and usually many more, since it is multidimensional. Another example of a natural plant association is red maple (*Acer rubrum*), witch hazel (*Hamamelis virginiana*) and spice bush (*Lindera bezoin*), of which the latter two are large shrubs. Beneath them could be mountain laurel (*Kalmia latifolia*), an evergreen able to capture the subdued light of the woodland, and on the woodland floor, dog-tooth violet (*Erythronium americanum*) and turk's-cap lily (*Lilium superbum*). An Asian example is a canopy of ginkgo trees with an understory of dove tree (*Davidia involucrata*). The shrub component might be *Rhododendron lutescens* and the woodland floor composed of *Cardiocrinum* and *Primula helodoxa*. The woodland garden is built up in this way with compatible plants, either natural associates, as in the examples above, or plants that are

Developing Specialized Habitats

Imagine visiting a number of gardens and finding the same plant combinations in every case. You might begin to recognize certain patterns caused by the copying and borrowing of ideas. One way to be original is to specialize, using groups of plants that are of particular interest. Geographical groupings, such as Chinese, Himalayan, Appalachian, etc., is just one example. Another could be special groups of plants — camellias or deciduous azaleas, for instance. A woodland garden specializing in hardy lilies or meconopsis would be enchanting. There is no limit to the possibilities.

In a large garden there is scope for several species areas, particularly if the site has varying topography that can accommodate the habitats preferred by each.

Working with a Flat Site

One of the natural features that gives a garden site the potential for dramatic interest is changes in level. If the site has no natural undulation, cutting valleys and using the excavated material to make hills is an age-old method of achieving drama. On a modest scale, moving earth can be very useful in improving the design as well as providing various habitats for plants with differing requirements On an ambitious scale it can be very costly and can cause problems with drainage and slippage unless well planned by a professional.

native to areas with a similar climate. The possible combinations are limitless and offer a fertile field for study in making woodland gardens that are at the same time beautiful and interesting from a biogeographical point of view.

It may take several years for suitable conditions to develop on a raw site, and other plants may fill the void until necessary conditions of shade are met.

For instance, the authors developed a new woodland garden from a raw site with a theme drawn from the deciduous forest of the eastern United States. Until the shade canopy had formed, there was too much sun for woodland plants. A temporary underplanting of rudbeckias and gaillardias formed a spectacular ground cover for several years until there was enough shade for the azaleas, trilliums and erythroniums that were to carpet the woodland floor. As the shade increased, the sun-lovers gradually lost ground to the inheritors of the woodland kingdom.

A barrier of conifers on the windward side of a garden is an advantage. If the site has a slope that gives protection from the prevailing wind, conifers can be planted on the high ground, and the wind will be diverted over the garden site. Keep in mind that a random, partly broken screen planting dissipates the force of the wind and is preferable to a solid row. Sloping sites are often superior, since drainage is usually better, and cold air will not accumulate on a sloping site. Solid plantings should be avoided at the base of slopes, as this may trap cold air. Similarly, low depressions tend to contain pockets of frost in calm, cold weather. A balance has to be struck between good air circulation and protection from wind. Ravine sites are ideal, provided the lower end is open to allow the drainage of cold air and excess water. The sheltered, shaded side of a ravine provides habitat for broad-leaved evergreens, while the more exposed side may be planted with hardy deciduous trees and shrubs. Seaside sites are often difficult because of exposure, but some of the best woodland gardens are near the temperature-moderating influence of the sea; here, multi-layered windbreaks can protect the garden from marine storms.

Adapting a Natural Woodland

Land development is the main threat to the shrinking natural world. Making a garden in an existing woodland is development of a kind, and should be done with sensitivity to the local environment. A careless approach to land-scaping may destroy valuable habitat nurtured during the slow growth of nature's systems.

Figure 11

Trees must be protected during construction and house-building activity. The root zone must be protected from compaction and from deposition of toxic materials such as cement. A large enclosure (*left*) is more effective than merely shielding the individual trunk, as it protects the root zone from damage from power equipment moving on the site.

Combining Native and Exotic Plants

When introducing exotic plants to a natural woodland, the gardener must weigh the new plants' cultural needs against the long-term welfare of the native plants. Plants foreign to the woodland often require more water than natives and providing this may be harmful to existing trees. For example, in warm, dry parts of California, evergreen oaks often dominate the woodland. Species of California lilac (*Ceanothus*), rock rose (*Cistus*), bush anemone (*Carpenteria*) and manzanita (*Arctostaphylos*) would be appropriate choices for the understory. Attempting to grow rhododendrons or other plants of the moist woodland would require massive amounts of extra water during the warm summer months — an economically and aesthetically unsound practice. Eventually, the health of the original plant community would be undermined.

Established native woodland may appear to offer the ideal garden environment for a wide range of shade-loving plants, but this may not always be the case. The natural woodland consists of a tightly knit community of plants. Competition for light, moisture and nutrients may be severe and introduced plants may lack the competitive edge of more robust native species.

Another competitive factor to consider is light. The sun is the driving force in growing plants, and in some cases, almost no light reaches the forest floor. An example is the western climax forests of coastal redwood (*Sequoia sempervirens*) and western red cedar (*Thuja plicata*). Here the shade is so dense that there is almost no vegetation on the forest floor. A few spindly shrubs struggle upward toward the light. Even ferns must fight for survival in the gloomy depths. In the eastern deciduous forest, large areas may be densely treed with highly competitive species such as sugar maple. The dense shade cast by these trees, coupled with a thick mat of surface roots, often makes it difficult to establish introduced woodland plants.

Developing a Specialized Habitat

The author developed a woodland garden from a natural woodland in southern Ontario, Canada, to provide a habitat for a collection of rhododendron species and hybrids. The dominant trees were red oak (*Quercus rubra*) and white pine (*Pinus strobus*). High-limbed and deep-rooted, these species are noted for their tolerance of a rich understory of woodland plants. However, in this case, a dense understory of sugar maple had become established, which shaded out most shrubs except on the woodland fringe. The woodland flora contained large drifts of *Trillium grandiflorum* and *Erythronium americanum*, species that finish most of their yearly growth in the spring, before the full foliar development of the deciduous trees and shrubs. These precious native plants were preserved, but the adaptation of the woodlot to a woodland garden required some thinning of the maples and other competitive trees and shrubs. The work was done in the winter when the frozen ground protected the small plants on the woodland floor from compaction. In less environmentally sensitive areas of the woodland, the stumps of the felled trees were removed. This operation broke up the competitive matrix of roots and permitted the planting of many new shrubs, mainly rhododendrons and companion plants. Magnolias, dogwoods and witch hazels were planted to form a new understory.

Before commencing work in an existing woodland, however meagre its flora, take an inventory of all the trees, shrubs and plants. Man-made or altered woodlots in which the original flora has largely disappeared may be landscaped with less concern for the ecology than pristine wooded lands that have a rich and varied flora. The destruction of a pristine woodland habitat may be too great a price to pay for a garden, however promising the prospect may seem. In such cases, it is best to leave the woodland alone.

Occasionally, windfall, fire or flood in a mature forest may open up clearings, which support a more varied flora than densely shaded woodland. These natural events inject new life into the woodland and offer opportunities for introducing new plants.

When applied intelligently, the hand of the gardener can also enhance the plant community through thinning and disturbance of the habitat. Such intervention, however, should be limited to gentle modification of the natural influences of light, shade and competition. The desired effect will be achieved more slowly but with greater refinement than if attempted through drastic alteration of the landscape.

Allowing machinery of any kind beneath large trees almost invariably leads to habitat destruction. In cold climates, thinning and alteration of the woodland is best done in the dead of winter, when the frozen earth protects tender roots and shoots of herbaceous plants. Another opportunity exists in late summer, when woodland plants are again dormant and the dry soil is firm. At this time unwanted shrubs can be removed without unnecessary damage to the surrounding plants. The earth exposed by these operations should be quickly covered with a mulch of leaves to prevent the invasion of weeds.

An automatic or semi-automatic irrigation system can be valuable to the new woodland garden, as it can be used to provide a constant, even supply of moisture for optimum growth. But the installation of an underground irrigation system may be destructive to the roots of established trees and should be avoided near fine old trees. One way to lessen the damage is to install the pipes beneath a carefully planned system of pathways, avoiding the use of heavy excavating equipment. The trenches opened for this purpose may also serve as drainage channels, if they are filled to the surface with gravel or sand. These trenches will normally follow the lowest lines through the woodland, avoiding large trees and particularly valuable stands of native plants.

A vital consideration in any landscaping that involves moving earth or altering drainage patterns is the water table. Minor changes may be disastrous, particularly for established trees. A rise in the water table may destroy root systems by depriving roots of oxygen. Lowering the water table may cause a slow decline through drought stress. Building up the soil surface over the roots of established trees is usually fatal to the tree.

Perhaps the most common mistake in adapting a woodland is in taking too timid an approach to the removal of surplus trees. It is impossible to grow a wide range of ornamental plants under a dense, unbroken canopy of foliage. There should be plenty of clear sky between the major trees, allowing sunlight to penetrate to the woodland floor.

Deciding which trees to cut down is not easy. Certainly no trees should be felled until all the alternatives and opinions have been considered. Diseased and declining trees should be removed first, followed by less desirable species that are coarse and shallow-rooted. If the stumps can be removed without damaging the remaining trees or the woodland carpet, it is advisable to do so, particularly in areas where *Armillaria* root rot is prevalent. *Armillaria*, also known as honey fungus or shoestring fungus, lives on decaying wood in the soil and can infect living plants. This disease can be fatal to a wide range of trees and shrubs that are planted in infected ground. The presence of black shoestring-like threads beneath the soil surface is a sign. Fawn-colored mushroom-like fruiting bodies are produced above the soil surface.

A common mistake is to attempt planting exotic plants in the woodland without adequate soil preparation. The fine fibrous roots of rhododendrons and many related plants cannot compete with the coarse roots of some forest trees. Large planting holes must be prepared and some of the smaller invading tree roots removed. Healthy trees will not be harmed by the removal of a reasonable quantity of root fiber, providing the large anchor roots are not severed near the main trunk.

Do not remove the natural curtain of vegetation at the woodland edge. The shrubby undergrowth and low tree limbs act as a windbreak, protecting the trees within and preventing the wind-tunnel effect that is found under the canopy of unprotected woodland. If desirable tree species are badly placed in relation to a preconceived garden plan, consider adjusting your design, rather than removing the trees. Rigid adherence to plans is not always appropriate in the woodland garden.

In large woodland tracts, a cellular approach to design may be in the best interests of the woodland and the garden plan. This method involves the removal of groups of trees to form clearings, leaving large areas of the woodland untouched. It has the advantage of preserving existing habitat while offering good, well-lit planting areas for introduced plants. The method also offers the possibility of removing groves of inferior species while preserving the desirable trees and reducing damage to the roots throughout the site.

Preplanting Preparation

The preparation of planting sites by means of deep digging, drainage, placement of organic matter, soil amendment (where necessary) and fertilizing is very important to the rapid development of the young woodland garden.

To the professional gardener, nothing is more depressing than to see trees and shrubs condemned to die through inadequate soil preparation. The greatest single factor is soil compaction. Earth-moving equipment may leave behind severely compacted soil, but under natural, undisturbed conditions, the leaching of minerals through the soil over decades or centuries may cause hardpan layers to form beneath the surface. Both compaction and hardpan severely restrict the root development on which all growth depends. Simple hand digging may not be enough. Using equipment such as a Rototiller or backhoe, the soil should be broken up to a depth of 18 inches (45 cm) and large quantities (up to 25 percent of the soil mass) of leaf mold or peat moss worked in. This keeps the soil open and permits deep root penetration. The garden will then be healthy, fast-growing, and drought-resistant. Before undertaking any deep digging, clearly mark the position of underground services. Electrical, gas, sewer, water or drainage lines are easily forgotten until an accident occurs.

The use of mechanized digging equipment is a great advantage in preparing planting sites, even in woodland. However, it should be used carefully. A few moments of carelessness may destroy the roots of trees that have shaded the land for centuries. Any kind of mechanical equipment must be kept at least 10 feet (3 m) away from the trunks of trees.

Woodland Gardening on Alkaline Soils

Making a woodland garden on alkaline soil poses some special problems. Many of the finest ornamental plants taken for granted in gardens with acid soil are denied to gardeners working with alkaline soil. This includes most members of the rhododendron family, and magnolias and camellias may also be difficult or impossible to cultivate. Moreover, alkaline soil tends to be associated with areas of relatively low rainfall. Alkaline soils, particularly of the heavy clay variety, are very difficult to modify by organic or chemical means because of their dense mineral character. Strongly alkaline soils occur on level terrain or in low-lying alluvial areas where calcareous (limey or chalky) material tends to accumulate. These conditions make it difficult to create the varied woodland mosaic that is possible in more acid habitats.

The presence of large numbers of leguminous plants may indicate alkaline soil. Locust (*Robinia*), honey-locust (*Gleditsia*), Siberian pea (*Caragana*) and even clover and its relatives are indicator plants, perhaps not singly, but certainly in unison. Other lime-loving plants are clematis, viburnum, *Berberis*, the Judas tree (*Cercis siliquastrum*), hawthorns, yew, forsythia, buddleias, Spanish broom (*Spartium junceum*), hellebores, pulsatillas and hypericums. (Lime-tolerant might be a better way to describe these plants, as most of them grow quite well in mildly acid soils also.)

Most plants grow well within quite a wide pH range. The ideal range for a woodland garden is more or less between pH 5.5 and 6.5. In soils below pH 5.5, some plants may not be able to absorb certain nutrients.

Iron may be unavailable in alkaline soils, and since it is also an important component of chlorophyll, the symptom of its deficiency is chlorosis, a yellowing, mainly on the young growth. The best way to avoid iron deficiency before it makes an appearance is the addition of plenty of organic matter, such as decayed leaves or peat. A more immediate method is the use of an organic form of iron, such as iron chelate or granular iron sulphate, as a foliar spray or soil treatment.

Acidifying alkaline soil by mixing sulphur or iron sulphate with the soil mass may make it possible to grow ericaceous plants, such as heathers and rhododendrons, where they are not normally found. But this should be attempted only where the soil is not strongly alkaline; if there is a large amount of calcium carbonate in the topsoil, the alkalinity will reassert itself, particularly where the water used for irrigation is alkaline.

The most successful gardeners do not attempt to make major alterations to the soil but work with the natural soil of the site, improving and enriching its natural properties and planting adapted lime-tolerant species. But don't hesitate to experiment — try out different plants and don't rely completely on conventional wisdom. While it is true that a greater range of plants can be grown in moderately acid soil conditions than alkaline, the latter need be no obstacle to planting a woodland garden.

Organic matter is the key to success. Most well-drained soils will sustain a wide range of plants if plenty of organic matter is incorporated.

Alkaline soils are often fine-textured and sometimes poorly drained because the water cannot percolate easily between the fine plate-like particles. The situation can be improved by adding coarse sand, organic matter or compost to make the texture more open.

In alkaline soils, the decomposition of organic matter is accelerated, as the higher pH favors bacterial and fungal activity. Sphagnum peat moss is acid, fluffy in texture and resists decay. Spread it up to 6 inches (15 cm) deep over the soil. Several inches (8 cm) of coarse dry sand on top helps integrate the peat moss into the soil. A power Rototiller is the best tool for this job.

Never cultivate clay soils when wet in spring or fall. In late summer the dry soil is more easily pulverized. This can be followed by planting in the fall or the following spring.

Plants that grow well in alkaline soil are marked with ◆ in the plant lists for Chapters 3 to 6 and in the Authors' Favorite Plants.

Woodland Gardening in Difficult Climates

The making of woodland gardens in the prairies or semi-arid regions such as the American Southwest poses special problems. Summer heat, winter cold and wide seasonal and diurnal temperature fluctuations are part of living in these regions. Such conditions make gardening a challenge.

For gardeners in the interior areas, all garden operations must be precisely timed. Transplanting must be done well before fall frosts freeze the soil, or postponed until the spring thaw. Protective mulching is done after a few early frosts have hardened plant tissues, but there is little point in mulching after the soil is deeply frozen.

Feeding of plants must be more carefully adjusted to the seasons in cold climates than in mild ones. There is some evidence that fertilizing just prior to freeze-up and before applying mulch is beneficial. Semi-dormant plant tissue absorbs nutrients to be used when growth starts in the spring.

Fall-applied fertilizers should contain about twice as much potassium as nitrogen and phosphorus. Potassium facilitates cell wall permeability, which allows movement of dissolved nutrients into the cell. This creates an antifreeze effect that reduces the plant's susceptibility to cell rupture by freezing.

Gardeners in the interior regions are, of necessity, a hardy, persistent breed, but even they are forced to spend several months a year in semi-hibernation from their normal activities. Once the long-awaited but brief springtime arrives, temperatures soon soar to summer levels. Shade becomes the most valuable ally of gardeners who aspire to grow a wide range of exotic plants.

Environmental differences are accentuated by low rainfall and a climate that is inhospitable to mesophytic plants (those with relatively broad leaves and no special adaptation to conserve moisture). Most of the popular woodland plants of the mild, moist regions fall into this category. However, there is a wide range of resilient hardy plants, native and exotic, with which to furnish woodland gardens in harsher habitats. As to the natives, one need only look around for inspiration. Northern gardeners, when visiting the Southwest, are spellbound by the beauty of trees such as the desert ironwood (*Olneya tesota*) or the several kinds of palo verde (*Parkinsonia* or *Cercidium* spp.). These have a distinct, uncompromising beauty that is in perfect harmony with the desert environment. In north-central regions, groves of aspen and willows provide shelter and sustenance for smaller plants and wildlife. In the far north, black spruce, birch and lodgepole pine form the canopy.

The open, central parts of the United States and Canada once contained large tracts of natural woodlands. Agriculture, clearing for grazing and fire have depleted these to the point that trees are often confined to river valleys and steep mountain slopes. These remnant forests are often sought after as places for human dwellings. Because of the severity of the climate, the woodlands are slow-growing and fragile. They need protection and renewal if they are to remain healthy and self-sustaining. Like small groups of endangered animals, the woodlands may lack the ability to renew themselves. Conscientious gardeners can assist nature's processes by planting native species.

Resist the temptation to introduce nonadapted species that require constant watering and pampering. Hardy native species have adapted to the local conditions over long periods of time, and these should be used as the basis of the garden.

When choosing exotics, study other regions of the world that have a similar climate. Pinpoint areas that correspond in latitude, altitude, seasonal cycles, temperatures and annual rainfall. For example, Siberia has been a rich source of plants for the prairie regions. Good examples are Russian olive (*Elaeagnus angustifolia*) and Siberian pea tree (*Caragana arborescens*). In warm, dry climates, Australian *Eucalyptus* may find a place in the canopy. Innovative nursery operators and horticulturists at local arboreta and botanical gardens have studied these factors; seek their advice.

Plants that do well in dry inland areas nearly always have deep or wide-spreading root systems that seek out natural moisture. They may also have small leaves or thick, waxy leaf coverings that reduce evaporation. Some plants, such as palo verde (*Parkinsonia* or *Cercidium* spp.), have the ability to shed their leaves in hot, dry periods. This is summer dormancy, the opposite of the normal leaf drop in temperate climates. Both these adaptations help the plant survive periods of weather that are unfavorable for growth. These qualities are called "xerophytic," an apt word borrowed by landscapers to denote a style of gardening called xeriscaping. This simply means working in harmony with an arid environment by choosing plants that, once established, do not need supplemental water beyond what nature provides.

In all parts of America the lowest temperature reached is the major factor determining the kind of plants grown. On the other hand, a winter chill of insufficient duration limits the cultivation of north-temperate plants in the Deep South. Hence, in warm, temperate areas, oranges grow better than pears. In the South, the capacity of plants to tolerate heat becomes as important a factor in gardening as cold tolerance in the North. Altitude has a profound effect on climate. A rule of thumb often quoted is that every 1,000-foot (300-m) rise in elevation is equivalent to a 300-mile (500-km) gain in latitude to the north.

Plants appropriate to dry climates are marked with ✳ in the plant lists for Chapters 3 to 7 and in the Authors' Favorite Plants.

The Canopy

CHAPTER THREE

*I*N NATURE, the ecological succession of a real woodland may take many lifetimes to develop, even hundreds of years. A cultivated woodland garden, on the other hand, can be made in less than a decade with the right choice of trees.

The foliage canopy of the dominant trees determines what plants make up the woodland beneath. A continuous canopy may cast too much shade or a sporadic one too little. A good rule of thumb is to admit 50 percent of the sunlight. This is about the same as the typical lathhouse of a nursery, a structure that simulates protected woodland conditions. In the landscape, trees should be widely spaced to allow sunlight to reach the woodland floor and the plantings arranged so that shade is provided during the heat of the day. The quality of the shade is also important. Dappled sunlight admitted by light-textured trees is preferable to the continuous shade cast by conifers or deciduous trees with large, overlapping leaves. Keep in mind that more shade may be needed in warm, sunny climates than in cloudy maritime or montane areas, although in such localities, the preferred garden plants may be more sun-tolerant. Finally, the site must be considered. Southern slopes will need more shade than northern exposures, and plants growing in moist soil are usually more sun-tolerant than those on dry sites. Look at nearby wooded sites to help determine appropriate light levels for the garden.

Many naturally wooded sites are too deeply shaded for woodland gardens and require thinning of less desirable, harshly competitive trees. Fine-textured trees, or those with pinnate leaves, are preferred when other factors are equal. Trees that may exceed 50 feet (15 m) in height should be planted in urban areas only after a thorough analysis of the long-term consequences. Big trees can be a liability, and they are expensive to maintain properly or remove. In the city garden, small woodland areas can be made beneath trees of moderate size, such as Asian dogwood (*Cornus kousa*), trident maple (*Acer buergerianum*), dove

PRECEDING PAGE: The garden canopy is inspired by the wild forest. *Picea breweriana* in the Siskiyou mountains of California.

tree (*Davidia involucrata*) or the many species of *Magnolia* and mountain ash (*Sorbus*). If these trees are encouraged to grow swiftly, a canopy will form within a few years. In the meantime, sun-loving shrubs and flowers can grow beneath them. In this way, the woodland garden can evolve gradually as a kind of natural succession in response to increasing shade.

The High Canopy

The planting of a woodland canopy depends on what species are hardy in the area. The main criterion is that the choice be made from species that have proven hardy over several decades. Nothing is more disappointing than the loss of the canopy after some years of growth because of an unforeseen failure of adaptation to the climate. Keep in mind that there is often considerable variation in hardiness between geographical races or strains of a species. If you are gardening in the warm south, select plants from a southern source. Plants for northern gardens should be selected from stock that originates in northern latitudes or at higher altitudes. It is better to plant a mixed selection of trees, some native, some exotic, including a few conifers, for variety of form and texture.

Place major canopy trees carefully to provide shade in appropriate places. It is sometimes helpful, as a guide, to place tall stakes where the trees are to be planted, moving these around until the desired spacing is obtained in relation to the direction and angle of the sun at its zenith.

SELECTING DECIDUOUS TREES

Some important criteria for the selection of canopy trees are that they be deep-rooted and possess foliage that is not excessively dense. Beeches and the large maple species are generally unsuitable because they form a thick, impenetrable mass of surface roots. Most oaks, particularly the red oak group, are among the best. The red oak (*Quercus rubra*) is the most widely planted oak. The scarlet oak (*Q. coccinea*) is similar and somewhat finer in texture; the cultivar 'Splendens' is especially fine. The elegant willow oak (*Q. phellos*) has small leaves that provide a light canopy and a fine-textured mulch when they fall. *Quercus cerris* (turkey oak) and the allied *Q. acutissima* from China are somewhat slower growing, eventually producing trees of picturesque outline and interesting texture. In the more southerly latitudes, evergreen oaks such as the live oak (*Q. virginiana*), the Mediterranean holly oak (*Q. ilex*) and the Californian coast live oak (*Q. agrifolia*) give year-round shade and provide habitat for various epiphytes such as Spanish moss and *Polypodium* ferns. Evergreen oaks give a fine sense of permanence and sculptural mass to the landscape.

Oaks have all the qualities of a good canopy tree. Plants beneath the canopy benefit from the oaks' deep roots and filigree foliage, which allows sufficient light to penetrate to the woodland floor. We have emphasized oaks for these reasons, but also because there is such a wide range of species adapted to greatly varying local conditions, from the cold north to the warm south.

Large-leaved maples, such as the Norway maple (*Acer platanoides*) and the sycamore maple (*A. pseudoplatanus*), are less suitable, but their hardiness and adaptability may be useful on difficult sites. The shade cast by these species is dense and their roots are apt to be very competitive.

Among the trees suitable for alkaline and clay soils are ash (*Fraxinus* spp.). These have beautiful pinnate foliage that, in some species, yields pleasant autumn colors. Most species of *Fraxinus* grow very large, often with tall, straight trunks that branch out into an elegant canopy high above the ground. The European ash (*Fraxinus excelsior*) has given rise to several worthy cultivars. A favorite among these is the golden ash (*F. excelsior* 'Jaspidea'). The leaves are tinged yellow in spring and autumn and the winter twigs are bright yellow. For the best effect, this cultivar should be planted with a background of conifers. The manna ash (*F. ornus*) is a tree of moderate size, rarely exceeding 50 feet (15 m). When in flower, it resembles a large white lilac, to which it is related. All ash species are noted for their tough, resilient character and freedom from disease. They are used as street trees in difficult urban conditions across North America. More suggested trees for alkaline conditions can be found in the plant list for this chapter, marked with ◆.

The deciduous trees of the canopy can do more than provide shade. Good fall color, attractive form or interesting bark can add immeasurably to the woodland scene. For example, sweet gum (*Liquidambar styraciflua*) has attractive foliage and good autumn color. Both succeed in either sandy or organic, acidic soils.

See the plant list at the end of this chapter for other fine canopy trees that may be suitable to your particular site.

CHOOSING CONIFERS

If oaks are rated highest in the deciduous broadleaf category, then pines are the leaders in the evergreen coniferous group. Most pines are valued for their strong,

A high canopy of white pine and red oak in Ontario, Canada.

A canopy of Douglas fir and Japanese maple in the understory of a Pacific Northwest garden.

rugged stature and longevity. Depending on the soil type and depth, they are relatively deep-rooted and tolerant of plants grown beneath them. With age, the canopy of a pine is broad and high, making it more suitable as a shade tree than the narrow, pyramidal form of many other conifers. A well-grown Scots pine (*Pinus sylvestris*) has few peers; the blue-green foliage and orange bark of mature trees are superb. The cultivar 'Argentea' (silver) is particularly fine. The lower limbs should be removed in stages as the tree grows. This encourages the development of a smooth trunk with the characteristic orange-brown bark.

The Japanese red pine (*Pinus densiflora*) also has attractive bark. Some of its cultivars have interesting foliage, such as the one known as the dragon's eye, 'Oculus-Draconis'. All these are two-needled pines. The five-needled pines include some of the best ornamental conifers, often used to accent and contrast with deciduous plants. There is no better tree as an accent on a high promontory than the Japanese white pine (*P. parviflora*). The horizontally spreading branches and tufted foliage cast a dappled shade. A low planting enhances the architectural quality of the pine's picturesque branching habit. The ideal underplanting is dwarf azaleas and rhododendrons. Moss-covered rocks and dwarf ferns are also appropriate.

Pines are among the most cold tolerant and heat tolerant of conifers. Jack pine (*Pinus banksiana*) is hardy to Zone 1, and Aleppo pine (*P. halepensis*) to Zone 9. In the southern states, pines, together with evergreen oaks, are indispensable canopy trees. Longleaf pine (*P. palustris*), loblolly pine (*P. taeda*) and slash pine (*P. elliottii*) are all adaptable to a fairly wide range of conditions where mild winters and hot, humid summers dominate the climate. In mixed stands with evergreen oaks, they form a woodland of great aesthetic appeal that epitomizes the landscape of the South. However, on their own, the effect of pines is apt to be rather monotonous.

In the western rain-shadowed areas of the interior, from British Columbia to California, ponderosa pine (*Pinus ponderosa*) and other conifers form open woodlands. The experience of walking through a scented pine woodland on a warm spring day is without equal. Adding plants with fragrant foliage or flowers enhances this delightful sensory effect.

In large gardens where light shade is desired, Himalayan white pine (*Pinus wallichiana*) is a good choice in milder areas. This elegant species is not tolerant of extreme cold or heat, even in the Pacific Northwest. White pine (*Pinus strobus*) is a hardy alternative.

We have dwelled on the merits of pines because, like oaks, there is a wide range of species adapted to varying conditions. They also form a lighter canopy — unless widely spaced, many conifers, such as *Thuja* species, hemlock, spruce and fir, do not admit sufficient light through the canopy. Deciduous conifers, such as larch (*Larix* spp.), bald cypress (*Taxodium distichum*) and dawn redwood (*Metasequoia glyptostroboides*), have light, airy foliage and are very good canopy trees. Suitable conifers, including some of the deciduous species such as larch, are described on the plant list at the end of this chapter.

The Second Tier

The second tier of trees beneath the high canopy makes up the main fabric of the woodland. These trees are planted as much for their own intrinsic interest as they are for the shade they provide. They include magnolias, dogwoods, Asian maples, and a host of other trees of moderate size that provide a pageant of colorful interest throughout the year. Some gardeners specialize in one or two genera, particularly if space is limited, and this gives a definite flavor to the garden. Magnolias, for example, offer the choice of large trees, such as *Magnolia kobus* var. *borealis*, or shrubby plants, such as *M. sieboldii*. In the maple clan, there are a great number of small species from the Orient to enrich the woodland with varied texture, from the bold foliage of *Acer japonicum* 'Aconitifolium' to the filigree delicacy of *A. palmatum* 'Dissectum'.

Interesting bark is another consideration. *Acer palmatum* 'Senkaki' has brilliant coral-colored bark. The "snake-bark" maples, most of Asian origin, are good plants for semi-shade, though most of them grow quite large, including the North American native, *A. pensylvanicum*. The Asian species of maple are supreme because of their large number and widely varying character. Particularly good are *A. forrestii* and *A. davidii*. The paperbark maple (*A. griseum*) has intense autumn color and remarkable ruddy orange peeling bark. All these maples enjoy semi-shade and well-drained but moist, acidic soil.

The second-tier trees, more than any other element, determine the textural quality of the woodland garden; choosing wisely is vital to the long-term development of the landscape.

Interesting Trees for Temperate Areas

In mild temperate areas, the choice for second-tier trees is very wide. *Stewartia* has camellia-like flowers in June. *Styrax*, the snowbell tree, of which there are several species, has dainty white flowers in mid-June. The epaulette tree (*Pterostyrax hispida*), so named for its attractive fringe-like flowers, is an easily cultivated and rapid-growing tree of moderate size. Four of the five species of the silverbell tree (*Halesia*) grow in the southeastern American states. This elegant tree offers various sizes and growth habits. The tree named for Benjamin Franklin, *Franklinia alatamaha*, can be added to this select group of fine specimens. The redbud tree should not be overlooked; *Cercis canadensis* is the best-known species and is a good tree for a sunlit woodland clearing. The Texan variety *C. texensis* is more heat tolerant, and the western redbud (*C. occidentalis*) makes a large shrub or small tree best suited to the conditions of northern California and southern Oregon.

Trees to Avoid

Some tree species, because of factors such as dense shade, competitive shallow roots, susceptibility to pests or even toxic qualities, are best avoided. The horse chestnut (*Aesculus hippocastanum*) and most members of the walnut family, such as the black walnut (*Juglans nigra*), secrete toxic substances that inhibit many understory plants. The leaves of these species should not be used as mulches.

Elms have an extraordinary capacity to remove all moisture from the soil within their reach. Plants growing under elms may suffer severely in summer. The susceptibility of many true elms (*Ulmus*) to Dutch elm disease further argues against their use in garden settings. These trees and the related Caucasian elms (*Zelkova*) also seed themselves freely throughout the landscape. This may also be said of the larger species of maple, such as *Acer platanoides*, *A. pseudoplatanus*, *A. saccharinum* and the bigleaf maple (*A. macrophyllum*), a tree of large and noble proportions. In humid, high-rainfall areas, old bigleaf maples are often beautifully festooned with epiphytic mosses, lichens and ferns. This can be a considerable asset to the overall beauty of the woodland garden. Perhaps it is one of those trees that is best avoided, but those who inherit a specimen cherish it.

Most beeches, poplars, alders, willows and the larger maples are shallow rooted; these and the majority of birches should not be used as canopy trees because of their invasive root systems.

The tree of heaven (*Ailanthus altissima*) is often spurned because of the rank odor of the flowers on male trees. It also suckers profusely if its roots are disturbed. However, this tree grows quickly and the interesting, bold pinnate foliage may be useful for providing temporary shade until slower-growing trees are large enough to cast shade.

Trees for the Woodland

❀ = scented flowers   ✳ = suitable for dry places   ◆ = suitable for alkaline soils

BOTANICAL NAME	COMMON NAME	ZONE	NOTES ON CHARACTER

Large Trees (over 50 ft [15.2 m]): Deciduous

BOTANICAL NAME	COMMON NAME	ZONE	NOTES ON CHARACTER
Acer cappadocicum	harlequin maple	6	Attractive leaves turn yellow in the fall.
Acer cappadocicum 'Aureum'	golden harlequin maple	6	Leaves emerge yellow, turn green in summer. Good fall color.
Acer platanoides ◆	Norway maple	5	Robust tree casting dense shade. Tough and adaptable. Good fall color
Acer pseudoplatanus ◆	sycamore maple	6	Attractive large tree for any soil. Good in exposed locations. Cultivar 'Brilliantissimum' is a smaller version with striking shrimp-pink new foliage; 'Prinz Handjery' is medium sized, slow growing with purple-backed leaves.
Acer rubrum	red maple	3	Noted for its adaptability to wet sites. Red flowers in spring and good fall color. Good cultivars are 'Autumn Blaze' and 'Sunset'
Aesculus chinensis ◆	Chinese horse chestnut	6	Large tree. Susceptible to late spring frosts.
Aesculus indica ◆	Indian horse chestnut	7	Magnificent tree bears white flowers in large panicles. Requires a moist site.
Aesculus indica 'Sydney Pearce' ◆	Indian horse chestnut	7	A free-flowering form of the species with denser panicles.
Ailanthus altissima	tree of heaven	4	Legendary for its adaptability to difficult city conditions. Pinnate leaves and reddish fruit.
Alnus glutinosa 'Imperialis'	black alder	3	Deeply lobed leaves are a feature of this tree.
Betula albosinensis	Chinese paper birch	5	Tawny-colored peeling bark is attractive. Small leaves allow light to penetrate canopy.
Betula maximowicziana	monarch birch	5	Fast-growing open-branched tree with large leaves and racemose female catkins.
Betula pendula	silver birch	2	A tree of graceful weeping habit. Silvery white trunk. Susceptible to borers.
Betula utilis var. *jacquemontii*	Himalayan white birch	6	Stark chalk white bark is superior to that of other white birches. Vigorous upright growth habit in youth, spreading later.
Castanea mollissima	Chinese chestnut	4	Fuzzy edible nuts plentiful in autumn.
Catalpa bignonioides ❀ ◆	Indian bean tree	4	Wide-spreading tree with heart-shaped leaves and white tubular flowers in summer. Needs plenty of room. 'Aurea' is a smaller form with clear yellow leaves. Late to leaf out.
Fraxinus angustifolia	narrow-leaved ash	6	A rounded tree suitable for drier sites. Purple fall color.
Fraxinus excelsior 'Jaspidea' ◆	golden ash	4	Beautiful gold-colored twigs and autumn color.

LEFT: Japanese maple often reaches a size large enough to form the canopy in a small garden.

▷

BOTANICAL NAME	COMMON NAME	ZONE	NOTES ON CHARACTER
Fraxinus pennsylvanica	red ash	3	Stately tree with an open crown. Gray, furrowed bark.
Fraxinus velutina ✳ ◆	Arizona ash	6	Resilient and versatile. Not suitable for rainy areas.
Ginkgo biloba	maidenhair tree	4	Unique fan-shaped leaves with parallel veins turn clear yellow in the fall. Pollution tolerant.
Gleditsia triacanthos var. *inermis* ◆	thornless honey locust	4	Large tree with fernlike foliage. Good for dry sites. Bears curiously twisted brown pods.
Kalopanax septemlobus	castor-aralia tree	5	Stoutly branched tree with large palmate leaves and fiercely spined branches.
Larix gmelinii	Dahurian larch	2	Deciduous conifer from Russia. Very hardy. Succeeds in cold, moist sites.
Larix kaempferi	Japanese larch	4	Reddish shoots and glaucous or gray-green leaves. Tolerant of acidic, poorly drained soils.
Larix laricina	American larch	2	Very hardy, deciduous conifer. Bright green needles turn golden yellow in fall.
Liquidambar formosana	Formosan gum	7	The three-lobed leaves emerge plum purple, become green, turn crimson in the fall.
Liquidambar styraciflua	sweet gum	5	Pyramidal tree, retaining its maple-like foliage late into the fall. Good in moist sites. Spectacular fall color.
Liriodendron chinense	Chinese tulip tree	7	Much like its American cousin (*L. tulipifera*) but with narrower-waisted leaves and smooth trunk.
Liriodendron tulipifera	tulip tree	4	Towering tree with saddle-shaped leaves. Flowers are borne high in the branches. Yellow fall color.
Magnolia acuminata	cucumber tree	4	Large tree with oval leaves and warty cucumber-like fruit with red seeds.
Magnolia dawsoniana ◆	Dawson magnolia	7	Flowers are borne before the leaves emerge in early spring. Sensitive to early frosts.
Magnolia hypoleuca		6	Large leaves and scented bloom with purple-red stamens. Fruit brilliant red.
Magnolia sargentiana var. *robusta*		7	Large pink flowers are borne before the leaves. Forms a multistemmed tree.
Magnolia sprengeri 'Diva'	Sprenger magnolia	7	Rosy pink flowers are held erect on the branches in April.
Magnolia tripetala	umbrella tree	4	Huge ribbed leaves with tapering bases are held at the apex of the shoots. Attractive fruit.
Magnolia × *veitchii*	Veitch magnolia	7	A vigorous hybrid between *M. campbelli* and *M. denudata*. Blush pink flowers in April.
Metasequoia glyptostroboides	dawn redwood	5	Deciduous conifer of rapid growth and graceful habit. Fernlike foliage and rusty brown stems. Likes moist sites.
Nothofagus antarctica	southern beech	8	Delicate branching and small leaves allow light to reach understory. Leaves fragrant when young.
Nothofagus obliqua ◆	southern beech	8	Deciduous tree from Chile and Argentina. Small leaves.
Oxydendrum arboreum	sorrel tree	5	Slender tree valuable for its white flowers in late summer followed by scarlet autumn tints.

▷

BOTANICAL NAME	COMMON NAME	ZONE	NOTES ON CHARACTER
Paulownia tomentosa ❁ ◆	princess tree	5	A spectacular flowering tree with panicles of purple foxglove-like flowers. Bold, fuzzy leaves.
Platanus racemosa ✴	California sycamore	7	Attractive bark and maple-like leaves on large, heat and wind tolerant tree.
Prunus serotina	black cherry	3	The largest of cherries, with glossy dark foliage turning yellow in fall. Good on sandy soils.
Quercus cerris	Turkey oak	6	An attractive, elegant, and fast-growing oak of large size.
Quercus coccinea	scarlet oak	4	Excellent woodland shelter canopy tree. Open branching habit and red fall color.
Quercus coccinea 'Splendens'	Knaphill oak	4	A form of the scarlet oak with intense autumn coloration.
Quercus macrocarpa	burr oak	2	Rugged-looking tree that tolerates wet soil.
Quercus palustris ◆	pin oak	5	Pyramidal and low-branching tree in youth, later spreading. Not for dry soils.
Quercus phellos	willow oak	5	Narrow linear leaves are unlike other oaks. Pyramidal shape when young, later spreading.
Quercus robur	English oak	5	Long-lived wide-spreading tree with small leaves. Excellent woodland shelter tree.
Quercus rubra	red oak	3	Fast-growing tree requiring moisture and fertile soil to do well. Deep rooted.
Quercus × turneri	Turner's oak	7	Semi-evergreen tree clad with leathery, dark green leaves. Demand low-grafted trees.
Robinia pseudoacacia ❁ ✴ ◆	black locust	3	Large tree bearing clusters of pendulous fragrant white flowers in June. Casts open shade, but large size and suckering habit make it inappropriate for smaller gardens.
Sophora japonica ✴	Japanese pagoda tree	5	Pinnate leaves cast an open shade. Flowers creamy white in late summer. Drought resistant.
Taxodium distichum	swamp cypress	4	Deciduous, bright green, fine-textured, feathery foliage. Grows well in extremely wet conditions, even submerged.
Zelkova serrata	sawleaf zelkova	5	This elmlike tree with smooth gray bark is wide spreading and pest resistant.

Large Trees: Broad-leaved Evergreen

Eucalyptus gunnii	cider gum	8	Silver-green, lance-shaped leaves and peeling bark. Very fast growth. One of the hardier eucalypts.
Magnolia grandiflora ❁	southern magnolia	7	Outstanding ornamental species for its glossy leaves and lemon-scented white flowers. Numerous cultivars offered differing mainly in leaf size and indumentum coloration.
Magnolia virginiana ❁	sweet bay	5	Semi-evergreen species bearing lovely scented blossoms all summer.
Nothofagus dombeyi	southern beech	8	Large evergreen tree with small leaves.

▷

ABOVE, L TO R: *Franklinia alatamaha, Magnolia DeVos-Kosar* hybrid 'Susan', *Pinus wallichiana*

RIGHT: Dawn redwood (*Metasequoia glyptostroboides*). Filigree foliage provides dappled shade.

◁ *Trees for the Woodland*

BOTANICAL NAME	COMMON NAME	ZONE	NOTES ON CHARACTER
Quercus agrifolia ✳	California live oak	9	Spreading tree valuable in dry climates. Susceptible to armillaria root rot.
Quercus ilex ◆ ✳	holly oak	8	Fine evergreen with masses of dark green foliage. Withstands drought and coastal conditions.

Large Trees: Coniferous Evergreen

BOTANICAL NAME	COMMON NAME	ZONE	NOTES ON CHARACTER
Abies amabilis	Pacific silver fir	5	Makes a beautifully symmetrical tree in cool, moist climates. Cones a rich purple color.
Abies grandis	grand fir	6	Large forest tree with oppositely ranked needles. Rapid grower on cool, moist sites.
Abies koreana	Korean fir	5	Slow-growing tree producing attractive blue cones when young.
Abies pinsapo	Spanish fir	6	Succeeds in acid or alkaline soils. Stiff green or blue-green blunt needles surround the branches.
Abies procera 'Glauca'	noble fir	6	Blue form of this species. Trees bear the largest cones of any fir. For cool, moist sites.
Cedrus atlantica 'Glauca' ◆	blue Atlas cedar	6	Striking blue foliage on stiff branches. Tolerates drought and severe pruning. Needs large space.
Cedrus deodara	deodar cedar	7	Weeping branch tips give this tree a graceful habit. Drought resistant.
Cedrus libani ssp. *brevifolia* ◆	Cyprus cedar	7	Compact growth makes this a good tree for smaller spaces. Drought resistant.

▷

BOTANICAL NAME	COMMON NAME	ZONE	NOTES ON CHARACTER
Cedrus libani var. *stenocoma* ◆	cedar of Lebanon	6	Slender conical form when young. Hardier than the species.
Chamaecyparis nootkatensis	Nootka cypress	5	Attractive conifer with pendulous branches. Prefers a moist site.
Chamaecyparis nootkatensis 'Pendula'	weeping Nootka cypress	5	Strongly weeping conifer with attractive, bright green, fernlike foliage.
Cupressocyparis × *leylandii* ◆	Leyland cypress	7	Good windbreak for edge of woodland. Fast growing.
Cupressus macrocarpa ◆	Monterey cypress	8	Excellent in maritime locales for windbreak.
Cryptomeria japonica	Japanese cedar	7	Columnar evergreen tree with dagger-shaped needles. Bark peels in strips. Many forms available.
Picea breweriana	Brewer's spruce	7	Graceful spire decked with vertical curtains of branches. Seed-grown plants develop the nicest form.
Picea mariana	black spruce	3	Very hardy small spruce. Attractive purple cones. Grows well in cold, swampy areas.
Picea omorika	Serbian spruce	4	A very narrow, short-branched tree becoming a slender tapering spire.
Picea smithiana	Himalayan spruce	7	Resembling *P. breweriana* with shorter pendulous branches.
Pinus contorta ✳	shore pine	7	Good species for poorly drained, peaty soils. Withstands coastal conditions. The related lodgepole pine (ssp. *latifolia*) is taller growing and is better adapted to drought and colder climates (Zone 3).
Pinus densiflora	Japanese red pine	4	Like a Scots pine with reddish trunk and bright green needles. Tolerates poor, sandy soils. Rapid growth.
Pinus flexilis ✳ ◆	limber pine	4	For cold-winter regions. Wind tolerant.
Pinus monophylla ✳ ◆	one-needle pinyon	5	Excellent medium-sized pine for dry, high-elevation areas.
Pinus nigra ◆	Austrian pine	5	Strong, dark-foliaged conifer. Casts a dense shade.
Pinus pinaster ◆	maritime pine	7	Unexcelled for its adaptability to coastal conditions, tolerating poor, sandy soils. Rapid growth.
Pinus strobus ◆	eastern white pine	3	Imposing tree when mature but susceptible to pine blister rust. Remove all currant bushes nearby.
Pinus strobus 'Pendula' ◆	weeping white pine	3	Effective weeping form with drooping branches.
Pinus sylvestris ◆	Scots pine	2	A variable species of picturesque beauty. Very hardy and adaptable to poor soils. Reddish trunk.
Pinus sylvestris 'Aurea' ◆	golden Scots pine	3	Form of the Scots pine with green needles that turn an attractive shade of yellow in winter.
Pinus tabuliformis ◆	Chinese pine	6	Hardy tree with persistent cones, often forming a broad flat crown at maturity.

▷

BOTANICAL NAME	COMMON NAME	ZONE	NOTES ON CHARACTER
Pinus wallichiana	Himalayan white pine	7	Beautiful glaucous blue needles are long and droop from the branches. A graceful, fast- growing tree.
Pseudotsuga menziesii	Douglas fir	6	An imposing forest giant with furrowed bark and long mastlike trunk. Can take summer drought.
Sequoia sempervirens	redwood	7	One of the world's tallest trees. Likes ample moisture and space. Attractive bark and foliage.
Sequoiadendron giganteum	giant sequoia	6	A dense pyramid with branches to the ground becoming very tall with a massive trunk. Needs full sun.
Tsuga canadensis	eastern hemlock	4	The hemlocks are generally shade tolerant under large deciduous trees except for the Carolina (*T. caroliniana*) and mountain (*T. mertensiana*) kinds, which are slower growing, compact trees. The western hemlock (*T. heterophylla*) is a forest giant from the Pacific Northwest, and grows best in similar temperate climates.

Small to Medium-sized Trees (15 to 40 ft [4.5–12 m]): *Deciduous*

Acer buergerianum	trident maple	6	A small, bushy tree with three-pointed leaves, which are held late into the fall.
Acer capillipes		5	This tree has attractively striated branches and three-lobed leaves borne on red leaf stalks.
Acer circinatum	vine maple	5	Good for massing; brilliant fall colors. Attractive green stems.
Acer crataegifolium 'Veitchii'	hawthorn maple	6	Slender tree with small leaves. Snake-bark maple from Japan.
Acer davidii	David's maple	6	Compact maple with white-striped bark and unlobed leaves.
Acer davidii ssp. *grosseri*		6	Small snake-bark maple. Requires moist, semishaded position.
Acer griseum ◆	paper bark maple	5	Beautiful tree with peeling orange-brown bark. Good fall color.
Acer japonicum 'Aconitifolium'	cutleaf Japanese maple	6	Small tree with deeply dissected leaves. Brilliant red-orange fall color.
Acer shirasawanum 'Aureum'	full moon maple	6	Leaves remain golden green all summer. Can scorch in hot sun.
Acer palmatum var. *heptalobum*	Japanese maple	6	Outstanding orange to red fall color.
Acer palmatum 'Senkaki'	Japanese maple	6	Brilliant coral-barked maple. Very effective in winter.
Acer palmatum 'Shin Deshojo'	Japanese maple	6	Deep red spring foliage turns reddish green. Good fall color.
Acer pectinatum ssp. *forrestii*	Forrest's maple	7	Uncommon snake-bark maple with three-lobed leaves.
Acer rufinerve		6	Handsome snake-bark maple from Japan.

▷

BOTANICAL NAME	COMMON NAME	ZONE	NOTES ON CHARACTER
Acer spicatum	mountain maple	3	Hardy shrubby maple with good fall color.
Acer tataricum ssp. *ginnala*	Amur maple	3	Small maple bearing fragrant flowers in spring and red fall color. Very hardy.
Aesculus flava ◆	yellow buckeye	4	Bears erect panicles of yellow flowers in May and June.
Aesculus pavia 'Atrosanguinea' ◆	red buckeye	5	Darker red flowers distinguish this form of the red buckeye.
Aesculus turbinata ◆	Japanese horse chestnut	6	Stiffly branched tree with large five to seven-part leaves and resinous buds.
Albizia julibrissin ◆	silk tree	6	Low and wide-spreading tree with finely dissected leaves. Pretty pink flowers in summer. Requires good drainage and a warm, sunny location.
Alnus hirsuta var. *sibirica*	Manchurian alder	4	Multistemmed, spreading small tree with attractive leaves and persistent woody fruit.
Asimina triloba	pawpaw	5	Attractive foliage and curious flowers borne on the stems. Fruit edible.
Carpinus caroliniana	American hornbeam	3	Small bushy tree of slow growth. Fall color ranges from orange to scarlet.
Cercidiphyllum japonicum ◆	katsura tree	5	Attractive heart-shaped leaves. Good fall color. Good for moist sites.
Cercis canadensis	Canadian redbud	5	Bright green leaves and showy flowers. Flowering poor in cool coastal climates. 'Forest Pansy' has rounded leaves that remain red all summer and attractive rose-colored flowers in spring.
Cercis occidentalis ✽	western redbud	8	Rose pink flowers in April. Heart-shaped leaves. difficult to transplant.
Cercis siliquastrum ◆	Judas tree	6	Very showy flowering display before leaves emerge in spring. Rosy purple flowers. Best in sun.
Chilopsis linearis ✽	desert willow	8	Attractive pink flowers in spring. Tolerant of desert heat.
Chionanthus virginicus	fringe tree	4	Magnificent for its pure white fragrant flowers in pendent clusters that cover the tree in June.
Chitalpa tashkentensis ✽	mountain chitalpa	8	Hybrid between *Catalpa bignoniodes* and *Chilopsis linearis*. Medium-sized deciduous tree tolerant of light shade.
Cladrastis kentukea (*lutea*)	American yellowwood	3	Yellow flowers in June. Bright green foliage turns yellow in the fall.
Cornus alternifolia	Pagoda dogwood	3	Flat-topped small tree with alternate leaves. Attractive layered form. The variegated form is most beautiful.
Cornus controversa	Giant dogwood	6	Resembles *C. alternifolia* with tiered branching. The variegated form is popular.
Cornus 'Eddie's White Wonder'	white wonder dogwood	6	A cross between *C. nuttallii* and *C. florida*. Weeping branch tips and large white flower bracts.
Cornus florida	eastern flowering dogwood	6	Small understory tree. Attractive flowers from white to red. Susceptible to anthracnose leaf blight.

▷

ABOVE, L TO R: Redbud (*Cercis canadensis*), Giant dogwood (*Cornus controversa*), *Magnolia* × *soulangiana* 'Picture'

◁ *Trees for the Woodland*

BOTANICAL NAME	COMMON NAME	ZONE	NOTES ON CHARACTER
Cornus florida 'Rubra'	red eastern dogwood	6	Red-flowered form of the eastern dogwood. Can succumb to anthracnose if not controlled.
Cornus kousa ◆	Kousa dogwood	6	Outstanding tree with star-shaped white flower bracts in June followed by red fruits. Disease free. Variety *chinensis* is a more vigorous and larger-flowered form.
Cornus mas ◆	Cornelian cherry	4	Very effective in early spring for its yellow flowers. Red cherrylike fruit is edible.
Cornus nuttallii	Pacific dogwood	7	Largest bracts of any dogwood. Flowers in midspring. Susceptible to anthracnose leaf blight.
Corylus colurna	Turkish hazel	4	Pyramidal tree bearing edible nuts enclosed in a leafy husk.
Crataegus crus-galli ❂ ◆	cockspur thorn	4	Flat-topped small tree with glossy leaves and white flowers in June. Fruit and fall color are red.
Crataegus laevigata ◆	English hawthorn	5	Rugged adaptable tree. Picturesque form when older.
Crataegus monogyna ◆	May tree	5	Smallish tree for sunny location. White flowers in May.
Crataegus × *lavallei* ◆	Lavalle hawthorn	6	Compact medium-sized tree. Showy red fruit. Dark glossy leaves.
Crataegus × *mordenensis* 'Toba' ◆	Toba hawthorn	5	Hardy tree with interesting horizontal branching. White flowers aging pink in late spring.
Crataegus pinnatifida ◆	hawthorn	6	Large-leaved hawthorn with white flowers in late May.
Davidia involucrata ◆	dove tree	6	Lovely rough-barked tree bearing enormous white bracts in May. Heart-shaped leaves and shaggy, tan-colored bark make this an effective tree at all seasons.

▷

BOTANICAL NAME	COMMON NAME	ZONE	NOTES ON CHARACTER
Elaeagnus angustifolia ✿ ✳	Russian olive	2	Very hardy tree with striking narrow silvery foliage and highly fragrant but inconspicuous flowers.
Tetradium daniellii	Euodia	5	Attractive wide-spreading pinnate-leaved tree.
Fraxinus ornus ◆	manna ash	5	Handsome tree with luxuriant foliage. Showy large panicles of white flowers are held above the foliage.
Glyptostrobus pensilis	Chinese swamp cypress	8	Deciduous conifer from China related to the swamp cypress. Needles turn reddish before falling.
Halesia carolina	snowdrop tree	5	Bears lovely pendulous snowdroplike flowers in spring. Fast-growing. *H. monticola* is similar but grows larger, with bigger flowers and fruits.
Idesia polycarpa ✿	Iigiri tree	8	Interesting tree with red-stalked, catalpa-like leaves. Fragrant yellow flowers followed by showy red fruit on female plants.
Koelreuteria paniculata ◆	goldenrain tree	6	Superb small tree. Rugged form. Showy yellow flowers followed by attractive inflated fruit.
Laburnum anagyroides ✳ ◆	common laburnum	5	Yellow, drooping flower clusters. Good for dry, sunny locations.
Laburnum × watereri 'Vossi' ◆	golden chain tree	5	Showiest of the laburnums. Good drainage essential.
Magnolia campbellii		8	A magnificent species from the Himalayas forming a large tree. Sensitive to early spring frosts.
Magnolia cylindrica		6	A small tree with flowers quite similar to those of *M. denudata*
Magnolia fraseri	Fraser magnolia	5	Large leaves are carried at the ends of the branches. Large flowers in May or June.
Magnolia denudata ◆	Yulan magnolia	5	Conspicuous flower buds open from March to May make this a very showy tree. Susceptible to late frosts.
Magnolia kobus ◆	Kobus magnolia	5	Round-headed medium-sized tree covered with white blossoms in late spring.
Magnolia kobus var. *borealis* ◆	northern Kobus magnolia	4	A more robust form of *M. kobus* that is slow to flower when young.
Magnolia liliiflora	lily magnolia	6	A large bush or small tree flowering after the leaves develop. Many named forms available.
Magnolia liliiflora 'Nigra'	purple lily magnolia	6	Remarkable for its large, very dark purple flowers borne in late May.
Magnolia salicifolia	anise magnolia	6	This species blooms on naked stems in April. The bark emits a pleasant scent if bruised.
Magnolia sieboldii ✿	Oyama magnolia	7	The fragrant flowers hang on long stalks. Multistemmed.
Magnolia sinensis ◆	Chinese magnolia	7	White, fragrant flowers develop on stalks in June. Will grow in alkaline soil.

▷

BOTANICAL NAME	COMMON NAME	ZONE	NOTES ON CHARACTER
Magnolia wilsonii ◆	Wilson magnolia	7	The white flowers with a ring of red stamens are borne on pendent stalks in May. Multistemmed.
Magnolia × soulangiana	saucer magnolia	5	This single or multistemmed tree flowers in April and May. Many named forms available.
Malus baccata ◆	Siberian crab	5	Hardy small tree for sunny location. White flowers and yellow or red fruit.
Malus ionensis ◆	prairie crabapple	5	Crabapple trees affected by fungal diseases in high rainfall areas.
Nyssa sinensis	Chinese tupelo	7	Upright tree with good red or yellow fall color.
Nyssa sylvatica	black tupelo	5	Good for poorly drained sites. Intense red autumn tints.
Ostrya virginiana	ironwood	4	Attractive leaves and pendent hoplike fruits in the fall. Low branching. Shade tolerant.
Parrotia persica	Persian parrotia	7	Wide-spreading, low-branched tree with flaking bark and good autumn color.
Populus tremuloides ✱	quaking aspen	2	Good for prairie regions. Leaves flutter in the wind and turn golden yellow in fall. Fast growing.
Populus wilsonii	Wilson's poplar	5	An Asiatic poplar with stout branches and firm leaves with red midrib and stalk. Fast growing.
Prunus avium ◆	gean	5	The double-flowered cultivar 'flore Plena' is showier in bloom.
Prunus × blireana ◆	plum	5	Compact small tree. Pretty, double pink flowers.
Prunus mume ❀	Japanese apricot	6	A small tree bearing multitudes of lovely pale to dark rose fragrant blossoms in late spring. Best in a sheltered place.
Prunus padus 'Watereri' ◆	bird cherry	5	Spreading tree with showy racemes of white flowers in spring.
Prunus sargentii ◆	Sargent cherry	5	Splendid tree for beauty of blossom in April and scarlet autumn tints.
Prunus serrula ◆	birch bark cherry	5	Shining, coppery brown, peeling bark is very notable, especially in winter. Not showy in flower.
Pyrus calleryana ◆	Callery pear	6	For sunny, warm location. White flowers; good autumn color.
Quercus acutissima	sawtooth oak	6	A medium-sized oak suitable for smaller spaces. Native to China and Japan.
Quercus garryana	Garry oak	7	Open crown and deep roots make an ideal shelter for woodland plants that are tolerant of dry conditions.
Rhamnus purshiana	cascara	6	Small tree with smooth grayish bark and prominently veined leaves. Bark has medicinal value.
Robinia pseudoacacia 'Frisia' ◆	golden false acacia	4	Outstanding form with golden yellow leaves throughout the summer. Good for dry sites.
Robinia × ambigua 'Idahoensis' ◆	Idaho locust	3	Fast growth and magenta-rose flowers in spring. Good tree for the Great Basin region.

▷

ABOVE, L TO R: Golden ash (*Fraxinus excelsior* 'Jaspidea'), Birchbark cherry (*Prunus serrula*), Chinese tupelo (*Nyssa sinensis*)

RIGHT: Chinese mountain ash (*Sorbus hupehensis*) produces abundant crops of attractive berries.

◁ *Trees for the Woodland*

BOTANICAL NAME	COMMON NAME	ZONE	NOTES ON CHARACTER
Sorbus alnifolia ◆	Korean mountain ash	5	Compact tree with alderlike leaves and gray bark. White flowers and orange-scarlet fall color.
Sorbus aria ◆	whitebeam	5	Its entire leaves are coated beneath with a white felt. White flowers and red fruits in fall.
Sorbus aucuparia ◆	mountain ash	3	Feathery foliage, white flowers, and showy red fruit are its attributes. Easily grown.
Sorbus aucuparia 'Edulis' ◆	Moravian mountain ash	3	Upright form with larger fruit suitable for making jam and jelly.
Sorbus cashmiriana ◆	Kashmir mountain ash	6	Bears large pink-tinted flowers in May, followed by white fruit that persists on the tree all winter.
Sorbus commixta ◆	Korean mountain ash	6	Lustrous red fruit and good fall color distinguish this mountain ash from Japan and Korea.
Sorbus 'Joseph Rock' ◆	Rock's mountain ash	6	Small tree with pretty flowers and primrose yellow fruits. Crimson, purple and scarlet autumn color.
Sorbus folgneri 'Lemon Drop' ◆		6	Leaves are covered beneath with a silvery felt. Fruit yellow and semipendulous.
Sorbus hupehensis ◆	Chinese mountain ash	6	Sea green foliage turns crimson red in autumn. Showy white or crimson-pink fruit.
Sorbus sargentiana ◆	Sargent mountain ash	6	Stiff-branched tree with large leaflets and orange-scarlet fruit. Good fall color.
Sorbus vilmorinii ◆	Vilmorin mountain ash	5	Elegant, spreading tree with fine pinnate foliage and dense clusters of pink fruit.

▷

BOTANICAL NAME	COMMON NAME	ZONE	NOTES ON CHARACTER
Stewartia pseudocamellia	Japanese *stewartia*	7	Tree of great beauty for its flaking bark, white camellia-like blossoms in summer, and red fall color.
Styrax japonicum ✳	Japanese snowbell	5	Graceful small tree laden with pendulous pure white blossoms in June.
Styrax obassia ❀	Fragrant snowbell	6	Beautiful for its hanging white fragrant flowers. Best viewed against a dark background.
Tamarix chinensis ✳	salt cedar	7	Attractive flowers. Looks best when cut back regularly. For sunny location. Unequalled for resistance to wind and saline soils. Should be planted with caution in Southwest, where it has become an aggressive weed.
Tetracentron sinense		7	Handsome, rare tree bearing slender catkins of yellowish flowers in summer.
Ulmus pumila ◆	Siberian elm	2	Valuable in prairie regions for its hardiness and drought tolerance. Resistant to Dutch elm disease.

Small to Medium-sized Trees: Broad-leaved Evergreen

BOTANICAL NAME	COMMON NAME	ZONE	NOTES ON CHARACTER
Arbutus menziesii ✳	Pacific madrone	7	Peeling bark reveals smooth, red branches. Drought resistant. Best planted young and not disturbed.
Cercocarpus montanus var. *glaber* ✳	mountain ironwood	9	Interesting texture. Small leaves. Good on warm southern slopes.
Cordyline australis ❀	cabbage tree	9	Tropical-looking multistemmed tree with graceful, arching, long lance-shaped leaves. Terminal panicles of fragrant white flowers.
Eucalyptus pauciflora ssp. *niphophila*	snow gum	8	The hardiest eucalypt. Peeling bark, red young stems, and glaucous blue leaves are most attractive.
Ilex × *altaclerensis* 'Camelliifolia'	Highclere holly	7	Pyramidal tree with glossy evergreen leaves and red berries in winter.
Ligustrum lucidum ❀	Chinese glossy privet	7	Small evergreen tree for a woodland clearing. White panicles of fragrant flowers are borne in autumn.
Lithocarpus densiflorus	tanbark oak	7	Oak-like tree, pyramidal in youth, later spreading. Bark rich in tannin.
Magnolia delavayi ❀ ◆	Delavay's magnolia	9	Bold gray-green leaves and fragrant flowers in summer distinguish this tree. *Magnolia grandiflora* is a better choice for colder areas.
Maytenus boaria	mayten tree	8	Graceful small tree with narrow evergreen leaves held on pendent branches.
Olea europea ✳	olive	9	The true olive grown for its fruit. Tough, adaptible tree with dense crown of gray-green leaves.
Olneya tesota ✳	desert ironwood	9	Beautiful slow-growing tree with pinkish lavender flowers. Can take desert heat.

▷

BOTANICAL NAME	COMMON NAME	ZONE	NOTES ON CHARACTER
Parkinsonia florida ✷	blue palo verde	9	Fast-growing desert tree smothered in yellow flowers in spring. Small blue-green leaves are shed early, revealing intricate branching habit.
Prunus lusitanica ✿ ◆	Portugal laurel	7	Hardy, small spreading evergreen tree with attractive and fragrant white flower spikes in late spring.
Quercus acuta	Japanese evergreen oak	7	Bright green leaves with a tapering point are handsome. Grows faster in southern gardens. *Q. myrsinifolia* is similar.
Quercus chrysolepis ✷	canyon live oak	7	Slow-growing, round-headed tree with whitish bark. Noble tree good for dry-summer areas.
Quercus glauca	ring-cupped oak	8	A handsome bushy tree with glaucous, green-backed, prominently veined leaves.
Schinus molle ✷ ◆	peppertree	9	Elegant fine-textured tree with weeping branches. Extremely tolerant of pollution and neglect.
Trachycarpus fortunei ◆	windmill palm	8	Among the hardiest of palms. Bold fan-shaped leaves and coarse fiber-clad trunk. Exotic looking.
Umbellularia californica ✷	California bay	7	The aromatic foliage of this American relative of the bay laurel (*Laurus nobilis*) is used as a spice. Prefers moist soil but withstands drought. Thrives in sun or shade.

Small to Medium-sized Trees: Coniferous Evergreen

BOTANICAL NAME	COMMON NAME	ZONE	NOTES ON CHARACTER
Cunninghamia lanceolata	China fir	8	Medium-sized conifer with large, glossy, green awl-shaped needles. Requires shelter.
Cunninghamia lanceolata 'Glauca'	blue China fir	7	Very effective glaucous blue form of the China fir. Hardier than the species.
Cupressus arizonica ✷	Arizona cypress	8	Columnar conifer of medium size. Dwarf cultivars available.
Cupressus himalaica v. *darjeelingensis*	Kashmir cypress	9	Among the most beautiful of conifers. Graceful pendulous branches of blue-gray foliage. Regrettably tender.
Cupressus duclouxiana	Yunnan cypress	7	Tree of conical habit with reddish bark and elegant habit. Rare.
Juniperus scopulorum ✷ ◆	Rocky Mountain juniper	4	Round-topped at maturity with reddish brown bark. Very good for dry, sunny sites.
Juniperus scopulorum 'Tolleson's Weeping' ◆		4	Beautiful weeping form of the Rocky Mountain juniper. Grey-green foliage. Most striking.
Picea jezoensis var. *hondoensis*	Hondo spruce	4	Symmetrical Japanese spruce. Purplish red young cones contrast nicely with foliage.
Picea mariana 'Aurea'	golden black spruce	3	Graceful variant of the black spruce with golden yellow needles.
Pinus aristata ✷	bristlecone pine	4	Small tree well adapted to cold, dry conditions.
Pinus bungeana	lacebark pine	4	Low-branching tree from China. Flaking bark exposes the creamy-colored inner bark. Slow growing.

▷

BOTANICAL NAME	COMMON NAME	ZONE	NOTES ON CHARACTER
Pinus densiflora 'Oculus-draconis'	dragon eye pine	4	Yellow spots give each whorl of needles the appearance of two yellow rings on green background.
Pinus densiflora 'Umbraculifera'	umbrella pine	4	Multistemmed tree forming a flat-topped umbrella shape. Very attractive.
Platycladus orientalis ◆	oriental arborvitae	5	Rangy but interesting form when older.
Saxegothaea conspicua	Prince Albert yew	7	Unusual bushy conifer from Chile with peeling bark and small leaves. Slow growing.
Sciadopitys verticillata	Japanese umbrella pine	5	Elegant plant with thick fleshy needles clustered at branch ends like the spokes of an umbrella.
Taxus baccata 'Dovastoniana' ◆	Westfelton yew	7	Long-lived, slow-growing small trees. Wide-spreading becoming broader than high. Poisonous seeds and leaves.
Taxus cuspidata	Japanese yew	4	A more erect replacement for the English yew for colder climates. Reddish bark.
Tsuga diversifolia	Japanese mountain hemlock	5	Slow-growing, shade-tolerant conifer. Young shoots bright yellow-green.
Tsuga mertensiana	mountain hemlock	6	A beautiful compact-growing hemlock with a narrow pyramidal crown. Not for dry areas.
Tsuga sieboldii	southern Japanese hemlock	5	Slow-growing tree with drooping branches. Rare.

The Understory

*I*F THE CANOPY is the architecture that frames the landscape space, the shrubs that form the understory define and decorate that space. The openings between shrubs can be described as landscape rooms, the floor of which is the woodland carpet of low-growing plants.

As the dominant landscape feature, a shrub layer of broad-leaved evergreens, such as rhododendrons and camellias, is particularly powerful. For this reason this chapter focuses on rhododendrons and provides a separate plant listing for this genus at the end of the chapter. This is not to suggest that these plants are indispensable and that gardens would be less beautiful without them. In areas where climate or soil conditions make it difficult or impossible to grow them, viburnums are one alternative. There are even a few evergreen kinds.

In selecting the shrubs that compose the understory of the woodland garden, the amount of shade determines the main groups of plants. Shrubs requiring much sunshine, such as lilacs and most rose species, will not thrive in shade, but may succeed in the dappled light of open woodland. With some notable exceptions, such as rhododendrons, the best woodland shrubs are less flamboyant than sun-loving plants. But the adaptations to shade focus the eye on shape and form, rather than flower. One of the most obvious woodland adaptations is broad leaves that are held horizontally on an open, spreading habit of growth. This secures the maximum amount of light available under the canopy. Witch hazel (*Hamamelis virginiana*) and *Enkianthus campanulatus* are good examples. The airy, layered effect has an elegant quality, in contrast to the shapeless habit of many commonly grown flowering shrubs.

Evergreen plants are at an advantage in the woodland because they can use light over a much longer period of the year. The lustrous foliage and flowers of evergreen plants last longer under the protection of the canopy. Because of this, evergreen plants may have a competitive advantage over deciduous plants in the southern parts of the continent. In the north, broad-leaved evergreens

PRECEDING PAGE: *Skimmia japonica*, an evergreen shrub bears flowers and fruit at the same time.

may be limited by severe winters, except for small leathery-leaved shrubs such as false daphne (*Chamaedaphne calyculata*) and bog laurel (*Kalmia polifolia*).

Gardeners in milder areas have a wide selection of exotic evergreens to choose from. Camellias, for example, came from the forests of southwest China. These species and their hybrids have graced woodland gardens for over a century. The hardier hybrids of *Camellia japonica* are popular in southern gardens, being well adapted to warm, humid summers and cool winters. Zone 7 is the limit of their hardiness, but this extends to the 49th parallel at Vancouver, British Columbia, and much farther north along the coast. The best camellias for woodland gardens are C. *sasanqua*, C. *saluenensis* and C. *reticulata*, but these species are not as hardy as C. *japonica*. Fortunately, hardier hybrids exist between C. *saluenensis* and C. *japonica*. Of these hybrids, C. × *williamsii* 'Donation' is one of the best for Zone 8.

The silk tassel bush (*Garrya elliptica*) is an excellent plant for the woodland garden. A native of California, it can reasonably be expected to thrive where soil conditions are well drained, even dry, but where the climate is mild and fairly humid. The silk tassel bush is an attractive evergreen and bears its catkin flowers during the winter. These characteristics make it one of the more conspicuous woodland plants wherever it can be grown. Also winter-blooming are the Asian mahonias, such as *Mahonia lomariifolia* and *M. japonica*, and their hybrids 'Arthur Menzies' and 'Charity', which produce spectacular racemes of yellow flowers. Their bold, pinnate, evergreen foliage adds an exotic touch throughout the year.

Rhododendrons

Wherever rhododendrons can be grown, they are an important part of the woodland garden. Ranging from gigantic tree species to creeping, fine-textured plants, there is a kind for every niche in the landscape. For reasons of convenience, the big group of rhododendrons known as azaleas are often treated separately by growers. Although they are distinct in having fewer stamens in the flower than the other species of rhododendron, there is no botanical reason to retain the use of the old generic term. The cultivation of rhododendrons engenders such fierce loyalty among amateur and professional gardeners alike that there is a danger of overusing them to the exclusion of many other worthy woodland plants. A woodland crowded with rhododendrons is a spectacular sight during the season of their bloom, but at other times of the year the effect may be somewhat heavy and ponderous unless other plants of lighter texture are freely intermingled with

Massed deciduous azaleas in a north-facing, yet sunny border.

them. Examples are deciduous species of *Acer*, *Cornus*, *Enkianthus*, *Sorbus* and *Vaccinium*, and airy evergreens like *Azara* or *Trochodendron*. This is particularly true of the vast number of rhododendron hybrids, which tend to have a certain monotonous texture of foliage and an opulent display of bloom that may defeat the sense of naturalism so carefully cultivated beneath the woodland canopy.

Rhododendron species are more exacting in their cultural needs than the hybrids and often less spectacular in their floral display. But the diversity of their plant form, leaf shape, indumentum (leaf covering) and color is a never-ending source of wonder to gardeners who look a little beyond the showy display of the hybrids. Hybridizing nearly always dilutes the special character of species, a distinction that has resulted from countless generations of natural selection.

Until relatively recently, only a handful of species were available from nurseries, and these were often random, rather nondescript seedlings. It is now possible to obtain some of the finest forms of the species from specialist growers who have sought them out from their natural habitat and established collections in older gardens. The American Rhododendron Species Foundation in Federal Way, Washington, has also played a major role in encouraging the cultivation of the best species forms.

Owning a collection of fine rhododendron species is akin to owning a collection of fine art. Each specimen may be unique and worthy of conservation, like a rare artifact. The protected environment of a woodland garden is an ideal setting for a species collection. These plants are better displayed individually than as part of a massed display. The small-leaved lepidote (scaly-leaved) species are an exception and are effective massed in drifts. Most of these are dwarf or semi-dwarf and are invaluable for the front of plantings.

Large plants, such as *R. maximum*, *R. fortunei*, *R. rex* ssp. *fictolacteum* or the statuesque *R. calophytum*, need plenty of room — perhaps 20 feet (6 m) between them. However, immature plants can be planted closer together than this, with a view to thinning them out by transplanting after a few years have passed. Like some of the large Asian magnolias, these patricians of the rhododendron clan are slow to mature and flower. Make sure the young plants are propagated from superior horticultural forms or known wild sources. The initial cost is slightly higher than average, but the alternative is the possibility of great disappointment after waiting for many years for a plant to flower, only to find it is an inferior form. This principle applies not only to rhododendrons, but to all garden plants that may take some years to show their merit or lack of it.

The conditions under which rhododendrons are found growing naturally offer the best guide to their successful cultivation. The climate is not one of extremes, either summer heat or winter cold. The rainfall usually exceeds 30 inches (762 mm) and is reasonably well distributed throughout the year. For cultivated plants this will usually be supplemented with irrigation during the critical period from May to July, when new growth is made and flower buds are formed.

The soil should be acid (pH below 7) and organic rather than mineral, although well-drained sandy soil is suitable if amended with organic matter. The forested areas of the Northeast, Southeast, and Northwest contain the best habitats for rhododendrons in America. Local microenvironments exist in other areas where the right combination of conditions is found. The ideal place is a wooded, sloping site, oriented in such a way that the rhododendrons are protected from desiccating winds and summer heat.

Maintain mulch over the soil all year round. In summer, this will conserve moisture and maintain an even soil temperature, which is a characteristic of the natural forest. In winter, the mulch can be thicker, as this delays or prevents the frost penetration. The best mulch is decayed leaves — the leaf mold used by generations of gardeners. Leaf mold is prepared by stacking leaves for a year or more, turning the pile over occasionally, and adding some nitrogen fertilizer to accelerate their decay. When the partially decayed leaves are used as a mulch, there may be no need to use additional chemical fertilizers, as leaf mold releases nutrients gradually as it continues to decay. Other kinds of mulches may use up some of the nutrients in the soil. There are specially formulated fertilizers blended for rhododendrons, and these may be used where the growth is slow or when nutrient deficiencies occur.

In the Pacific Northwest, heavy winter rains may leach out nitrogen and other nutrients, with the result that in spring, plants look a little anemic. Small, carefully placed applications of special rhododendron fertilizer will correct these symptoms. Well-nourished rhododendrons will seldom be seriously affected by pests or diseases.

Success with rhododendrons depends to a large extent on choosing the hardiest, best-adapted species. A study of the kinds that succeed naturally in each locality will pay dividends. In Pennsylvania and adjacent states, the native R. *maximum* is a hardy, beautiful woodland plant that blooms later than most of the species and hybrids. In the Pacific Northwest, the native R. *macrophyllum* occupies diverse habitats ranging from bog and dense woodland to open hillsides. Yet this lovely species is seldom planted in gardens. The same may be said of the native azalea, *R. occidentale*. Gardeners are too often influenced by the easy availability of common exotic species and hybrids. We recommend that the natives be used more extensively. How else will the visitor from other places or other lands savor the particular botanical riches of the region?

In the eastern states, native species have been used extensively by modern American hybridizers. Much of this work has centered upon wild forms of the catawba rhododendron (*R. catawbiense*) and its white variety, *album*. This was necessary because of the need for winter-hardy hybrids. On the West Coast, where hardiness is less important, rhododendron breeding has largely been an extension of the work begun by British and European hybridizers. Some of the new hybrids are notable for their great size and bloom; others for intense colors that are an improvement on the old hybrids.

The great variation in size and shape of rhododendrons makes it possible to arrange them in interesting landscaping groups. Large plants form the center of these groupings with smaller, finer-textured plants beneath and around them. In the colder areas, there are very few species that attain the proportions of trees. *Rhododendron maximum*, under favorable conditions, might qualify. *Rhododendron fortunei*, a hardy species from eastern China, may also reach a large size in cultivation. In mild climatic areas, there are more choices; *R. calophytum*, hardy to Zone 7, is a favorite. Many large-leaved species are capable of reaching majestic proportions in milder areas. These species are successful where there is little frost penetration of the soil in winter and protection from desiccating or strong winds. Large-leaved rhododendrons require more moisture than other species because they are natives of the protected valleys where monsoon conditions affect the season of growth. Frequent overhead irrigation is recommended, particularly when new growth is appearing. In addition to *R. calophytum*, other hardy members of this group include *R. rex* ssp. *rex* and *R. rex* ssp. *fictolacteum*, but in North America, even these are limited to the very mildest areas. In the Northeastern states and the Great Lakes region, the old catawbiense hybrids remain the mainstay for general garden planting, but in the woodland, the native species should always be given a place. *Rhododendron catawbiense*, *R. maximum*, *R. minus*, and *R. minus* var. *chapmanii* are evergreen. Among the deciduous azaleas, *R. calendulaceum*, *R. canescens*, *R. periclymenoides*, *R. viscosum* and *R. vaseyi* lead the way. Many other native and exotic species may be appropriate; experiment to determine which species are best adapted to local conditions.

In the woodland, the filtered light has a special quality that brings out the subtlety of form and color of many rhododendrons. Muted yellows, creams and white, with only the occasional emphasis of a strong red, are very effective. Blues, lavenders and purples are particularly outstanding in the shade, adding depth and the illusion of distance to the garden. Outstanding is *Rhododendron augustinii*, a large, small-leaved shrub with beautiful blue-lavender flowers in April and May. The best form of this is 'Electra', with violet-blue flowers. In this color range, and hardier, are cultivars such as 'Lee's Dark Purple', 'Boursault' and 'Everestianum'. The cultivars of *Rhododendron ponticum*, which include 'Purple Splendor', 'Blue Peter', and 'Blue Ensign', are less hardy. One of the finest is 'Arthur Bedford', which has large lavender flowers with a deeper blotch. It is a fine foliage plant, fast growing and capable of reaching the dimensions of a small tree.

The group of species related to *Rhododendron ponticum* are hardy, resilient, and occupy a special place in North American gardens. The native members of this group — *R. catawbiense*, *R. maximum* and their cultivars — are the mainstay in colder gardens. *Rhododendron caucasicum* is a rare species, seldom seen in gardens, but it has yielded some fine hybrids. In sheltered locations, these have the surprising habit of opening some of their flowers in midwinter. Two such hybrids are 'Christmas Cheer' and 'Rosa Mundi'.

Rhododendron smirnowii is another member of the Ponticum group. A very hardy species from the Caucasus Mountains, it most closely resembles such Asian species as *R. yakushimanum* and its subspecies *makinoi*. This and other species allied to *R. yakushimanum* are fine foliage plants with thick, felty indumentum under the leaves. They are quite sun tolerant, except where hot summers prevail, and generally belong in the open clearings of the woodland. The *Taliensia* subsection of rhododendrons, which are mostly found in southwestern China, possess a similar quality of foliage. They are less hardy than the foregoing species and best suited to the mild climate of the Pacific Northwest. *Rhododendron wiltoni* is a leading representative of this group.

Nearly all the Asian lepidote (scaly-leaved) rhododendrons with their small leaves require shade when grown in American gardens. This fact sometimes surprises gardeners who are aware of the exposed montane habitat of many dwarf species. It should be remembered that summer temperatures at subalpine altitudes are relatively low and that there is usually abundant moisture beneath the soil surface. The opposite of these conditions may prevail in many American gardens, even in the Pacific Northwest. A soil-cooling mulch of decayed leaves is essential. The most

Rhododendron × 'Fraseri', a hybrid of *R. canadense*.

commonly grown lepidote species is *R. impeditum*. It is easy to propagate and grows quickly under nursery conditions. Unfortunately, it seems to lack durability in the open landscape — the brittle stems often die back, spoiling the neat, compact form. *Rhododendron fastigiatum* is another dwarf lepidote species, more flexible in stem growth as well as in garden adaptability. The best forms have flowers of a pleasing true blue. Most of the dwarf lepidote group have an engaging habit of producing a second season of bloom in the autumn. Their predominant flower color is blue-purple, but a few species have flowers of an attractive purplish plum color. *Rhododendron saluenense*, *R. campylogynum* and *R. calostrotum* belong in this category. These are montane plants of the Sino-Himalaya and succeed best in the moist climate of the Pacific Northwest, although even there they must have supplemental summer watering.

As a group, the lepidote rhododendrons have an enormous geographical range. With such a large genetic pool, there is scope for experimentation by selecting hardier plants from large batches of seedlings. Propagation by seed is easy, and extensive drifts of small plants can be planted to give a mass effect. Superior clones are readily grown from summer cuttings.

Where winters are mild and the humidity is high, evergreen azaleas can be planted in large intermingling drifts. There is a bewildering array of varieties in the Kurume clan. Most have a similar fine texture, and there is a danger of monotony unless the height and plant habit is alternated in small groups of plants. There are some delightful dwarf cultivars, such as *Rhododendron indicum* 'Balsaminiflora', and some with fine-textured leaves, such as *R. kiusianum*. These are good plants for placing near the woodland path where they may be seen at close range. Some of the American native azaleas that bloom quite late, such as *R. prunifolium*, are useful to help extend the season of floral interest.

Hydrangeas

A rhododendron planting is apt to be dull after midsummer unless it is interplanted with other shrubs. Hydrangeas fill the gap admirably. These are plants for semishade, enjoying the same conditions as rhododendrons. The Asian species are temperate plants that do not tolerate extremes of temperature. The cool-summer areas of Zone 8 suit them best, but microclimates may exist in colder areas where they should be tried. To many, *Hydrangea* means the large mopheaded style of bloom, so familiar in gardens and as a florist's potted plant, and at one time affectionately known as hortensias by an older generation of gardeners.

The popular mopheads and lacecaps of gardens, in an almost infinite range of horticultural varieties, are all derived from essentially one Asian species, *Hydrangea macrophylla* — meaning large-leaved. An idea of what the original species looked like can be had by looking at the variety *normalis*, a lacecap type. The mopheads were a development from this type of plant. Some of the more interesting cultivated varieties are named in honor of people, such as 'Marechal Foch' and 'General Vicomtesse de Vibraye'. The color of the flowers of most hydrangea cultivars varies according to the pH of the soil. In acid soils they tend to be blue, but on alkaline soils, or if they are limed, will be pink. The blue color is caused by the uptake of aluminum from the soil; when the soil is alkaline, the aluminum cannot be assimilated by the plant and the flowers will be pink. Iron sulphate can be used to increase the intensity of blue coloring.

The flower heads, if harvested before the colors fade, make attractive dried specimens. The lacecaps are closest to the wild type, with fertile flowers on the inside of the head surrounded by a ring of sterile flowers. There are several beautiful cultivars, including 'Blue Wave', 'White Wave' and 'Mariesii'.

Hydrangea serrata resembles *H. macrophylla* but is smaller and less coarse. It is reported to be hardier and more drought resistant than other species. With water restrictions likely to become a fact almost everywhere, these are valuable qualities. 'Bluebird' is a favorite lacecap cultivar derived from this species.

Hydrangeas are not generally distinguished for the quality of their foliage, but *H. aspera*, first collected from Nepal, is worth growing for this quality alone. *H. villosa* is closely related, and is thought of by plant connoisseurs to be the doyen of the genus. Both specific names refer to the felty feel and look of the leaves and stems. They are big plants and when sited in partly shaded locations are more resistant to drought. *Hydrangea aspera* is said to be tolerant of alkaline soil. The flowers of both species are an exquisite clear blue, sometimes pink.

The American oak-leaved hydrangea (*H. quercifolia*) is a medium-sized, sprawling shrub with white flowers. Its attractive oaklike leaves turn red in the autumn. Another American species, *H. arborescens*, produces large billowing masses of white bloom that lend a pleasant cooling effect on warm summer days. The common name, hills of snow, fits well. These are hardy to Zone 5. See Chapter 6 for details on the climbing species *H. anomala* and *H. petiolaris*.

Shrubs for the Woodland

❀ = scented flowers   ✳ = suitable for dry places   ◆ = suitable for alkaline soils
PLANT HEIGHT CODE (HT):   s = small (under 3 ft [1 m])   m = medium (3–9 ft [1–3 m])   t = tall (more than 9 ft [3 m])

BOTANICAL NAME	COMMON NAME	HT	ZONE	NOTES ON CHARACTER

Coniferous Shrubs

BOTANICAL NAME	COMMON NAME	HT	ZONE	NOTES ON CHARACTER
Athrotaxis laxifolia	Summit cedar	m	8	Fine-textured foliage and elegant branching habit.
Cephalotaxus harringtonia var. *drupacea*	Japanese plum yew	m	6	Upright plant with elegant drooping branching habit.
Cryptomeria japonica	Japanese cedar	m	6	Many dwarf cultivars available combining compact growth with elegant habit. Pest free.
Juniperus chinensis ✳ ◆	Chinese juniper	s	6	Suitable ground cover for dry sunny location.
Juniperus deppeana ✳ ◆	alligator juniper	t	9	Blue-gray needles. Excellent for hot dry climates. Attractive checked bark looks like alligator hide.
Juniperus horizontalis ✳ ◆	horizontal juniper	s	3	Ground cover for dry, open woodland. Very hardy.
Juniperus × media 'Pfitzeriana' ✳ ◆	Pfitzer juniper	s	5	Vigorous hybrid juniper good for covering sunny banks. Golden forms available.
Juniperus sabina ✳ ◆	Savin juniper	s	3	Vivid green color. Hardy and dependable for cold areas. Needs sun.
Juniperus squamata ✳ ◆	singleseed juniper	s	6	Needs well-drained soil and sunny location. Good selected forms available.
Microbiota decussata	Russian cypress	s	3	Good ground cover and tolerant of shade. Foliage turns bronzy in cold weather.
Picea mariana 'Nana'	dwarf black spruce	s	3	Dwarf cultivars suitable as accent plants for sunny locations in cooler climates.
Picea orientalis 'Gracilis'	dwarf oriental spruce	m	5	One of the best spruces for Zone 7 and warmer gardens.
Pinus strobus 'Nana'	dwarf white pine	m	3	Dense foliage. Will grow large in time. Susceptible to blister rust.
Platycladus orientalis	oriental arborvitae	m	5	Hardy and resilient shrub. Cypress-like foliage. Prefers sun.
Podocarpus alpinus	Tasmanian podocarp	s	7	Fine-textured foliage resembles that of *Taxus*. Attractive red fruit. Best in sunny location.
Podocarpus macrophyllus	Buddhist pine	m	8	Broad-leaved conifer suitable for warmer areas. Sun or shade. Upright habit, with dark green foliage.
Saxegothaea conspicua	Prince Albert's yew	m	7	Shade tolerant and slow growing. Resembles *Taxus*.
Sequoia sempervirens 'Adpressa'	dwarf redwood	s	6	Prostrate form, tolerant of shade. Prune to maintain dwarf character.
Taxus baccata 'Repandens'	dwarf English yew	m	6	Excellent prostrate yew suitable as a ground cover for sun or dense shade.
Taxus baccata 'Dovastoniana'	Westfelton yew	t	6	Wide-spreading, large shrub with horizontal branches and graceful weeping branchlets. 'Dovastoniana Aurea' has gold-edged leaves.
Taxus cuspidata ◆	Japanese yew	m	5	Similar to *T. baccata*, but hardier.
Taxus × media ◆	hybrid yew	m	5	Many forms available. Hardy. Useful for screening at the woodland edge.

▷

ABOVE, L TO R: *Abeliophyllum distichum*, Red buckeye (*Aesculus pavia*)

◁ *Shrubs for the Woodland*

BOTANICAL NAME	COMMON NAME	HT	ZONE	NOTES ON CHARACTER
Thuja plicata 'Filiformis'	threadleaf red cedar	m	6	Tough, shade-tolerant cultivar. Drought resistant.
Thujopsis dolobrata	Hiba arbovitae	m	6	Shade-tolerant shrub with bold, scaly foliage. Eventually attains a large size.
Torreya grandis	Chinese nutmeg-yew	m	8	Rare plant with spine-tipped needles and attractive texture. Shade tolerant.
Taxus canadensis	Canada yew	s	4	Low spreading shrub.
Taxus brevifolia	Pacific yew	m	6	Slow-growing large shrub or small tree with dark green foliage and attractive reddish peeling bark.

Deciduous Shrubs

BOTANICAL NAME	COMMON NAME	HT	ZONE	NOTES ON CHARACTER
Abelia × *grandiflora* ◆	hybrid abelia	m	6	Fine-textured shrub with pink flowers over a long season.
Abelia schumannii		s	6	Floriferous shrub with long flowering season. Flowers lilac-pink.
Abeliophyllum distichum ✿	white forsythia	s	5	Fragrant white flowers during February. The cultivar 'Roseum' is a fine, pink-flowered form.
Abutilon vitifolium ◆	flowering maple	m	9	Mauve, mallow-like flowers carried in profusion May–July. Leaves grayish-green, maple-shaped. Needs sun.
Acer circinatum 'Little Gem'	dwarf vine maple	s	5	Dwarf form suitable for small gardens. Orange fall color.
Acer palmatum 'Dissectum'	cutleaf Japanese maple	s	5	Low, mounded form with arching, decumbent stems. Good fall color. Needs summer moisture.
Aesculus californica	California buckeye	t	7	Eventually large, broad-spreading shrub. Fragrant white flowers held erect in summer.
Aesculus parviflora	bottlebrush buckeye	m	5	Spectacular white flowers with red anthers held in abundant panicles. Good fall color.
Aesculus pavia	red buckeye	m	5	Attractive foliage and crimson flower spikes in June.

▷

BOTANICAL NAME	COMMON NAME	HT	ZONE	NOTES ON CHARACTER
Alangium platanifolium		m	9	Unusual foliage shrub bearing white lily-like flowers in June. Rare and tender.
Amelanchier alnifolia ◆	Saskatoon berry	m	2	Hardy, white-flowered shrubs with small, rounded leaves. Good fall color.
Amelanchier canadensis ◆	shadblow serviceberry	m	3	As for *A. alnifolia*. Grows especially well in wet soils.
Amorpha fruticosa ✳ ◆	false indigo	m	5	Pinnate leaves and purple-blue flowers in July. Drought tolerant, prefers sun.
Aralia elata	Chinese angelica tree	t	5	Suckering shrub with thick, spiny stems and huge twice-pinnate leaves. White flower spikes in August, followed by black fruit.
Aronia arbutifolia	red chokeberry	m	4	Attractive shiny leaves, gray beneath. Showy red fruit. Good for moist soils.
Aronia melanocarpa	black chokeberry	s	4	Noted for its hawthorn-like flowers in spring, clean shiny foliage, black berries and outstanding fall color.
Berberis amurensis ✳ ◆	Amur barberry	s	6	Colorful berries and good fall color. Spiny stems. Tolerates poor, dry soil.
Berberis morrisonensis ◆	Mt. Morrison barberry	s	6	Compact shrub with small leaves that turn scarlet in fall. Fruit red, showy.
Berberis thunbergii ◆	Japanese barberry	s	6	Compact habit, bright red berries and good fall color. 'Atropurpurea' is a good purple-leaved form.
Betula nana	dwarf birch	s	3	Dwarf birch with glandular stems and neat, rounded leaves. Succeeds in boggy soils.
Buddleja alternifolia ❀ ◆	butterfly bush	t	5	Large shrub with fragrant lilac flowers loved by butterflies.
Buddleja davidii ❀ ◆	butterfly bush	t	6	Showy white to purple arching panicles in summer are heavily scented and attract butterflies. Needs sun. Prune hard each spring.
Buddleja × *weyeriana* ◆	hybrid buddleia	m	6	Yellow to apricot globose flowers borne from summer to autumn.
Callicarpa bodinieri	beauty berry	m	6	Grown chiefly for its metallic violet blue berries, which attract birds. Plant in groups to assure fruit production.
Calycanthus floridus ❀	Carolina allspice	m	5	Aromatic leaves and curious brownish-red flowers in summer. Shade tolerant, of easy cultivation.
Calycanthus occidentalis ❀	California allspice	m	6	As for *C. floridus*, but with larger leaves and flowers.
Caragana arborescens ✳ ◆	Siberia pea shrub	t	2	Attractive filigree foliage and pale yellow flowers. For sunny spot. Good in poor, dry soil.
Caragana pygmaea ✳ ◆	dwarf pea shrub	s	3	Small, drought-tolerant shrub with yellow flowers in spring-summer.
Caryopteris × *clandonensis* ◆	bluebeard	s	7	Small, spreading shrub with bright blue flowers in summer.
Chaenomeles japonica ◆	lesser flowering quince	m	5	Ornamental shrubs grown for their glorious early spring show of red, orange and white flowers. Of easy culture, they grow well in sun or shade. Many cultivars offered under *C. speciosa* and × *C. superba*, mostly differing in the color of their flowers.
Chimonanthus praecox ❀	wintersweet	m	6	Winter-flowering shrub with sweetly scented yellow translucent flowers. Interesting sandpapery leaves.
Chionanthus retusus	Chinese fringe tree	t	6	Profusion of snowy white flowers in July on older plants. Best in areas with hot summers and cool to cold winters.

▷

BOTANICAL NAME	COMMON NAME	HT	ZONE	NOTES ON CHARACTER
Chionanthus virginicus ✿	American fringe tree	t	5	American counterpart to *C. retusus*, with larger leaves and mildly fragrant white flowers.
Clerodendrum trichotomum✿◆	harlequin glorybower	t	7	Vigorous shrub with fetid leaves and extremely fragrant white flowers in maroon calyces in August and September, followed by china blue berries. Variety *fargesii* is more floriferous and hardier (Zone 7) than the type.
Clethra alnifolia ✿	sweet pepperbush	s	4	Good show of scented, erect, white flower panicles in August. Suitable for moist soils. Suckering habit.
Clethra delavayi ✿		t	7	Magnificent floral display from abundant, large white panicles held horizontally in July and August. Rare and worth seeking.
Coriaria terminalis	coriaria	s	7	Interesting subshrub with translucent red fruits. Good fall color. Variety *xanthocarpa* has yellow fruit.
Cornus alba	Tatarian dogwood	m	3	Useful thicketing shrub succeeding well in wet or dry soils. The young stems are an attractive red in winter.
Cornus alternifolia 'Argentea'	alternate-leaved dogwood	m	3	One of the most beautiful variegated shrubs. Foliage silver-variegated. Attractive horizontal branching pattern. Other good cultivars also offered.
Cornus controversa	giant dogwood	t	5	Large shrub or small tree with extremely graceful, pagoda-like horizontal branching. Cream flowers in May. 'Variegata' is a slower-growing form with attractive silver-marginated leaves. Resistant to the dogwood leaf blight affecting *C. florida*.
Cornus stolonifera 'Flaviramea'	golden-twig dogwood	m	4	Suckering shrub with bright yellow shoots in winter. Very effective when planted with the red-stemmed *C. alba*. Good on moist sites.
Corylopsis glabrescens	Japanese winter hazel	m	5	Beautiful display of primrose yellow flowers carried abundantly on drooping tassels in April.
Corylopsis pauciflora ✿	buttercup winter hazel	m	6	Sweetly scented yellow flowers in March. Small leaves, pink when emerging.
Corylus avellana 'Aurea' ◆	gold hazel	t	5	Large spreading shrub festooned with long pendulous catkins in February–March. Needs ample room in partial shade.
Corylus avellana 'Contorta'◆	corkscrew hazel	m	4	Curiously contorted stems are a feature in winter. Catkins provide added show in season. Slow growing. Needs sun.
Corylus maxima 'Purpurea'◆	purple filbert	t	4	Large, spreading shrub with purplish leaves. Shade tolerant.
Cotinus coggygria ✳	smoke bush	t	6	Medium to large shrub thriving in poor soil. Purple-leaved cultivars need full sun to develop best color.
Cotoneaster bullatus ◆	bullate-leaved cotoneaster	t	6	Handsome and distinctive for its attractively corrugated leaves, which turn red-orange in autumn, and abundant red fruit.
Cotoneaster horizontalis ◆	rockspray cotoneaster	s	5	A low, spreading shrub with attractive arching stems with herringbone branching pattern. Good autumn color and red berries that persist into winter.
Cotoneaster lucidus ◆		m	4	Hardy, black-fruited cotoneaster used for hedging in colder climates, but more attractive in its natural unpruned form. White to pink flowers in spring. Excellent fall color.

▷

BOTANICAL NAME	COMMON NAME	HT	ZONE	NOTES ON CHARACTER
Cotoneaster multiflorus ◆		m	5	This extremely floriferous, spreading shrub makes the best floral display of the cotoneasters (May). Red fruit.
Cotoneaster zabelii ◆		m	7	Arching growth habit, red fruit. One of the few cotoneasters to color yellow in the fall.
Daphne blagayana ❀ ◆		s	7	Dwarf shrub of prostrate habit with heavily scented creamy white flowers in March and April.
Daphne mezereum ❀ ◆	February daphne	s	5	Deliciously fragrant, purple-red flowers appear on leafless stems in late winter. The red fruit that follows is poisonous.
Decaisnea fargesii		m	6	Tropical-looking long pinnate leaves provide exotic character. Curious metallic blue seed pods.
Deutzia × *kalmiiflora* ◆	deutzia	m	5	Showy pink or white flowers on arching branches.
Disanthus cercidifolius		m	7	Resembling a witch hazel in habit, with leaves like *Cercis*, this shrub is distinguished by its superb crimson fall color. For moist position.
Edgeworthia chrysantha ❀	paperbush	m	8	Interesting on account of its fragrant yellow flowers in March and remarkably flexible stems that can be tied into a knot! Used in Japan to make paper for currency. Needs sheltered sunny location.
Elaeagnus commutata	silverberry	m	2	Valued for its silvery foliage and very fragrant yellow flowers borne in June. Very hardy.
Eleutherococcus sieboldianus	five-leaf aralia	m	4	Tropical-looking shrub with palmate leaves and spiny stems. Good as bold accent. Grows well in sun or shade.
Elsholtzia stauntonii ❀	mint shrub	s	5	Small subshrub valued for its late show of lilac-purple panicles from August to October. Leaves emit a mintlike odor when crushed.
Enkianthus campanulatus		m	5	Easy-to-grow plant of great refinement. The shrub is festooned with drooping racemes of orange-yellow flowers in spring. Good fall color.
Eucryphia glutinosa	brush bush, nirrhe	t	7	This Chilean shrub makes a great show in August when covered with white blossoms, most attractive to bees. Upright branching habit and orange-red fall color.
Euonymus alatus	winged spindle bush	m	3	Noted for its outstanding autumn color, with leaves turning crimson-pink. The showy, persistent red fruit splits open to reveal the orange seeds inside. Best to plant in groups to assure fruit production.
Euonymus bungeanus		t	6	Arching growth habit with yellow flowers in June, followed by creamy pink fruit. Best in areas with hot summers.
Euonymus planipes		t	5	Large shrub with showy autumn color display. Conspicuous red fruit is abundantly produced.
Euonymus verrucosus	warty euonymus	m	5	Intriguing warty branches, good fall color, and orange-red fruit are among its attributes.
Exochorda giraldii	pearl bush	m	6	This shrub is loaded with large papery white flowers in May. Arching stems. Variety *wilsonii* is a larger-flowered form.

▷

ABOVE, L TO R: *Enkianthus campanulatus, Hamamellis mollis*

◁ *shrubs for the Woodland*

BOTANICAL NAME	COMMON NAME	HT	ZONE	NOTES ON CHARACTER
Forsythia ovata ◆	Korean forsythia	s	5	Compact growth and early amber-yellow flowers set this species apart from its coarser relations. For sunny spot.
Fothergilla gardenii ✿	witch alder	s	5	Showy bottlebrush-like fragrant flowers composed of white stamens appear in April and May. Good fall color.
Fothergilla major ✿		s	5	Similar to *F. gardenii* but with leaves glaucous beneath. Outstanding fall color.
Franklinia alatamaha ✿	Franklin tree	t	5	Now extinct in the wild, this American shrub bears camellia-like white flowers in late summer. Best flowering occurs after hot summers.
Fuchsia magellanica ◆	Magellan fuchsia	s	7	Vigorous subshrub with arching stems studded with purple-red flowers from summer to frost. In colder areas it can be treated as root-hardy perennial.
Genista cinerea ✱ ◆	broom	t	7	Large shrub for sunny location with bright yellow flowers in summer. Good on poor, dry soils.
Hamamelis × intermedia ✿	hybrid witch hazel	t	6	Hybrids derived from crosses between *H. japonica* and *H. mollis*, valued for their winter-blooming habit. Flower color ranges from pale yellow to deep coppery red, depending on the cultivar. Good fall color. All witch hazels look best when planted against an evergreen background.
Hamamelis japonica ✿	Japanese witch hazel	m	6	Wide-spreading shrub carrying yellow flowers from December to March. Excellent fall color.
Hamamelis mollis ✿	Chinese witch hazel	t	5	A large, spreading shrub with large, soft hairy leaves that color a rich yellow in the fall. Large, sweetly scented yellow flowers in winter perfume the air for a considerable distance. Arguably the best of the witch hazels and deserving of place wherever it can be grown. 'Pallida' and 'Brevipetala' are two good cultivars.

▷

ABOVE, L TO R: *Hydrangea aspera, Hydrangea serrata* 'Blue Bird'

◁ *Shrubs for the Woodland*

BOTANICAL NAME	COMMON NAME	HT	ZONE	NOTES ON CHARACTER
Hamamelis vernalis ✸	Ozark witch hazel	m	5	American species with upright branching habit and profusion of small reddish flowers early in the new year.
Hamamelis virginiana ✸	Virginian witch hazel	t	4	Noted for flowering from September to November, earlier than other witch hazels. Flowers small, yellow, and mildly fragrant.
Holodiscus discolor	ocean-spray	m	7	Attractive plumes of white feathery flowers in June and July. Withstands drought well.
Hydrangea arborescens ssp. *arborescens*	hills-of-snow	s	5	Snowy white flowers are borne in summer on this American native of lax habit. For moist soils. 'Annabelle' is a popular cultivar.
Hydrangea heteromalla		t	6	This shrub has exfoliating bark and dark green leaves that are whitish beneath. The large white lacecap-type flowers are borne in July. 'Snowcap' is a fine cultivar.
Hydrangea macrophylla	hortensia	m	6	Variable group of cultivars with large flower heads in summer. Color ranges from white to blue and near red. Flower color is affected by soil pH. For best growth provide ample summer water. Old flowering stems should be thinned and cut back in early spring. Recommended cultivars include: 'Blue Wave' (blue), 'General Vicomtesse de Vibraye' (blue), 'Marechal Foch' (pink to blue), 'Mariesii' (pink), 'Miss Belgium' (red) and 'White Wave' (white).
Hydrangea quercifolia	oak-leaved hydrangea	m	5	Interesting lobed, oak-like leaves that color intensely in the fall. Large white flowers in summer.
Hydrangea sargentiana	Sargent's hydrangea	m	7	Shrub with stout bristly stems with peeling bark and large velvety hispid leaves. Flattened corymbs of tiny China blue flowers are surrounded by white ray florets. Excellent in light shade under trees.
Hydrangea serrata	lacecap hydrangea	m	5	Spreading shrub to 2m (6ft) with flat-topped flowers in blue or pink. Hardier than *H. macrophylla*. Best forms include 'Blue Bird' (pale blue or pink) and 'Preziosa' (pink to crimson).

▷

BOTANICAL NAME	COMMON NAME	HT	ZONE	NOTES ON CHARACTER
Hydrangea villosa ◆		m	7	Graceful shrub with arching habit. Flowers pink or blue, changing to purple. Shade tolerant.
Ilex decidua	possum haw	m	5	Good show of bright orange-red berries that persist through winter. Glossy leaves.
Ilex serrata	Japanese winterberry	m	6	Interesting twiggy habit and attractive red fruit on female plants. 'Xanthocarpa' has yellow berries, 'Leucocarpa', white.
Ilex verticillata	winterberry	m	3	Especially suited for swampy places, this holly has showy red fruit. Best when massed, including a male plant to assure fruit production.
Jasminum nudiflorum ◆	winter jasmine	s	5	Bright yellow tubular flowers decorate its arching green stems from November to March, depending on the season. Best with sun, and periodic cutting back. Great bank cover.
Kerria japonica ◆	kerria	m	4	Suckering shrub sending up many arching green stems covered in May with bright yellow flowers. 'Pleniflora' is the vigorous, double-flowered form.
Lagerstroemia indica	crape myrtle	t	9	Abundant clusters of white, pink, lavender, red or bluish flowers on large panicles during summer. Attractive exfoliating bark and privet-like leaves. Flowering poor in cool summer climates.
Leycesteria formosa ✹	Himalayan honeysuckle	m	7	Fast-growing, suckering shrub with delicately scented purplish-white flowers borne in late summer.
Ligustrum chenaultii	Chenault privet	t	7	Distinctively long, glossy, pointed semi-evergreen leaves. Large white flower panicles in late summer.
Lindera benzoin ✹	spice bush	t	4	Dense shrub with aromatic twigs and leaves. Fragrant, small yellow flowers in April. Good fall color and showy red berries on female plants. Excellent growth on wet soils.
Magnolia 'De Vos' and 'Kosar' hybrids ✹		m	6	Valuable group of American hybrids between *M. liliiflora* and *M. stellata*, combining the best attributes of each parent. Erect branching habit and abundant white to deep pink fragrant tulip-like flowers.
Magnolia liliiflora magnolia	lily-flowered	m	6	Spreading shrub with dark green, ovate leaves and tulip-shaped flowers, flushed purple on the outside, in April. Flowers appear intermittently all summer. 'Nigra' has deeper purple flowers and is more compact.
Magnolia × *loebneri*		t	6	A hybrid group derived from *M. kobus* crossed with *M. stellata*, with white to pink fragrant flowers in April. Two outstanding selections are 'Leonard Messell' with lilac-pink flowers, and 'Merrill', white.
Magnolia sieboldii ✹	Oyama magnolia	t	7	Large shrub with lemony-scented, downfacing white flowers from May to August. The crimson fruit clusters are very showy.
Magnolia sieboldii ssp. *sinensis* ✹		t	7	Spreading shrub with nodding white flowers with prominent red staminal cone. Flowers fragrant, borne in June.
Magnolia × *soulangiana*	saucer magnolia	t	6	Multistemmed large shrub with large, tulip-shaped, white flowers, stained purple at the base. Flowers in April and May. Tolerant of urban conditions and of easy culture. Many cultivars are offered.

▷

BOTANICAL NAME	COMMON NAME	HT	ZONE	NOTES ON CHARACTER
Magnolia stellata ❁	star magnolia	s	5	Compact-growing, popular garden shrub with many-petalled, fragrant flowers borne in March. Interesting hairy winter buds.
Magnolia wilsonii ❁ ◆	Wilson magnolia	t	6	Wide-spreading shrub or small tree bears fragrant white saucer-shaped pendulous flowers each with a ring of crimson stamens in May and June.
Malus sargentii ◆	Sargent's crab apple	m	5	Shrubby crab apple with abundant white flowers with golden stamens in April, followed by showy red fruit in fall. 'Rosea' is a shell pink-flowered form.
Menziesia ferruginea	rustyleaf	s	6	Small shrub related to *Pieris*, with pink flowers in May. Interesting peeling bark.
Myrica gale	bog myrtle	s	2	Superb low shrub for growing in damp soils. Golden brown catkins are borne in April and May. Aromatic leaves and stems.
Paeonia lutea var. *ludlowii* ◆	shrub peony	m	7	A bold suckering shrub with deeply cut leaves and and large, golden yellow flowers, which open as the foliage is expanding in spring. A first-rate plant.
Parrotiopsis jaquemontiana		t	7	Upright habit with rounded leaves and flower clusters surrounded by showy white bracts in May. Yellow fall color.
Potentilla fruticosa ✳ ◆	shrubby cinquefoil	s	5	Low shrub with yellow flowers for sunny locations. Flowers borne over long summer season. White-, orange- and red-flowered cultivars available.
Prunus tenella ◆	dwarf Russian almond	s	2	Valuable for colder areas for its good show of bright pinkish-red flowers in April. 'fire Hlll' is an excellent form.
Prunus tomentosa ◆	Manchu cherry	m	2	Extremely hardy shrub with white flowers in April followed by red, edible fruits in summer.
Rhamnus frangula	alder buckthorn	t	3	Large shrub of dense habit and rapid growth. Lustrous green leaves and red fruit, changing to black; very ornamental when both colors are present. Yellow fall color.
Rhodotypos scandens	jetbead	s	5	Good foreground plant with white flowers May to July, followed by persistent jet-black fruit.
Rhus glabra ✳	smooth sumac	t	4	Suckering shrub or small tree with outstanding crimson fall color. Conical scarlet fruit is attractive all winter.
Rhus trilobata ✳	squawbush	m	5	Clumping habit useful as natural hedge or bank cover. Good yellow to red fall color. Very heat and drought tolerant.
Ribes lacustre	swamp gooseberry	s	3	Brown, bristly stems and red-green flowers on long hanging racemes. Excellent in wet position.
Rosa sp. ❁ ◆	rose	varies		Many roses are prized for their scented flowers. Species roses are better suited to woodland conditions than the hybrids. *Rosa chinensis* 'Mutabilis' (Zone 7) is an excellent shrub with showy yellow-orange, fragrant flowers borne over a long season. For sunny clearings.
Rubus cockburnianus		m	6	Interesting accent with its purplish arching, spiny stems covered with a bright white bloomy coating. Attractive ferny leaves. Very effective in winter.
Rubus spectabilis	salmonberry	m	6	Suckering shrub useful for naturalizing under trees. Deep pink flowers in April, followed by edible fruit. Excellent under trees. 'Flore-Pleno' is a double-flowered form.

▷

BOTANICAL NAME	COMMON NAME	HT	ZONE	NOTES ON CHARACTER
Salix aegyptiaca	musk willow	t	6	This willow is noted for its showy, bright yellow catkins in February. Leaves grayish. All willows grow well in damp places.
Salix fargesii	Farge's willow	m	7	Unusual shrubby willow with strong thick stems and large, deep green, glossy leaves. Catkins held erect. Shoots are an attractive reddish-brown with conspicuous, large, red buds.
Salix gracistyla	rose-gold pussy willow	m	5	Beautiful pussy willow bearing bright yellow catkins before the leaves in early spring. Very effective.
Salix repens	creeping willow	s	4	Effective dwarf shrubs forming dense clumps of silvery-green leaves. Showy, profuse catkins in spring.
Sambucus caerulea ✱	blue elder	m	5	Large shrub with interesting blue-green pinnate foliage and black fruit.
Sambucus canadensis	American elder	t	3	A bold plant for moist soils in woodland. Large, white, flat flower clusters in June and black, edible fruit in late summer. Coarse textured. Cv. 'Aurea' has yellow foliage and red fruit.
Sambucus nigra	European common elder	t	5	Similar to *S. canadensis*, with rough, fissured bark. There are many varieties, which are distinguished by various foliar and fruiting characters.
Sambucus racemosa 'Plumosa Aurea'	European red elder	m	4	One of the best golden-foliaged shrubs with deeply incised, golden pinnate leaves and yellow flowers.
Shepherdia canadensis ✱	buffalo berry	m	2	Bushy shrub with scaly, silvery leaves and red berries on female plants. Needs sun. Useful in cold, dry climates where other shrubs won't thrive.
Sophora davidii ✱	vetch sophora	m	6	Feathery pinnate leaves and blue-violet pea-like flowers in June. Grows well in poor, sandy soil.
Sorbaria tomentosa	false spirea	m	6	Vigorous shrub with handsome pinnate leaves. Stems surmounted by large, feathery white plumes in July and August. Likes moist soil.
Sorbus reducta ◆	dwarf mountain ash	s	5	Thicketing shrub up to 1 m (3 ft) high with red-petioled pinnate leaves and reddish-white fruits. Can be used as a large-scale ground cover in open areas.
Sorbus vilmorinii ◆	Vilmorin mountain ash	t	6	Spreading shrub of elegant habit with small, ferny, pinnate leaves that turn red and purple in fall. Rose-pink berries.
Spiraea × arguta ◆	garland spirea	s	4	Graceful shrub bearing masses of white flowers in flat clusters in May along slender, arching branches.
Spiraea japonica 'Anthony Waterer' ◆	Anthony Waterer spirea	s	5	Good dwarf shrub for edging paths with crimson flowers in late June. Plant in groups for effective mass effect.
Spiraea nipponica ◆	Japanese spirea	m	4	Long, arching stems bear white flowers along their upper sides in late May. Lovely sight when in full bloom.
Stachyurus praecox		t	6	Interesting shrub with reddish branches and ovate leaves. Graceful, drooping racemes of pale yellow flowers appear in late winter. *S. chinensis* has longer racemes and blooms later.

▷

ABOVE, L TO R: *Viburnum* × *bodnantense* 'Dawn', *Mahonia* hybrid 'Arthur Menzies'

◁ *Shrubs for the Woodland*

BOTANICAL NAME	COMMON NAME	HT	ZONE	NOTES ON CHARACTER
Staphylea holocarpa ◆	Chinese bladdernut	t	6	Trifoliate shrub grown for its conspicous bladder-like fruit capsules. White or pink flowers in April.
Stephanandra incisa	lace shrub	m	5	Fine-textured plant with graceful, zig-zag stems bearing greenish-white flower panicles in June. Good fall color.
Stewartia malacodendron	Virginia stewartia	t	7	Large shrub with attractively mottled bark and ovate leaves. Flowers white, camellia-like, with purple stamens, in July and August. For moist, loamy, acid soil. Difficult to transplant. *S. ovata* is similarly good, and hardier to Zone 6.
Symphoricarpos albus	snowberry	m	3	Thicketing shrub with pinkish-white flowers in June and showy white berries lasting well into winter. Will grow in dense shade under trees. *S. orbiculatus* is similar, with rose-purple berries.
Symplocos paniculata	sapphire berry	t	6	Large, densely branched shrub bearing beautiful turquoise fruit. Plant both sexes to assure fruiting.
Syringa meyeri ✿ ◆	Meyer lilac	m	5	Compact shrub with lilac-purple flowers in early summer.
Syringa microphylla ✿ ◆	small-leaved lilac	t	5	Fine-textured shrub with fragrant pink flowers.
Syringa patula ✿ ◆	Korean lilac	m	5	Flowers lilac, white within; early summer. This species and the preceding two are the best lilacs for smaller gardens because of their moderate size.
Syringa pekinensis ✿ ◆	Peking lilac	t	6	Large shrub with abundant fragrant cream flowers in summer.
Syringa × *prestoniae* (cultivars) ✿ ◆	Preston lilac	t	4	Flowers rose-white to deep lilac or magenta, depending on cultivar. Hybrid developed in Canada for improved hardiness.
Syringa reticulata ✿ ◆	Japanese tree lilac	t	5	Eventually a small tree with exfoliating bark. Richly scented panicles of creamy white flowers in summer.

▷

BOTANICAL NAME	COMMON NAME	HT	ZONE	NOTES ON CHARACTER
Syringa yunnanensis ✿ ◆	Yunnan lilac	t	6	Fragrant pale pink flowers, aging to white. Will grow in partial shade.
Vaccinium corymbosum	swamp blueberry	m	3	Dense, thicketing branching habit with small leaves turning vivid shades of red in fall. White, urn-shaped flowers in May, followed by edible blue berries.
Vaccinium membranaceum	thin-leaved bilberry	m	6	Smaller than *V. corymbosum*, with brilliant scarlet fall color.
Vaccinium parvifolium	red huckleberry	m	6	Finely branched erect shrub with green branchlets bearing pinkish flowers in May, followed by tart, red fruit. Excellent in deep shade under trees.
Viburnum betulifolium ◆	birch-leaf viburnum	t	5	Outstanding over winter when its arching branches are weighed down with bright red fruit. White flowers in June. Plant in groups to ensure fruiting.
Viburnum × bodnantense ✿ ◆	Bodnant viburnum	m	6	Upright branching shrub with tightly packed clusters of fragrant, rosy flowers through late autumn and winter.
Viburnum × carlcephalum ✿ ◆	fragrant snowball	m	4	Compact shrub producing rounded flower clusters of very fragrant pink flowers in May. Good fall color. 'Cayuga' is a cross with *V. carlesii* of more compact form with white flowers.
Viburnum carlesii ✿ ◆	Korean spice viburnum	m	4	Clusters of deliciously fragrant, white flowers, pink in bud, grace this rounded shrub in April. Black fruit and good fall color. 'Aurora' and 'Diana' are good selections.
Viburnum cassinoides ◆	withe-rod	m	2	Hardy and pretty shrub with cream flowers in June. Showy red fruit, turning black, and vivid crimson fall color.
Viburnum dilatatum ✿ ◆		m	5	Rounded, toothed leaves and heavily scented white flowers in May. Abundant red fruit, persistent.
Viburnum farreri ✿ ◆	Farrer's viburnum	m	6	Distinctive winter-flowering shrub with toothed leaves. The white, scented flowers, pink in bud, appear from November through winter.
Viburnum × juddii ✿ ◆	Judd's viburnum	s	6	Similar to *V. carlesii* with sweet-scented, pinkish flowers in April.
Viburnum lantana ◆	wayfaring tree	t	3	Shade-tolerant shrub with white flowers. Fruit red/black, attractive to birds.
Viburnum opulus ◆	cranberry bush	t	4	Spreading shrub with maple-like leaves which turn purplish-red in autumn. Hydrangea-like flower clusters of white flowers in June, followed by showy red berries that last into winter. Good for moist sites. Many good cultivars to choose from.
Viburnum opulus 'Nanum' ◆	dwarf cranberry bush	s	4	Dwarf bush suitable for foreground massing or by margins of a pond. Good red fall color. Flowering is infrequent.
Viburnum opulus 'Roseum' ◆	snowball bush	m	4	Popular, hardy shrub with large snowball-shaped heads of creamy, sterile flowers.
Viburnum plicatum ◆	double-file viburnum	m	6	Beautiful, wide-spreading shrub with horizontal branching habit. The white flower clusters are borne in two rows along the top of the branches, in May and June. Good fall color. 'Grandiflorum' has larger flower heads with pink-tinged white florets. Cultivar.
Viburnum plicatum 'Sterile' ◆	Japanese snowball	m	6	This form, with its large, ball-shaped clusters of sterile florets, makes a conspicuous show for several weeks.

▷

BOTANICAL NAME	COMMON NAME	HT	ZONE	NOTES ON CHARACTER
Viburnum setigerum ◆	tea viburnum	m	6	Attractive foliage of ever-changing hues; white flowers in July and orange fruit, becoming black.
Viburnum sieboldii ◆	Siebold viburnum	t	5	Large creamy-white flowers in spring are followed by long-lasting pink to red fruit. Leaves have fetid smell in spring and autumn.
Viburnum trilobum ◆	cranberry	m	2	Very hardy and shade tolerant. Red fruit attractive to birds. White flowers.
Vitex agnus-castus ✳	chaste tree	t	7	Aromatic shrub with compound leaves and showy terminal racemes of violet-blue flowers in late summer. Needs hot summers to flower well.
Weigela middendorffiana	Middendorf weigela	s	5	Compact shrub with peeling bark and attractive orange-spotted, yellow bell-shaped flowers in April. Upright habit.
Xanthoceras sorbifolium	shiny-leaf yellowhorn	t	6	Large, upright shrub with compound leaves. Showy, erect horse chestnut-like flower panicles of white flowers with a red eye appear in May. Best in a sunny clearing.
Zanthoxylum piperitum	Japan pepper	m	6	Compact shrub with interesting pinnate leaves that turn a bright yellow in fall. The small, reddish fruit contains seeds used as a pepper substitute in Japan.

Broad-leaved Evergreen Shrubs

BOTANICAL NAME	COMMON NAME	HT	ZONE	NOTES ON CHARACTER
Andromeda polifolia	bog rosemary	s	3	Dwarf shrub with narrow leaves, glaucous beneath. Pink flowers in May. Good for boggy clearings.
Arbutus unedo ✳	strawberry tree	m	8	Drought-resistant shrub with reddish-brown peeling bark and attractive bell-shaped white-to-pink flowers accompanied by strawberry-like fruit. Best in sunny spot.
Arctostaphylos columbiana ✳	hairy manzanita	m	7	Beautiful wine-red, smooth bark and grayish rounded leaves. Good for coastal locations in sunny position. Drought tolerant.
Arctostaphylos patula ✳	greenleaf manzanita	m	6	Similar to *A. columbiana*, but with sage-green, shining leaves, and hardier. Needs sun.
Arctostaphylos uva-ursi ✳	bearberry, kinnickinick	s	4	Rapidly spreading evergreen ground cover for sunny banks. Small, round leaves. Pink, urn-shaped flowers in spring, followed by red berries.
Ardisia japonica	marlberry	s	9	Small shrub producing glossy green leaves at the ends of its branches. Bright red berries appear throughout the year.
Artemisia tridentata ✳	sagebrush	m	5	Rounded bush with small, gray aromatic leaves. Drought tolerant. Suitable for open woodland in dry climate areas.
Aucuba japonica	spotted laurel	m	7	Superb shrub for deep shade with bold, serrated leaves, attractively splashed or spotted yellow in various cultivars. Female plants produce attractive red fruit.
Azara microphylla ✳◆	chinchin	m	8	Upright shrub with fine-textured sprays of tiny lustrous leaves. Yellow, vanilla-scented flowers appear in early March.
Azara serrata		m	9	Similar to *A. microphylla* but with larger leaves and showier yellow flowers in July, followed by white berries.

▷

BOTANICAL NAME	COMMON NAME	HT	ZONE	NOTES ON CHARACTER
Baccharis pilularis ✳	coyote bush	m	8	Perhaps the best ground cover for high desert regions. Good for holding banks. Cut back in early spring before growth begins, to maintain appearance.
Berberidopsis corallina	coral plant	m	9	Unusual scandent shrub with spiny-edged, heart-shaped leaves that are white beneath. Deep crimson flowers in drooping clusters in late summer.
Berberis buxifolia	Magellan barberry	s	7	Dome-shaped shrub with small, semi-evergreen spine-tipped leaves, white underneath. Yellow-orange flowers appear in April, followed by purple berries.
Berberis candidula	Chinese barberry	s	6	Dense rounded shrub with dark green leaves, silver beneath. Yellow flowers. *B. verrucosa* is similar.
Berberis darwinii	Darwin barberry	m	7	Beautiful spring-flowering shrub with bright orange flowers over a long period in spring. Small, holly-like leaves.
Berberis linearifolia		m	7	Notable for its brilliant orange-red flowers which appear in spring and sometimes in fall. Narrow, deep green, spine-tipped leaves.
Berberis × *lologensis*	Lake Lolog barberry	m	7	A hybrid between *B. darwinii* and *B. linearifolia*, combining the best features of both.
Berberis × *stenophylla*	rosemary barberry	m	6	Graceful shrub with arching stems clothed in yellow flowers in April. Various cultivars offered.
Bruckenthalia spiculifolia	spike heath	s	7	Attractive heath-like plant with rose-pink, bell-shaped flowers in June. For sunny, moist location and peaty soil.
Buxus microphylla ◆	Japanese boxwood	s	5	Dense, low shrub for foreground planting in sun or shade. Variety *koreana* said to retain green color better in colder zones.
Buxus sempervirens ◆	common box	m	5	Large shrub with small ovate leaves that thrives in sun or shade. Drought tolerant. Many dwarf and variegated forms are available.
Camellia japonica	common camellia	m	7	Beautiful flowering shrubs with lustrous, rounded leaves and large, white through red, single to double flowers in early spring, depending on cultivar. Best in light shade and on neutral to acid soils.
Camellia reticulata		m	9	More tender camellia with single pink flowers and thick, leathery leaves. A number of cultivars are offered.
Camellia sasanqua ✿	sasanqua camellia	m	8	Compact shrubs with smaller leaves than *C. japonica*, tolerating more sun. Flowers single or double, white to red, slightly fragrant, appear from October to February.
Camellia × *williamsii*		m	7	Hybrid between *C. japonica* and *C. saluenensis*, combining the good features of each. Easy to grow and vigorous, with rosy pink flowers. 'Donation' and 'J.C. Williams' are two of the best cultivars.
Carpenteria californica ◆ ✿	bush anemone	m	7	Beautiful, fragrant white anemone-like flowers with a central boss of yellow anthers appear in midsummer. Best in sunny position.
Cassiope		s	2	Prostrate shrub with white to red heathlike flowers. Requires moist, acid soil and open position. Most effective when massed.

▷

Fatsia japonica has a bold sub-tropical appearance.

◁ *Shrubs for the Woodland*

BOTANICAL NAME	COMMON NAME	HT	ZONE	NOTES ON CHARACTER
Cestrum parqui ❁	willow-leaved jessamine	m	10	Powerfully fragrant night-blooming shrub with yellowish green tubular flowers and willow-like leaves. Best in partial sun. *C. aurantiacum* has orange flowers; *C. elegans* is red. The latter two species have showier flowers but little fragrance.
Chamaedaphne calyculata	leatherleaf	m	2	Very hardy shrub tolerant of wet location.
Chamaerops humilis ✳	European fan palm	m	9	Clustering palm succeeding in poor stony soil. Green to blue fan-shaped leaves with sharp spines along leaf petioles.
Choisya ternata ❁ ◆	Mexican mock orange	m	8	Dense shrub with aromatic, dark glossy green leaves and orange blossom-scented white flowers in spring and early summer, sometimes again in fall.
Clerodendrum bungei ❁ ✳	Cashmere bouquet	t	8	Fast-growing, suckering shrub with large, ill-smelling leaves (only when crushed). Delightfully scented rosy red flowers in summer. Best in part shade.

▷

BOTANICAL NAME	COMMON NAME	HT	ZONE	NOTES ON CHARACTER
Cleyera japonica	sakaki	m	7	Japanese shrub with entire, dark green leaves crowding the branches, assuming reddish tones in winter. 'Tricolor' is a colorful variegated form.
Cotoneaster conspicuus ◆	wintergreen cotoneaster	m	6	Graceful arching stems laden with white flowers in June, followed by persistent red fruit. The cultivar 'Decorus' is a dwarf form suitable as ground cover.
Cotoneaster dammeri ◆	bearberry cotoneaster	s	5	Excellent ground cover for banks or under shrubs. White flowers and showy red berries. Spreads quickly by rooting stems. Cut back periodically to control height.
Cotoneaster franchetii ◆	Franchet cotoneaster	m	6	Orange-red berries and sage-green leaves. Semi-evergreen in colder zones. Graceful branching.
Cotoneaster microphyllus ◆	small-leaved cotoneaster	s	5	Low, mounding habit with stiff stems clothed in tiny, leathery dark green leaves. The scarlet berries are most attractive.
Cotoneaster rugosus ◆	rugose-leaved cotoneaster	m	6	Broad, arching habit with dark green leaves with deeply impressed veins above, white-woolly beneath. Pinkish-white flowers followed by red fruit.
Cotoneaster salicifolius ◆	willow-leaved cotoneaster	t	6	Long, pointed leaves held on graceful arching branches which become laden with bright red fruit in fall. 'Fructoluteo' has yellow fruit.
Cotoneaster sternianus ◆	Ward's cotoneaster	m	7	Very attractive shrub with sage-green leaves, silvery beneath. Flowers pink, followed by large, orange-red berries. Sold as *C. wardii* by many nurseries.
Cotoneaster × *watereri* ◆	Waterer's cotoneaster	t	6	Fast-growing hybrid with long, semi-evergreen leaves, arching stems and profuse red or orange fruits. Many named forms offered.
Crinodendron hookerianum	red lantern tree	m	9	Chilean shrub with dark green, serrated leaves and hanging, long-stalked, bell-shaped crimson flowers in May and June. Needs moist soil and partial shade.
Cytisus battandieri ✿ ✳ ◆	Moroccan broom	m	7	Sprawling shrub with silvery foliage and pineapple-scented blossoms. For sunny location only. Drought resistant.
Daboecia cantabrica	St. Dabeoc's heath	s	7	Neat, dwarf shrub suitable for massing. Showy rose-purple flower spikes from summer into late fall. Needs part sun and moist peaty soil.
Daphne arbuscula ✿ ◆		s	6	Procumbent shrub with clusters of rose-pink flowers in summer.
Daphne × *burkwoodii* ✿ ◆	Burkwood daphne	s	6	Hybrid, semi-evergreen shrublet with sweetly scented pink flowers in May and June, often again in fall.
Daphne cneorum ✿ ◆	garland flower	s	6	Grown for its fragrant, rose-pink flowers in April and May, which are borne in great abundance. Ensure soil is moist but well drained.
Daphne laureola ✿ ◆	spurge laurel	s	6	Unassuming small shrub valuable for planting in deep shade under trees. Drought tolerant. Fragrant, yellow-green flowers clustered under uppermost leaves in late winter. May become invasive in the Northwest.
Daphne × *mantensiana* ✿◆		s	6	Dwarf shrub valued for its fragrant, rose-pink flowers that appear over a long period from April through fall.

▷

BOTANICAL NAME	COMMON NAME	HT	ZONE	NOTES ON CHARACTER
Daphne odora ❀	winter daphne	s	7	Superbly fragrant on account of its reddish-purple flowers borne in late winter. The cultivar 'Aureomarginata,' with leaves narrowly marginated with yellow, is hardier than the type.
Daphne tangutica ❀ ◆		s	6	Small, compact shrub with very fragrant rose-purple flowers in May, followed by red fruits.
Daphniphyllum macropodum	Yuzuriha	t	7	Handsome foliage plant with long, rhododendron-like leaves with white undersides. Valuable for bold, subtropical effect.
Distylium racemosum		m	7	Spreading evergreen witch hazel-like shrub with glossy leaves and flowers, consisting of red stamens, in April.
Drimys winteri ❀ ◆	winter's bark	t	9	Large shrub with large, leathery bright green leaves, coated white beneath. Fragrant white flowers open in late spring.
Embothrium coccineum	Chilean firebush	t	9	Spectacular flowering shrub in May with tubular orange-scarlet flowers in profusion. Needs acid soil. Variety *lanceolatum* 'Norquinco Valley' is the hardiest (Zone 8), with semi-evergreen leaves.
Empetrum nigrum	black crowberry	s	3	Dwarf carpeting shrub with glossy black fruit. Useful as a ground cover in damp, peaty situations.
Erica arborea ❀	tree heath	m	8	Fine-textured, bright green, needle-like leaves and profusion of fragrant, white flowers in March–April. Variety *alpina* is the hardiest form (Zone 7).
Erica carnea ◆	spring heath	s	5	Good plant for massing in semishade. Small, bell-shaped flowers in shades of white to rose-red cover the plants from January to May, depending on variety. Many cultivars available.
Erica ciliaris	Dorset heath	s	7	Similar to *E. carnea*, but with gray, needle-like foliage and larger rosy-purple flowers. Needs moist, sheltered location.
Erica × darleyensis	Darley heath	s	6	Hybrid between *E. carnea* and *E. erigena*. Taller than *E. carnea*, with white to rosy-magenta flowers, depending on cultivar. Lime tolerant.
Eriobotrya japonica ❀ ◆	loquat	m	8	Bold foliage plant with dark green, leathery corrugated leaves. Flowers fragrant, white in late fall, followed by yellow edible fruit in warmer zones.
Eucryphia × intermedia	hybrid eucryphia	t	8	Upright, fine-textured shrub with white flowers in profusion in late summer, when few other shrubs are in bloom.
Eucryphia × nymansensis ◆	Nymans' eucryphia	t	8	Columnar growth habit with shining, olive-green leaves and large white flowers which adorn the branches in August. Culture as for *Rhododendron*.
Fatsia japonica	Japanese fatsia	m	7	Bold, maple-like leaves carried on stout stems, topped by large, white flower panicles in October. Prefers shade, as foliage may scorch in full sun.
Fremontodendron californicum ✳ ◆	flannel bush	t	8	Showy yellow blossoms appear over long period. Fast-growing and blooms young. Tawny-colored felt on leaves and stems may irritate skin.

▷

BOTANICAL NAME	COMMON NAME	HT	ZONE	NOTES ON CHARACTER
Gardenia augusta ❂	Cape jasmine	m	9	Glossy, leathery leaves and waxy, white flowers that emit a powerful perfume from spring to fall. Need summer heat to bloom well. For acid soils only.
Garrya elliptica ✳	silk tassel bush	m	8	Most attractive in January and February when draped with its long gray-green catkins. Leaves gray-green, holly-like.
Gaultheria procumbens	wintergreen	s	3	Charming, mat-forming plant with shiny leaves and white, bell-shaped flowers in May, followed by bright red berries in fall. For moist, acid soil.
Gaultheria shallon	salal	m	6	Thicketing shrub with attractive rounded, leathery leaves and pink, bell-shaped flowers in late spring. Vigorous spreader in moist, acid soil.
Heteromeles arbutifolia ✳	Christmas berry	m	9	Dense shrub with thick and leathery leaves and white flowers in June, followed by clusters of bright red berries from November to January, attractive to birds. Drought tolerant and will grow in sun or part shade.
Hypericum 'Hidcote'	Hidcote hypericum	s	6	Superb floral show from abundant golden-yellow flowers borne from July to October. Semi-evergreen shrub of compact habit, deciduous in cold winters.
Hypericum androsaemum	tutsan	s	6	Free-flowering semi-evergreen shrub with showy golden-yellow flowers from June to October, followed by red fruiting capsules.
Hypericum calycinum ◆	St. John's wort	s	6	Excellent ground cover for dry, shaded places. Large, bright yellow flowers in July. Cut back to ground level in late winter to control height.
Hypericum henryi ◆		m	7	Shade-tolerant shrub with yellow flowers in late summer.
Hypericum × moserianum ◆	gold flower	s	7	Good ground-covering shrub that will do well in the shade of trees. Reddish young shoots and yellow flowers all summer.
Ilex × altaclerensis	Highclere holly	t	7	As for *I. aquifolium*, with larger leaves and similar range of cultivars available.
Ilex aquifolium	English holly	t	7	Multitude of cultivars with different leaf shapes and colors, and fruit color, are suitable for growing as large shrubs. Tolerant of pruning.
Ilex crenata	Japanese holly	m	6	Dense, rounded habit with small, rounded leaves. Black berries. 'Convexa' has convex leaves and is a bit hardier.
Ilex glabra	inkberry	s	3	Tiny, glossy leaves and shining black fruit. Tolerant of damp sites. Female plants tend to turn purplish in cold winter areas.
Ilex latifolia	lusterleaf holly	t	7	Bold shrub with large, leathery leaves reminiscent of *Magnolia grandiflora*, with serrated margins. Fruit orange-red.
Ilex × meserveae	blue holly	m	6	Small, dark blue-green leaves on spreading stems. Best in open woodland, where *I. aquifolium* is not hardy.
Ilex pedunculosa	longstalk holly	m	5	Unholly-like with its entire, spineless, wavy leaves and long-stalked red fruit. Narrow upright habit.
Ilex pernyi	Perny holly	m	6	Glossy, small triangular-shaped spiny leaves on weeping stems make this a most attractive shrub. Red fruit.

▷

BOTANICAL NAME	COMMON NAME	HT	ZONE	NOTES ON CHARACTER
Ilex vomitoria	Yaupon holly	t	7	Small ovate leaves, glossy, deep green. Fruit red or yellow, abundant and persistent. Drought resistant.
Illicium anisatum ✿	star anise	m	8	Interesting shrub with aromatic, elliptic leaves and yellowish-green flowers in spring.
Illicium floridanum ✿	Florida anisetree	m	7	As for *I. anisatum* but with longer, aromatic leaves and many-petalled red flowers in July.
Itea illicifolia ✿	hollyleaf sweetspire	m	8	Unusual shrub with holly-like leaves and very graceful, long drooping racemes of fragrant greenish-white flowers in summer.
Jasminum fruticans ✿	jasmine	s	8	Jasmine with yellow flowers through summer and semi-evergreen trifoliate leaves.
Jasminum humile 'Revolutum' ✿	Italian jasmine	s	8	Dark green leaves and deep yellow tubular, fragrant flowers during summer.
Kalmia latifolia	mountain laurel	m	4	Medium-sized rhododendron-like shrub with glossy leaves and pink and white, or red flowers in June. Many cultivars offered. Requires acid soil.
Kalmia polifolia	bog laurel	s	2	Low, thicketing shrub with narrow, shiny leaves, silvery below and rose-colored flowers in May. Good for swampy or boggy places.
Leucothoe fontanesiana	drooping laurel	m	4	Graceful arching stems with long leathery green leaves turning shades of red or purple in autumn. White flowers in May. Excellent ground cover in acid soil.
Lonicera nitida	box honeysuckle	m	7	Small-leaved shrub of arching, twiggy habit, with white, fragrant flowers and blue fruit. Withstands clipping well.
Lonicera pileata	privet honeysuckle	s	5	Semi-evergreen shrub with small leaves that emerge an attractive bright yellow-green color. Useful as ground cover in shade.
Mahonia aquifolium ◆	Oregon grape	m	5	Dark green, pinnate leaves with holly-like leaflets that turn various shades of bronze in the fall. Yellow flowers in spring, followed by grape-like blue fruit in fall. For sun or shade.
Mahonia japonica ✿	leatherleaf mahonia	m	6	Attractive bold spine-tipped compound leaves and terminal racemes of yellow flowers in late fall to early spring. Sold as *M. bealii* by many nurseries.
Mahonia lomariifolia		m	8	Dramatic pinnate foliage on little-branched stems. Deep yellow flower racemes in winter, followed by blue fruit.
Mahonia × media ✿		m	7	Hybrid between *M. japonica* and *M. lomariifolia*, of compact habit, with long racemes of yellow flowers in winter. 'Charity' and 'Arthur Menzies' are two good selections.
Mahonia nervosa ◆	Cascades mahonia	s	5	Attractive pinnate leaves and upright yellow flower spikes in late spring. Spreads by underground runners and is excellent for dry, shady locations. Drought resistant.
Mahonia repens ◆	creeping mahonia	s	5	Similar to *M. nervosa* but with matte blue-green leaves. Effective as a ground cover in shady, dry locations.
Mahonia × wagneri 'Moseri' ◆	hybrid Oregon grape	m	6	The apple-green pinnate leaves are shades of orange, green and red through winter. Coloration best developed with exposure to sun.
Michelia figo ✿	banana shrub	m	9	Magnolia-like shrub bearing numerous creamy-yellow, shaded brownish purple flowers with a powerful fruity fragrance along the stems in spring.

▷

BOTANICAL NAME	COMMON NAME	HT	ZONE	NOTES ON CHARACTER
Mitchella repens	partridge berry	s	4	An excellent fine-textured evergreen ground cover for beneath trees in moist, peaty soil. Foliage turns shades of red in autumn.
Nandina domestica	heavenly bamboo	m	7	Elegant, bamboo-like shrub with attractive compound foliage that turns shades of red in autumn. Terminal panicles of white flowers in summer followed by red berries. 'Nana Purpurea' is a good dwarf form.
Nerium oleander ✳	oleander	m	9	Staple flowering shrub for desert climates. Many color forms available. Plant is poisonous if eaten.
Osmanthus × *burkwoodii* ❀◆	Burkwood osmanthus	m	7	Shrub of compact habit with small, dark, shiny green oval leaves and fragrant tubular white flowers in profusion during April.
Osmanthus delavayi ❀ ◆	Delavay osmanthus	m	7	A lovely shrub bearing profuse, fragrant, pure white, tubular flowers in April.
Osmanthus fragrans ❀ ◆	sweet olive	m	9	Neat shrub with glossy leaves and inconspicuous but powerfully sweet flowers with an apricot-like fragrance in spring and early summer.
Paxistima myrtifolia	Oregon boxwood	s	5	Dwarf shrub of neat habit with tiny leaves and four-sided stems. Good for moist, shaded locations. *P. canbyi* is hardier (Zone 4). Its leaves turn bronze with cold weather, and it is more tolerant of dry sites.
Photinia davidiana ◆	Christmas berry	m	7	Narrow-leaved, spreading shrub with white flowers in June, and buff crimson berries carried in pendent clusters through winter.
Photinia serratifolia ❀ ◆	Chinese photinia	t	8	Upright shrub with handsome leathery, toothed leaves that emerge a showy coppery-red color. White flowers in April are followed by red fruit.
Phyllostachys aurea	golden bamboo	m	6	Yellow-stemmed running bamboo with dense foliage. Drought resistant, but best with ample moisture.
Phyllostachys aureosulcata	yellow-groove bamboo	m	7	Distinctive bamboo with yellow grooved canes. Less dense than *P. aurea*.
Phyllostachys bambusoides	timber bamboo	t	8	One of the tallest of the hardy "timber bamboo" species. Trim lower foliage to expose attractive green canes. Best allowed to form large grove in moist site.
Phyllostachys flexuosa	zig-zag bamboo	m	7	Graceful thicketing bamboo with wavy canes and edible young shoots. Good for screening.
Phyllostachys nigra	black bamboo	m	8	Distinctive black canes distinguish this clumping bamboo. Tall canes have graceful arching habit. *P. nigra* var. *henonis* has taller, arching green canes.
Phyllostachys viridiglaucescens	sweet-shoot bamboo	m	7	Yellowish green canes carry drooping clumps of silver-backed leaves.
Pieris 'Forest flame'	forest flame pieris	m	7	Superb shrub with bright red new growth and large terminal panicles of white flowers in early spring.
Pieris floribunda	mountain pieris	m	4	Hardiest *Pieris* species from eastern U.S. with upright, not pendent, ivory-white flower clusters in early spring.

▷

BOTANICAL NAME	COMMON NAME	HT	ZONE	NOTES ON CHARACTER
Pieris formosa var. *forrestii*	Chinese pieris	t	8	Handsome, large shrub with scarlet young growth and heavy panicles of white, fragrant flowers.
Pieris japonica	lily of the valley bush	m	5	Dense habit with shiny tapering leaves and drooping clusters of white flowers in April. Many cultivars to choose from. Needs shade in colder zones.
Pittosporum tobira ✿ ◆	mock orange tobira	m	9	Lustrous rounded leaves and creamy white, orange-scented flowers in May. Best in partial sun.
Pleioblastus auricoma	variegated bamboo	m	7	Bamboo with purplish stems and attractively variegated leaves. Good, less vigorous species that does well in shade.
Pleioblastus humilis		s	6	Spreading bamboo useful as a ground cover under trees. Leaves green. Aggressive spreader.
Pleioblastus pygmaea	dwarf fern-leaf bamboo	s	6	Excellent ground-covering bamboo forming dense carpet of green leaves on short canes under 1 m (3 ft).
Pleioblastus simonii	Simon bamboo	m	7	Attractive foliage on clumping olive-green stems. Can be used as informal screen or hedge.
Pleioblastus variegatus	dwarf white-stripe bamboo	s	6	Low-growing bamboo forming thickets of zig-zag stems clothed in white-striped leaves.
Prunus lusitanica ✿ ◆	Portugal laurel	t	7	Large shrub to small tree with dark green, undulate leaves on red stalks. Flowers borne on upright racemes, fragrant, in June, followed by dark purple cherry-like fruit.
Pseudosasa japonica	Metake or arrow bamboo	m	7	Running bamboo with erect clumps of green canes carrying long-tailed, relatively wide leaves.
Pyracantha (cultivars) ◆	firethorn	m	6	Robust shrub with arching branches. White spring flowers followed by spectacular show of red, orange or yellow berries.
Rhaphiolepis indica	India hawthorn	s	9	White to crimson-pink flowers over a long season from fall to spring. Rounded, compact growth habit. Many varieties offered.
Rhaphiolepis umbellata	Yeddo-hawthorn	s	7	Thick, leathery rounded leaves and white, mildly fragrant flowers in late spring, followed by black fruit.
Rhododendron — see separate list				
Rhus ovata ✱	sugar bush	t	8	Leathery leaves. Pink flowers are followed by reddish hairy fruit coated with sugary excretion.
Ruscus aculeatus	butcher's broom	s	7	Stiffly branched shrub making clumps of spine-tipped thick cladodes (flattened stems) resembling leaves. Bright red berries where both sexes planted. Will grow in deep shade.
Sarcococca humilis ✿	sweet box	s	7	Small, thicketing shrub with shiny, tapering leaves and very fragrant white flowers in late winter followed by shiny black berries. *S. hookeriana* and *S. ruscifolia* are similar, the latter with red berries. All are good in deep shade.

▷

BOTANICAL NAME	COMMON NAME	HT	ZONE	NOTES ON CHARACTER
Sasa palmata	palmate bamboo	m	6	Large leaves spread fingerlike from bright green canes. Rampant spreader, so not for small gardens. The form *nebulosa* has purple blotched stems.
Sasa veitchii	Kuma-Zasa bamboo	s	7	Dense growth of purplish canes with wide leaves withering along margins in winter, providing variegated effect through winter.
Shibataea kumasasa	okame-zasa	s	7	Dwarf bamboo of compact, leafy habit on zig-zag, brownish canes. Best on moist soils.
Simmondsia chinensis ✳	jojoba	s	9	Nice foliage texture. Stands pruning well. Likes heat and sun. Female plants bear edible fruit.
Sinarundinaria nitida	fountain bamboo	m	6	Elegant bamboo with thin, purple canes arching at the top bearing delicate, narrow leaves.
Skimmia japonica ✿	Japanese skimmia	s	7	Rounded shrubs with bright green leaves, white, fragrant flowers in April, followed by bright red fruit on female plants. The variety *reevesiana* is lower growing, with perfect flowers, so every plant bears fruit.
Thamnocalamus spathaceus	umbrella bamboo	t	7	A clump-forming, non-invasive bamboo with elegant slender stems and small leaves. Thrives in woodland shelter.
Trochodendron aralioides	wheel tree	t	7	Attractive foliage plant with whorled, diamond-shaped, apple-green, leathery leaves and curious green flowers in summer. Attractive tiered branching habit.
Vaccinium ovatum	evergreen huckleberry	m	7	Dense growth habit with small, box-like leaves that emerge a bright coppery red color. White to pink flowers in May, followed by edible black berries.
Vaccinium vitis-idaea	mountain cranberry	s	3	Valuable for ground cover on moist, acidic soils. Small leaves, at first tinged red or orange. Pinkish flowers in May, followed by sour red berries.
Viburnum × burkwoodii ✿	Burkwood viburnum	m	5	Semi-evergreen shrub with shining, ovate leaves, brownish-felted below, and highly fragrant clusters of pinkish-white flowers from January to May, depending on season.
Viburnum cinnamomifolium		t	8	Attractive, lustrous three-nerved leaves on upright plant like a larger *V. davidii*. Flowers white in May, followed by blue-black fruit.
Viburnum davidii ◆	David viburnum	s	7	Versatile shrub of compact habit with dark glossy green, three-nerved leaves. Flowers white in June, followed by metallic blue fruit. Plant several to assure fruit is produced. Useful as large-scale ground cover.
Viburnum henryi ✿ ◆	Henry viburnum	m	7	Stiffly branched shrub with narrow, glossy leaves and white, fragrant flowers in large panicles in June. Fruit red, turning black.
Viburnum odoratissimum ✿	sweet viburnum	t	9	Large, lustrous dark green, oval leaves and fragrant, conical panicles of white flowers. Fruit is red, becoming black.
Viburnum propinquum		s	8	Resembling *V. davidii* in habit, but with narrower, three-nerved dark green, glossy leaves and black fruit.
Viburnum rhytidophyllum ◆	leatherleaf viburnum	t	5	Large shrub with long, crinkled leaves coated thickly with grayish-brown wool beneath. Showy red to black fruits. Makes a bold feature, space permitting.
Viburnum tinus ◆	laurustinus	m	8	Valuable winter-flowering species with pink to white flower clusters from November to April, followed by metallic blue, then black fruit in summer. More drought tolerant than most viburnums.

Rhododendron canescens, the Florida pinxter flower and *Primula japonica*.

Select List of Rhododendron Species

❀ = scented flowers   ✳ = suitable for dry places   ◆ = suitable for alkaline soils
PLANT HEIGHT CODE (HT): s = small (under 3 ft [1 m])   m = medium (3–9 ft [1–3 m])   t = tall (more than 9 ft [3 m])

The reader may think it strange that there are few rhododendron hybrids in the plant tables. All gardeners would agree that they should be well represented in the woodland garden. However, there are so many good sources of information (see bibliography) that to list the numerous hybrids would be superfluous. Instead, a selected, abbreviated list of rhododendron species (with a few outstanding forms) is included.

The rhododendrons are divided into evergreen and deciduous kinds in the list. For many years, the old category of Azalea has not been recognized. However, the deciduous kinds formerly called Azalea are listed separately. The popular evergreen species known as "Kurumes" or "Japanese azaleas" are found in the evergreen category.

SPECIES NAME	COMMON NAME	NATIVITY	HT	ZONE	NOTES ON CHARACTER
Evergreen species					
aberconwayi		Yunnan	m	7	Small, neat leaves and compact form.
adenogynum		Yunnan, Sichuan, SE Tibet	m	7	Compact plant with leathery, dark green leaves with heavy indumentum.
adenopodum		E. Sichuan and Hubei	m	6	Hardy plant with pink flowers, related to *R. smirnowii*.
ambiguum		Sichuan	m	6	Hardy, resilient lepidote species with pale yellow flowers.
arboreum		Kashmir to Bhutan	t	8	Superb true red flowers. Hardy only in milder areas.
arboreum 'Sir Charles Lemon'		Garden Origin	m	8	Spectacular foliage plant with cinnamon-colored indumentum on leaves and pink to red flowers.
arboreum var. *album*		Kashmir to Bhutan	t	8	Hardier than red-flowered forms.

▷

SPECIES NAME	COMMON NAME	NATIVITY	HT	ZONE	NOTES ON CHARACTER
argyrophyllum		Sichuan	t	8	Attractive growth habit with silvery underside to leaves and blush pink flowers.
augustinii		Tibet to Hupeh	m	7	Tall lepidote species with small aromatic leaves and beautiful lavender to blue flowers. Best in shade.
augustinii 'Electra'		Garden Origin	m	7	One of the best forms for its startling violet-blue flowers marked with yellow.
auriculatum ✿		Hupeh	t	8	Large shrub with distinct leaves noted for its late show of white, fragrant blooms in July and August.
baileyi		SE Tibet, Bhutan	s	7	Dwarf lepidote species with unusual purple-red flowers.
balfourianum		Yunnan, Szechwan	m	7	Attractive plant with glossy, dark green leaves with gray undersurface and pale rose, spotted flowers.
barbatum		Nepal, Sikkim, Bhutan	m	8	Large, spreading shrub with attractive peeling bark and hairy leaves. Flowers crimson-scarlet, in March.
callimorphum		Yunnan, NE Burma	m	8	Medium-sized shrub of neat habit with crimson-blotched rose-colored flowers.
calophytum		Sichuan	t	7	Large shrub or small tree of noble character and impressively large, narrow leaves. Needs shade and shelter from wind. Flowers white to pink, borne in late winter. The hardiest large-leaved species.
calostrotum		NE Burma, Yunnan, Tibet	m	6	Compact lepidote species with grayish green leaves and large magenta-crimson flowers.
campanulatum		Garden Origin	m	8	A medium to large shrub with distinct leaves covered beneath with a suede-like felt. Flowers rose to lavender-blue.
campylocarpum		Nepal, Sikkim, Tibet	m	8	Small to medium-sized shrub noted for its clear yellow flowers in April and May.
campylogynum	Myrtilloides group	Burma, Tibet, Yunnan	m	7	A low-growing, dainty shrub with small lustrous leaves, blue beneath. Waxy, plum-colored flowers. Good for sunny clearings along woodland paths.
catawbiense		Allegheny Mts., USA	t	4	Very hardy medium to large species tolerant of exposure. A parent of many hybrids. Flower purple to pink or white; June.
ciliatum ✿		Bhutan, SE Tibet, E Nepal	m	8	Beautiful, small rounded shrub with peeling bark and conspicuous ciliate leaves. Large, nodding, fragrant rosy pink flowers; March.
cinnabarinum		Nepal, Sikkim, Bhutan	m	8	Choice, medium-sized, upright shrub with ovate, spicy-scented leaves. Flowers tubular, red. 'Roylei' is one of its best variants.
cinnabarinum	Concatenans group	SE Tibet	m	8	As for *R. cinnabarinum*, but flowers apricot-yellow.

▷

SPECIES NAME	COMMON NAME	NATIVITY	HT	ZONE	NOTES ON CHARACTER
concinnum		Sichuan	m	7	Medium-sized lepidote shrub with funnel-shaped, purple flowers.
dauricum		N. China	m	5	Partly deciduous. Flowers violet pink in early spring. Hardy.
davidsonianum		Sichuan, Yunnan	m	8	Robust shrub with lanceolate leaves. Flower color variable, from soft pink to purplish-rose, often spotted. 'Caerhays Pink' is a good pink form.
decorum ❁		W. China, NE Burma	m	7	Large shrub bearing fragrant white flowers in May.
diaprepes ❁		Yunnan, SE Tibet	m	8	Small tree with light green leaves to 1 ft (30 cm). Fleshy, slightly scented white flowers appear in late June.
dichroanthum		NE Upper Burma, Yunnan	m	7	Dome-shaped shrub with leaves white-felted beneath. Flowers an unusual coppery-orange shade.
edgarianum		Garden Origin	s	6	Small shrub with scaly, sage-green leaves covered with lively, bright purple flowers in May.
falconeri ssp. *falconeri*		Sikkim, Nepal Bhutan	t	8	A large shrub or small tree requiring shelter. Leaves large, with deeply impressed veins above. Flowers cream-yellow, not borne on young plants.
fastigiatum		Yunnan	s	6	Dependable, dwarf lepidote shrub with lavender-purple flowers in April.
ferrugineum ◆	Swiss alpen rose	Pyrenees to Austrian Alps	s	5	Spreading shrub with small leaves and rose-crimson tubular flowers in late spring. Will grow in alkaline soil.
forrestii		SE Tibet, Yunnan, Burma	s	7	Prostrate, mat-forming plant with dark green, rounded leaves and large bell-shaped scarlet flowers in April. Needs constant soil moisture and shade.
fortunei ❁		Chekiang (E. China)	t	6	Large shrub with fragrant, funnel-shaped lilac-pink flowers in May. A good species to try in southern gardens due to its heat tolerance.
glaucophyllum		E. Nepal, Sikkim, Bhutan	s	7	Small shrub with glaucous, aromatic leaves. Flowers are bell-shaped, rose to lilac, appearing in late April.
haematodes		Yunnan	m	7	A dwarf species with beautiful form and foliage. Leaf indumentum is reddish brown. Flowers brilliant scarlet-crimson; May.
hanceanum ❁		Sichuan	s	7	Lepidote shrub of small size with bronzy-colored young growth and cream to pale yellow, mildly scented flowers in April.
hippophaeoides		Yunnan, Sichuan	s	5	Hardy, small lepidote shrub tolerant of very wet conditions. Lavender flowers appear in March and April.
hodgsonii		Nepal, Sikkim to Bhutan	t	8	Large, distinguished shrub with exfoliating bark and very handsome large leaves, gray felted beneath. One of the hardier large-leaved species. Flowers magenta on older plants.
impeditum		Yunnan, Sichuan	s	5	Dwarf shrub with small scaly leaves bearing purplish blue flowers in April. Suitable for sunny clearings. 'Exbury' is a good deep purple-flowered form.

▷

ABOVE, L TO R: *Rhododendron calophytum, Rhododendron cinnabarinum, Rhododendron × Loderi* hybrids

◁ *Select List of Rhododendron Species*

SPECIES NAME	COMMON NAME	NATIVITY	HT	ZONE	NOTES ON CHARACTER
indicum	Indian azalea	SW China, S. Japan	m	7	Small, dense, semi-evergreen azalea. Flower color ranges from red to scarlet. 'Balsaminiflorum' is a good form with double, salmon-pink flowers.
intricatum		Sichuan, Yunnan	s	6	Fine-textured dwarf lepidote. Flowers blue, in May.
kaempferi	Kaempfer azalea	Japan	m	6	Medium-sized shrub, semi-evergreen in mild areas. Flowers in May; color varies from salmon-red to rose-scarlet.
keiskei		Japan	m	5	Hardy semi-dwarf lepidote species. Abundant pale yellow flowers from March to May.
kiusianum 'Mt. Fuji'	Kyushu azalea	Garden Origin	s	6	Dwarf shrub with small oval leaves. This choice cultivar bears white flowers in May or June.
Ledum groenlandicum		Labrador tea	s	2	Dwarf shrub with aromatic leaves and white flowers in terminal clusters during late spring. Good on wet sites. For acid soil.
lepidotum		NW Himalaya Yunnan	s	7	A dwarf lepidote shrub with pink to purple, seldom yellow or white flowers in June. Lightly shaded location is best.
leucapsis		SE Tibet	m	8	An early-flowering, dwarf shrub with long hairy leaves and stems. Flowers whitish, with dark brown anthers; February or March. Needs shelter.
linearifolium ✿	spider azalea	C. & S. Japan	m	7	Spreading semi-evergreen shrub with densely hairy leaves. Flowers fragrant, pink-purple, April.
× *loderi* ✿		Garden Origin	t	7	Large fragrant white to pink flower trusses in May.
lutescens		Sichuan, Yunnan	m	7	Early-flowering Chinese species of medium height. Flowers primrose-yellow. Young leaves bronze-red. 'Bagshot Sands' is the best selection.

▷

ABOVE, L TO R: *Rhododendron maximum, Rhododendron tsariense, Rhododendron* 'Vinemount,' one of the author's hybrids

◁ *Select List of Rhododendron Species*

SPECIES NAME	COMMON NAME	NATIVITY	HT	ZONE	NOTES ON CHARACTER
macabeanum		Manipur	t	8	A large shrub with magnificent foliage, thriving in woodland shelter. Leaves to 1 ft (30 cm.), dark green, with impressed veins above, whitish tomentose beneath. Flowers pale yellow, blotched purple, April.
macrophyllum		B.C. to California	m	7	Medium to large shrub with rose-purple flowers, reddish spotted inside, appearing in May and June.
maximum	rose bay	E. North America	t	5	A very hardy, medium to large shrub with mildly fragrant white flowers, green spotted within. Although hardy, needs protection from cold winds.
minus var. *chapmanii*		SE United States	m	5	Small shrub endangered in the wild. Compact growth habit with pink flowers with greenish spots, and showy chocolate-colored anthers. Flowers in April and May.
moupinense		Sichuan, Kweichow	m	7	A desirable small, early-flowering shrub with bristly branches. Flowers white, pink, to rose, appearing in February or March. Needs shelter from cold east winds while in flower.
neriiflorum		Yunnan, SE Tibet, Burma	m	7	Beautiful medium-sized shrub with slender leaves, white underneath. Flowers scarlet to crimson, with large calyx colored like the corolla, in April and May.
niveum		Sikkim, Bhutan	m	7	Large, sturdy shrub with unique leaves covered in white indumentum, persisting and turning brown on older leaves. Flowers lavender-blue to purple, in April or May.
orbiculare		W. Sichuan	m	7	Medium-sized, dome-shaped shrub with unique rounded, heart-shaped leaves. Flowers rose-pink, in March and April. A first-class plant.

▷

SPECIES NAME	COMMON NAME	NATIVITY	HT	ZONE	NOTES ON CHARACTER
oreodoxa		Hupeh, Sichuan, Yunnan	m	7	Floriferous shrub of medium size. The pink flowers are red in bud, held when open in loose trusses, during March and April.
oreotrephes		Yunnan, Sichuan, Tibet	m	7	A large shrub noted for the bluish cast of its leaves and its free-flowering habit. Flowers mauve to rose, sometimes crimson spotted, during April and May.
pemakoense		SE Tibet	s	7	A dwarf, compact shrublet with tiny leaves smothered in outsized pink to purplish flowers. Flower buds susceptible to frost damage in cold gardens.
polycladum Scintillans group		Yunnan	s	6	Dwarf, lepidote shrub of upright habit with small leaves and blue to rose-purple flowers in April and May. One of the most reliable of the lepidote group.
proteioides		Yunnan, Sichuan, SE Tibet	m	7	Compact-growing plant with unique pattern of tight, rosetted leaves along the branches. Leaves have thick, woolly rufous coating underneath. Flowers cream with crimson spots, in April.
racemosum		Yunnan, Sichuan	s	6	A small, densely branched shrub valuable for open exposures. Abundant pink flowers, appear along the branches. Best when massed.
rex ssp. *fictolacteum*		Yunnan, Sichuan, SE Tibet	t	7	Large tree-like shrub with handsome large dark-green leaves coated with cinnamon brown felt beneath. Flowers white, in April and May. Hardy and desirable large-leaved rhododendron.
roxieanum		Yunnan, Sichuan	m	7	A slow-growing, compact shrub with narrow leaves coated with beautiful rusty-red indumentum. Flowers on older plants only; white, with rose flush, in April. Worth growing as a foliage plant alone.
rubiginosum		Sichuan, Yunnan, SE Tibet	m	7	Large shrub with oval, aromatic leaves with rusty-colored scales beneath. Flowers pink to lilac, brown spotted, in April and May.
rupicola		Yunnan, se. Tibet, Sichuan	s	7	Dwarf, spreading shrub with dark, glossy leaves, densely scaly below. Flowers deep purple to mauve, April–May. Variety *chryseum* has bright yellow flowers.
russatum		Yunnan, Sichuan	s	7	Compact growing shrub reaching about 3 ft (1 m). Flowers deep blue or violet during April and May.
saluenense		SE Tibet, Yunnan, Sichuan	s	7	Small, densely branched shrub covered in rich plum-purple flowers during April and May.
sanguineum		SE Tibet	m	8	A rather variable dwarf shrub with thick leathery leaves and large bright crimson flowers during May.
sargentianum		Sichuan	s	7	Dwarf, compact shrub. Leaves pungent when bruised. Flowers small, tubular, yellow or white; April.

▷

SPECIES NAME	COMMON NAME	NATIVITY	HT	ZONE	NOTES ON CHARACTER
sinograde		Yunnan, SE Tibet, Upper Burma	t	9	Large shrub or small tree grown for its impressive foliage. The huge, shining green leaves can be up to 3ft (1 m) long! Perfect for injecting a tropical atmosphere into the woodland.
souliei		Sichuan, Tibet	m	7	Medium-sized shrub with exquisite, nearly round leaves. Flowers white or light pink, in May or June.
stewartianum		SE Tibet, Upper Burma, Assam	m	7	Large shrub noted for the variable color of its flowers, ranging from white to yellow or crimson, appearing from February to April.
strigillosum		Sichuan	m	8	Beautiful medium-sized shrub with bristly shoots and long narrow recurved leaves. The crimson flowers are borne in February and March. Needs shelter. Subject to chlorosis in poorly drained soils.
sutchuenense		Sichuan, Hupeh	t	7	Big shrub with large, drooping leaves bearing magnificent large trusses of pale pink to rosy flowers in February and March. First rate.
thomsonii		Sikkim, Nepal, Bhutan, Tibet	m	8	A large shrub with conspicuous cinnamon-colored, peeling bark and rounded leaves. Flowers deep blood-red, with showy, persistent calyxes. Needs shelter.
trichostomum		Yunnan, Sichuan	s	7	Dwarf shrublet with small, aromatic leaves and terminal clusters of white or rose daphne-like flowers in May and June.
triflorum		E. Nepal, N. India, to Burma	m	7	Medium-sized shrub of upright habit with pretty peeling bark and lemon-yellow flowers in May.
tsariense		SE Tibet, Bhutan	m	8	Semi-dwarf shrub bearing delectable apple blossom pink flowers in May.
wardii		Yunnan, Sichuan, SE Tibet	m	8	Large shrub with rounded leaves and clear yellow flowers of exquisite form, color and character, in May.
williamsianum		Sichuan	m	6	Dome-shaped, wide spreading bush with heart-shaped, round leaves. New growth is bronzy-red. The bell-shaped pink flowers appear in April. Pest resistant. A first-rate plant.
wiltonii		W. Sichuan	m	7	A medium-sized shrub with beautiful foliage and pink flowers in May.
yakushimanum		Japan (Yakushima Is.)	m	6	Fine, compact shrub with silvery young growth, later becoming leathery, dark glossy green with dense brown tomentum beneath. Flowers apple-blossom pink, fading to white, in May.
yunnanense		Sichuan, Yunnan, and Burma	m	6	Hardy, free-flowering shrub of medium size with funnel-shaped pink flowers with darker spots in May.

Deciduous species

alabamense ❀	Alabama azalea	SE USA	m	6	Dainty, low deciduous species with white, fragrant flowers.
arborescens ❀	sweet azalea	E. USA	m	5	Tall-growing deciduous azalea with very fragrant flowers.

▷

◁ Select List of Rhododendron Species

SPECIES NAME	COMMON NAME	NATIVITY	HT	ZONE	NOTES ON CHARACTER
atlanticum ❀	coastal azalea	E. USA	s	5	Hardy, dwarf deciduous azalea with fragrant white to pinkish flowers.
austrinum	Florida azalea	SE USA	m	6	Large deciduous azalea with spectacular yellow to orange flowers.
calendulaceum	Torrey flame azalea	E. USA	m	6	Deciduous azalea to 10 ft (3 m). Vividly colored flowers ranging from yellow through orange-scarlet.
canadense ❀	rhodora azalea	Labrador to N. New Jersey	s	4	Small, moisture-loving deciduous azalea. Flowers rose-purple, in April.
canescens	Florida pinxter or azalea	SE USA	m	5	Charming, medium-sized deciduous azalea. Flowers white, pink-flushed, fragrant.
dauricum		NE Asia, Japan	m	5	Charming, early-flowering, semi-evergreen shrub bearing rosy purple flowers as early as January in mild seasons.
luteum ❀	Pontic azalea	Caucasus and E Europe	m	5	Deciduous azalea well known for its fragrant yellow flowers borne in May. Buds and young shoots are sticky.
mucronulatum		NE Asia, Japan	m	5	A hardy, small to medium-sized semi-evergreen shrub with bright rose-pink flowers appearing from January to March. 'Cornell Pink' is a choice selection.
occidentale ❀	western azalea	S. Oregon to S. California	m	6	Vigorous deciduous shrub with good fall color. Fragrant, white to pink flowers, tinged yellow to orange at the base, appear in early summer.
periclymenoides ❀	pinxter bloom azalea	E. United States	m	5	Medium-sized deciduous azalea flowering in May with fragrant, pink flowers with a red-tinged tube. Prefers a moist location.
prunifolium	plumleaf azalea	SW Georgia & E Alabama	m	6	Deciduous azalea of medium size remarkable for its late flowering in July and August. Flowers vermillion-red.
schlippenbachii	royal azalea	Korea and NE Manchuria	m	6	Medium- to large-sized deciduous azalea with whorled leaves turning orange and crimson in fall. The blush pink or white flowers appear before the leaves. A beautiful plant.
serpyllifolium	wild thyme azalea	C. & S. Japan	s	7	Small deciduous azalea-like shrub of dense, twiggy habit with tiny leaves. The small rose-pink flowers appear in April and May. This dainty plant should be planted near a path.
vaseyi	pinkshell azalea	North Carolina	m	5	Deciduous azalea of medium size. Red fall color. Pink or white flowers appear before the leaves in April.
viscosum ❀	swamp honeysuckle	E. United States	m	5	Summer-flowering azalea-type shrub of medium size. Flowers in June or July; white or pink, fragrant.
yedoense	Korean azalea	C. & S. Korea	m	5	Small deciduous azalea of spreading habit with good orange and red autumn color. Flowers lilac to purple, in May.

Plants of the Woodland Floor

*T*HE FLOOR OF the well-planted woodland garden is a carefully chosen mixture of compatible plants, which, because of their adaptation to shade, have a competitive advantage over coarser plants and weeds. In grouping the low herbaceous and woody plants together, the objective is compatibility among the plants in terms of a connected geographical origin or similar cultural needs. Asian primulas, rodgersias and meconopsis associate well together. An array of American woodland plants, including trilliums, erythroniums, sanguinarias and polygonatums, is a wonderful combination.

Herbaceous plants are often planted in drifts beside paths and in front of shrubs. A random, unstructured mix of diverse plants can also work well. After a few years, the natural conditions of the site will, by a sorting process, lead to a changed association of plants with dominant and lesser elements, just like a natural forest environment. The observant gardener will soon learn where interference is needed, where plants should be placed, and what plants would benefit by relocation to spots better suited to them.

PRECEDING PAGE: *Primula florindae*, in a moist spot beneath birches in a Quebec garden.

The prudent gardener will not be in an urgent hurry to plant the woodland floor. A period of war may need to be declared on some of the more aggressive native and foreign weeds, which, if uncontrolled, would overcome less assertive exotic plants. In some cases the natives need protection. It is a question of balance. Since native plants are the permanent and ultimate residents, they must be respected and not obliterated. The woodland floor is not a one-dimensional carpet, but a microcosm of the layered canopy structure above, and managing it requires considerable skill.

On the woodland floor, low shrubby plants can fill in between specimen shrubs such as rhododendrons, hydrangeas or camellias. A great number of small, fine-textured ericaceous plants originate from subalpine elevations in Asia. Their origin might suggest that full sun is appropriate, but experience shows that in the garden most of them are more successful under light wood-land shade with a northern or eastern exposure. Dwarf, small-leaved rhodo-dendrons such as *R. forrestii* and *R. campylogynum* are recommended, together with many Vaccinium and Gaultheria species. The American native winter-green (*Gaultheria procumbens*) is a good plant for sandy, organic soils in semi-shade. Most ericaceous plants will endure quite dry summer conditions if the humidity is high and they are shaded from the sun at its zenith.

Invasive Plants

Some herbaceous plant species should be treated with much caution because of their aggressive growth habits. False lily of the valley (*Maianthemum*), carpet bugle (*Ajuga*) and loosestrife (*Lysimachia*) spread rapidly, choking out more desirable plants. Wood anemones (*A. nemorosa* and *A. blanda*) are useful for deep shade since they leaf out and flower before the canopy reaches its midsummer density, but they are apt to be invasive, and there are better plants for less-shaded sites. One of the most rampageous plants is the common bluebell (*Hyacinthoides non-scripta*). A woodland carpet of bluebells is an attractive sight, but this fleeting spring effect is won at the expense of other less coarse species. Two curses of the woodland garden are common periwinkle (*Vinca minor*) and common ivy (*Hedera helix*). Both choke out the woodland floor, subduing all worthwhile plants. Ivy also climbs over and weakens shrubs and trees. Japanese honeysuckle (*Lonicera japonica*) and kudzu vine (*Pueravia lobata*) left unattended will smother a woodland in a few years. Blackberries (*Rubus* spp.) are also a problem on disturbed, open sites.

It is sad to see the demise of a woodland from the invasion of a foreign weed. Eradication must be ruthless and complete. A persistent program of physical removal, followed by a suitable fallow period to eradicate any regrowth, is the only way through this tangle once these plants become established.

Mosses festoon a maple tree in a Pacific Northwest rainforest.

The barberry family provides some good plants for the woodland floor. *Mahonia repens* and *M. nervosa*, native to the Pacific Northwest, are equally at home in sun or shade, provided the soil is reasonably moist. The thick, resilient leaves of these mahonias are masterpieces of plant architecture. The same strong, uncompromising quality is found, on a smaller scale, in herbaceous perennials such as the epimedium clan and Podophyllum species. The American may apple (*P. peltatum*) and the Asian *P. hexandrum* both have interesting leaves. Vanilla leaf (*Achlys triphylla*) spreads rapidly in leafy soil. These plants associate well with hepaticas, trilliums and erythroniums of American or Asian origin.

Primulas are meadow plants rather than plants of the woodland, but there are many species that are well suited to the banks of woodland streams and ponds or any spot where the moisture supply is abundant. The hardy cyclamens also have a place. *Cyclamen coum* flowers in spring, *C. hederifolium* in late summer. They require a gritty but organic soil in semishade, and they look well among rockwork, beside stone steps or on mounds and banks.

Ferns

Ferns are plants of ancient origin that contribute to the sense of mystery characteristic of the woodland garden. They range from the majestic royal fern (*Osmunda regalis*), ostrich fern (*Matteuccia struthiopteris*) and sword fern (*Polystichum munitum*), to the diminutive deer fern (*Blechnum spicant*) and parsley fern (*Cryptogramma crispa*), which are useful at the edge of the woodland path or in the rocky clefts of moss-covered rocks. In the Pacific Northwest forest, one of the most magnificent sights is an old maple clothed with moss, lichen and the epiphytic polypody fern (*Polypodium glycyrrhiza*). A similar image in the Deep South is live oaks colonized by the resurrection plant (*Selaginella lepidophylla*) and Spanish moss (*Tillandsia usneoides*). Epiphytes — non-parasitic plants that grow on other plants and obtain nutrients from rain, fallen debris, etc. — grow best where the climate is mild (Zone 7 or warmer) and humidity is high. Air plants prefer trees with thick, rough bark, such as maple (*Acer*), oak (*Quercus*) and black locust (*Robinia*). They are seldom found on conifers because the shade is too dense and conifer bark is too acid. Where conditions are suitable, it is worth the effort to attach ferns on little wads of sphagnum moss to crevices in the bark. Choose a spot that is semishaded but that receives as much rain as possible.

In the milder areas, evergreen ferns provide an interesting winter ground cover. Where the soil is too poor and shallow for ferns, one can encourage mosses, lichens and club mosses to cover the earth. These primitives of the plant kingdom contrast with more flamboyant flowering plants, compelling attention to the exquisite micro-communities of which they are a part.

Bulbs and Tubers

One of the great joys of the woodland garden is in observing its seasonal changes throughout the year. Some of these changes are dramatic, as in the brilliant color of autumn leaves or the explosion of spring bloom in massed plantings of rhododendrons. A more subtle change occurs when the delicate woodland flowers of spring and early summer appear. Many of these plants grow from bulbs and tubers, and their life cycle is ideally timed with the deciduous woodland: the flowering season and growth is complete before the leaf canopy obscures the sun. These plants will spread naturally on their own, but their numbers can be increased by dividing clumps after flowering.

Of all the plant families that carpet the woodland floor, the Liliaceae provides the richest selection. In the North American woodland, trilliums and erythroniums have pride of place. In well-prepared, leafy, spongy soil, they spread rapidly. *Trillium grandiflorum*, *T. erectum*, *T. sessile* and *T. ovatum* are easily grown and tolerant of quite dense shade. Dogtooth violets (*Erythronium* spp.) are plants of exquisite refinement. In colder areas, *E. americanum* and *E. albidum* should be tried first. The Eurasian *E. dens-canis* is the gem of the genus and probably hardier than generally supposed. The advantage of bulbous or tuberous plants is that they can be overwintered under mulches if their hardiness is suspect.

On the Pacific Coast, there is a wealth of native erythroniums. The easiest to grow (and obtain) are hybrids of *E. tuolumnense*. The cultivars 'Kondo' and 'Pagoda' are robust and spread quite rapidly. *Erythronium oregonum* is a large species with creamy white flowers. A pink species, *E. revolutum*, is rather scarce, but once established in the woodland, its flowering is a joyous annual event. Erythroniums are small, and some grooming of the woodland floor is necessary to show them to the best advantage.

The scillas and their relatives are a group of easily grown, rapidly spreading plants — sometimes to a fault. *Hyacinthoides non-scripta* is capable of taking over the entire woodland floor, but it may be suited to large gardens and associates

Plantain Lilies

Where conditions are too shaded for lilies, plantain lilies (*Hosta* spp.) are the best choice. They are valuable foliage plants for grouping along shady paths. A large number of species and hybrids are in cultivation, differing in size, leaf texture and markings.

well with large deciduous azaleas such as the Exbury hybrids and *Rhododendron luteum*. *Scilla bifolia* 'Rosea' is a charming small species that also spreads quickly. Siberian squill (*Scilla siberica*), glory-of-the-snow (*Chionodoxa luciliae*) and *Pushkinia scilloides* var. *libanotica* are good dwarf carpeting plants for the woodland floor.

Lilies

Most of the modern hybrid lilies are not generally successful woodland plants. Nearly all of them are better in full sun. This applies to the Asiatic hybrids and most of the trumpet types, including the golden aurelian strains. The Oriental hybrids (*Lilium auratum* × *L. speciosum*) should be attempted in fairly sunny woodland clearings. If they are kept isolated from other lilies and free of aphids (the principal virus vector), the effort is worthwhile, since there are few other bulbous plants that match them in spectacular beauty. Virus diseases often cause the decline of lily collections, and the presence of lilies in gardens is often ephemeral.

Of the trumpet species, *Lilium regale* seems to be the best survivor. *Lilium henryi*, a vigorous turkscap species with orange flowers, is hardy and disease-resistant. The cultivar 'Black Beauty' was obtained by crossing it with *L. rubrum*. The result of this mating is a flower color that is neither orange nor pink, but an unusual dark maroon shade. This robust hybrid is one of the best lilies for the woodland.

The finest woodland lilies are the American species and the martagons from Europe. *Lilium superbum* grows on tussocks in the moist woodlands of many eastern states and Canada. *Lilium michiganense* and *L. canadense* are similar in character, as is the western species, *L. columbianum*. All these species are perfectly in tune with the environment and aesthetic of the woodland garden. Grow them on little tussocks or mounds of leafy, gritty soil, slightly raised above the woodland floor. The martagons and their hybrids thrive with similar treatment, and generally are easier to grow than the American species. Their spotted flowers in subtle colors are lovely in dappled shade. The giant Himalayan lily (*Cardiocrinum giganteum*), a plant for milder regions, is capable of growing to 10 feet (3 m). It is magnificent beside a woodland stream.

Most lilies can be propagated by lifting and dividing the bulbs after flowering. There is no need to wait until the foliage dies down, as they will transplant well in August or September.

Himalayan Poppies

The Himalayan poppies (*Meconopsis*) are plants of the high meadows. Since the discovery of *M. betonicifolia* in 1886, this and several other species have become much sought after because of the purity of their blue flowers and handsome foliage. In cultivation, they seem to be most successful in the open woodland with well-drained, leafy soil. In these locations they may propagate naturally by seed or expansion of the clumps, but often their presence in gardens is rather fleeting, because most species are monocarpic, blooming only once and then dying, and those that are perennial may be short-lived. It is important to collect seed, which is produced in generous quantities, and grow a succession of young plants for replenishing the beds. Small *Meconopsis* plants are rather susceptible to damping off. Clean, pasteurized growing media should be used, and a careful watch kept for fungal infections that can have a devastating effect. Fungicides are a necessary standby in such cases. Slugs are apt to chew up young plants, particularly just after planting them out in the garden. These nocturnal raiders must be vigorously excluded until the plants are well established.

Meconopsis is hardier than is generally supposed. In cold areas of America, snow cover is important to winter survival, since the overwintering rosettes of foliage do not tolerate desiccation. Loose organic mulches of hay or evergreen boughs placed over the crowns may help. *Meconopsis* responds to feeding, and an annual mulch of rotted manure is beneficial and provides a hospitable bed for the seeds dispersed in late summer.

Meconopsis betonicifolia and *M. grandis* are perennial under favorable conditions of growth. Nip the flowerbuds of young plants in the first season. This encourages side shoots from the base.

The yellow-flowered species, *M. paniculata*, *M. integrifolia* and *M. villosa*, are easy plants to grow. The first two are monocarpic, the latter perennial. *Meconopsis napaulensis* bears red flowers. In gardens it hybridizes freely with *M. paniculata*, yielding a vigorous mixture of plants with yellow flowers variously tinted with red. Very pretty effects can be obtained by interplanting the blue primulas (*Primula alpicola* var. *violacea*, *P. capitata* and *P. nutans*) with these spectacular yellow poppies.

ABOVE: *Meconopsis* hybrids in a woodland clearing.

BELOW: Goatsbeard (*Aruncus dioca*) and fern associates in a Quebec garden.

ABOVE, L TO R: *Anemone blanda*, *Cyclamen repandum*, Willow gentian (*Gentiana asclepiadea*)

Plants for the Woodland floor

✿ = scented flowers   ✱ = suitable for dry places   ◆ = suitable for alkaline soils

PLANT TYPE CODE (PT): b = Bulb   ro = Rootstock   rz = Rhizome
                       c = Corm   t = Tuber   ss = Subshrub

PLANT HEIGHT CODE (HT): d = dwarf (under 12 in [30.5 cm])   m = medium (1–3 ft [0.3–0.9 m])   t = tall (more than 3 ft [0.9 m])

BOTANICAL NAME	COMMON NAME	ZONE	PT	HT	NOTES ON CHARACTER
Acanthus mollis ✱	bear's-breeches	8	ro	m	Bold-textured foliage and flowers.
Achlys triphylla	vanilla leaf	7	ro	m	Interesting leaf shape, shade tolerant.
Actaea rubra ◆	red baneberry	3	ro	m	Compound foliage. *A. alba* has white berries. Poisonous.
Adiantum pedatum	maidenhair fern	4	ro	m	Fine-textured deciduous fern.
Alchemilla mollis	lady's mantle	3	ro	d	Lime-green flowers.
Alstroemeria aurea ✿	Inca lily	7	ro	m	Orange-spotted tubular flowers. For sunny spot where it will spread.
Anaphalis margaritacea ✱	pearly everlasting	3	rz	m	Spreading perennial with grey foliage and papery white "everlasting" flowers.
Anemone blanda ◆	Greek anemone	6	t	d	Rapidly spreading, tolerant of heavy shade. White flowers. Cultivar 'Atrocaerulea' has blue flowers.
Anemone coronaria ◆	crown anemone	8	t	m	Tuberous plant with solitary scarlet, blue, white, pink or bicolored flowers in spring. Spectacular when drifted in various colors.
Anemone hupehensis ◆	Japanese anemone	6	ro	t	Good woodland plant with tall stems topped with dark pink flowers in late summer. Can be cut back when half grown to induce compact growth.
Anemone nemorosa ◆	European wood anemone	3	t	d	Vigorous, clump forming, shade tolerant.
Anemone sylvestris ◆ ✿		4	ro	m	Good plant for semishade. Flowers white, fragrant.

▷

BOTANICAL NAME	COMMON NAME	ZONE	PT	HT	NOTES ON CHARACTER
Anemonella thalictroides	rue anemone	4	ro	d	Fine texture, attractive blue flowers.
Aquilegia canadensis	columbine	4	ro	d	A fine ground covering plant with vibrant scarlet and yellow flowers.
Aquilegia 'McKana Hybrids'	columbine	4	ro	m	Attractive color range, shade tolerant.
Arisaema triphyllum	Jack-in-the-pulpit	4	t	m	Curious hooded flower, bold texture.
Aruncus dioicus ❁	goat's-beard	4	ro	m	Showy panicles of small white flowers in June. Compound leaves. Good in moist soil and partial shade.
Arum italicum	Italian arum	7	t	d	Shade tolerant. Attractive spikes of red/orange fruit.
Asplenium scolopendrium	hart's-tongue fern	3	ro	d	Tough evergreen foliage. Shade plant.
Astilbe chinensis 'Pumila'	dwarf astilbe	6	ro	d	Best of the astilbes. For a moist, sunny site.
Astilbe chinensis	Chinese astilbe	6	ro	m	Good near a pool or along a stream.
Astilbe × arendsii	hybrid astilbe	6	ro	m	Attractive flower spikes in a range of colors.
Astrantia major ◆	masterwort	6	ro	m	Curious papery white flowers. Grows well in semishade.
Athyrium felix-femina	lady fern	5	ro	t	Tall fern of pleasing texture. Prefers moist site.
Begonia grandis ssp. *evansiana*	hardy begonia	8	rz	m	A superb foliage plant. Emerald green leaves; purple behind. Needs moist soil and dappled shade.
Belamcanda chinensis	leopard lily	5	c	m	Pretty orange flowers in summer, followed by jet black seeds.
Bergenia cordifolia ◆	heartleaf bergenia	3	ro	m	Bold semi-evergreen plant of coarse texture for sun or shade. Pink flowers in early spring.
Bergenia purpurascens ◆	bergenia	5	ro	m	Leaves turn reddish in a sunny place.
Blechnum spicant	deer fern	6	ro	d	Rich-textured evergreen foliage.
Bletilla striata	ground orchid	8	b	d	Pink terrestrial orchid for a moist sunny place.
Brunnera macrophylla 'Dawson's White'	brunnera	4	ro	m	Attractive foliage.
Caltha leptosepala	white marsh marigold	3	ro	d	Spreads rapidly in moist soil. Good for edge of pool. White flowers.
Caltha palustris	marsh marigold	3	ro	m	For pond margins in moist soil. Flowers are bright yellow.
Caltha palustris 'Flore Pleno'	marsh marigold	3	ro	d	Double-flowered. Less aggressive than the type.
Calypso bulbosa	calypso orchid	2	b	d	Rare and endangered terrestrial orchid for a shaded, moist site. Do not collect from the wild; purchase plants from reputable source.
Camassia leichtlinii	Leichtlin camas	5	b	t	Bold foliage, blue flowers. For semishade.
Camassia quamash	common camas	5	b	m	Deep blue flowers. Needs sun. Not as tall as *C. leichtlinii*. Prefers to be dry after flowering.
Calochortus spp. ✳	mariposa lily	6	c	s	Elegant flowers. Best on sunny, summer-dry banks.

▷

BOTANICAL NAME	COMMON NAME	ZONE	PT	HT	NOTES ON CHARACTER
Cardamine diphylla	pepperroot	3	b	d	Shade-tolerant ground-covering plant.
Cardiocrinum giganteum ❀	giant Himalayan lily	6	b	t	Magnificent, bold heart-shaped leaves held on a tall, thick spike to 10 ft (3 m). White flowers.
Chionodoxa luciliae	glory of the snow	4	b	d	Rapidly spreading on a well-drained, moist site.
Chrysogonum virginianum	goldenstar	6	ro	d	Attractive aster-like plant for sunny places.
Claytonia virginica	spring beauty	5	b	d	Beautiful spring bulb for deciduous woodland.
Clintonia uniflora	queen cup	6	b	d	Attractive white flower followed by blue fruit.
Colchicum autumnale	autumn crocus	5	b	d	Impressive when massed in open woodland. Large pink flowers borne in late September.
Convallaria majalis ❀	lily of the valley	4	rz	d	One of the most fragrant woodland plants. White nodding flowers on upright flower spikes. Shade tolerant. Spreads by rhizomes.
Cornus canadensis	bunchberry	2	ro	d	Miniature dogwood flowers held above a compact carpeting plant. For moist shade.
Crocosmia cvs. ✳	montbretia	6	c	m	Cormous plant with iris-like leaves and showy flower spikes in late spring/summer. Flowers yellow to dark red, depending on variety.
Crocus ancyrensis	golden bunch crocus	4	c	d	Perfect for rocky outcrops in sun.
Crocus angustifolius	cloth-of-gold	4	c	d	Narrow leaves, golden yellow flowers in early spring.
Crocus chrysanthus	golden crocus	4	c	d	Interesting for its yellow blooms striped with brown.
Crocus korolkowii	Celandine crocus	6	c	d	Bright yellow flowers, easily grown.
Crocus medius		6	c	d	Autumn-blooming species. White flowers veined purple.
Crocus serotinus		6	c	d	Autumn-blooming. Flowers lilac with yellow throat.
Crocus sieberi		6	c	d	Early flowering, variable in flower color.
Crocus speciosus	showy crocus	5	c	d	Tolerant of a wide range of conditions and spreads freely. Flowers lilac-blue.
Crocus tommasinianus	Tommasini's crocus	5	c	d	Spreads rapidly. Flowers lavender to deep purple, spring.
Cryptogramma crispa ✳	parsley fern	4	ro	d	Tight, compact little fern for rocky places. Tolerates drought.
Cyclamen cilicium	sowbread	7	t	d	Mixture of grit and peat suit this plant. Autumn-flowering.
Cyclamen coum ◆	hardy cyclamen	7	t	d	Spring-flowering. Rosy red flowers. Easy to grow.
Cyclamen hederifolium ◆	ivy-leaved cyclamen	5	t	d	Choice, autumn-flowering. Spreads rapidly and is long lived.
Cyclamen repandum ❀ ◆	spring cyclamen	7	t	d	The last species to flower in spring. Fragrant flowers.
Cypripedium acaule	moccasin-flower	2	b	d	Exquisite terrestrial orchid. difficult to establish. For semishade.
Cypripedium calceolus ◆	yellow lady slipper	4	b	d	As above, flowers yellow. Don't collect wild plants.

▷

ABOVE, L TO R: Dogtooth violet (*Erythronium dens-canis*), *Erythronium americanum*, Japanese water iris (*Iris ensata*)

◁ *Plants for the Woodland Floor*

BOTANICAL NAME	COMMON NAME	ZONE	PT	HT	NOTES ON CHARACTER
Cypripedium californicum	lady slipper	7	b	d	Less hardy than related species. Flowers yellow-green.
Cypripedium montanum	mountain lady slipper	3	b	d	Attractive western species. Flowers purple.
Cypripedium reginae	showy lady slipper	3	b	d	The gem of the hardy orchids. Rare. Flowers pink, mottled white.
Dactylorhiza maculata	terrestrial orchid	6	t	d	One of the easiest orchids in cultivation. Spotted purple or white flowers.
Darmera peltata	umbrella plant	5	rz	m	Early, pale pink flowers are followed by bold leaves. Likes a moist location.
Dicentra canadensis	squirrel corn	4	ro	d	Rapidly spreading ground cover.
Dicentra formosa	western bleeding heart	5	ro	m	Good shade plant with pendent, jewel-like pink or purple flowers. A white form is also available. Can be invasive.
Dictamnus albus	gas plant	3	ro	m	Easily grown in semishade. Flowers white or pale purple.
Digitalis lutea	foxglove	5	ro	m	Biennial, less coarse than common species. Flowers yellow.
Digitalis ferruginea	rusty foxglove	7	ro	m	Brown, rusty red flowers.
Digitalis purpurea	common foxglove	4	ro	m	Tolerant of deep shade. Will naturalize itself.
Disporum hookeri var. *oreganum*	fairybells	7	ro	d	Elegant little wildflower. For shade.
Dodecatheon hendersonii	shooting star	7	b	d	Cyclamen-like flowers. Tolerant of wet soil.
Dracunculus vulgaris	dragon arum	8	t	m	Interesting aroid with curious flowers.
Dryopteris dilatata	wood fern	4	ro	d	Fine-textured fern that spreads rapidly.
Dryopteris erythrosora	Japanese shield fern	7	ro	d	Evergreen fern for moist, well-drained woods.
Dryopteris wallichiana		7	ro	d	Combines well with other Asian plants. Attractive foliage.

▷

BOTANICAL NAME	COMMON NAME	ZONE	PT	HT	NOTES ON CHARACTER
Epigaea repens	trailing arbutus	2	rz	d	Excellent creeping ground cover with fragrant, white-to-pink flowers in April. Good under pines and other difficult, shady positions.
Epimedium grandiflorum ◆	bishop's-hat	5	ro	m	Interesting-textured ground cover. Evergreen.
Epimedium pinnatum	Persian epimedium	5	ro	m	Tolerant of shade or sun.
Epilobium (Zauschneria) canum ✳	California fuchsia	7	rz	m	Good ground-covering perennial. Red tubular flowers attractive to hummingbirds. Good informal cover for sunny banks.
Eranthis cilicica ◆	winter aconite	6	t	d	Delightful harbinger of spring. Easily grown.
Eranthis hyemalis	winter aconite	4	t	d	For well-drained, woodsy soil. Yellow flowers.
Eremurus himalaicus ✿	Himalayan candle	3	c	m	Stately spikes of white flowers appear in late spring.
Erica carnea	winter heath	5	ss	d	Plant in peaty-sandy soil beneath the light shade of deciduous trees.
Eriogonum spp. ✳	buckwheat	6	rz	s	Tough mat-forming plants for dry, rocky places.
Erysimum linifolium ◆	shrubby wallflower	6	ss	m	Easily grown subshrub for sunny spot. Flowers purple or violet.
Erythronium albidum ◆	white fawn-lily	4	b	d	Ideal plant for naturalizing in woods.
Erythronium americanum ◆	dogtooth violet	4	b	d	Prefers well-drained, gritty soil. Flowers yellow, spotted brown or purple.
Erythronium dens-canis	European fawn-lily	3	b	d	Superb foliage, easy to grow. Rose to mauve flowers.
Erythronium oregonum	Oregon fawn-lily	5	b	m	One of the taller-growing species. Flowers cream with yellow center.
Erythronium revolutum	mahogany fawn-lily	5	b	d	Rare and beautiful pink-flowered species.
Erythronium tuolumnense	Tuolumne fawn-lily	5	b	m	This and its hybrids spread rapidly. Flowers bright yellow.
Euphorbia characias ✳ ◆		7	ss	t	Vigorous subshrub for sun or semishade. Attractive blue-green foliage. Subsp. *wulfenii* has showy yellow-green flowers.
Filipendula vulgaris ✿	meadowsweet	3	ro	t	Robust moisture lover for poolside.
Fritillaria imperialis ✿	crown imperial	5	b	t	Statuesque, easily grown fritillary with orange nodding flowers.
Fritillaria meleagris ✿	snake lily	3	b	d	Good plant for woodland rockery.
Fritillaria pudica ✿	chocolate lily	3	b	d	Unusual flower color, shade tolerant.
Galanthus elwesii	giant snowdrop	5	b	d	Easily grown bulb, indispensable in the woodland.
Galium odoratum	sweet woodruff	4	ro	d	Aggressively spreading ground cover, shade tolerant.
Galtonia candicans ✿	giant summer hyacinth	7	b	m	Summer-flowering bulb with tall spikes of pendent, creamy white flowers. Best in full sun.
Gentiana asclepiadea	willow gentian	6	ro	m	Tallest and most easily grown gentian. Azure-blue flowers.
Gentiana septemfida	crested gentian	3	ro	d	Grow in open sunny woodland clearings.
Gentiana sino-ornata	fall gentian	6	ro	d	Rich blue, needs perfect drainage, as do all gentians.
Geranium viscosissimum	cranesbill	4	ro	m	For a sunny spot near woodland edge.

▷

BOTANICAL NAME	COMMON NAME	ZONE	PT	HT	NOTES ON CHARACTER
Gilia aggregata ✳	scarlet gilia	7	ro	m	Brilliant red flowers. Thrives on dry slopes.
Goodyera oblongifolia	rattlesnake plantain	7	ro	d	Dainty terrestrial orchid. Easy to grow.
Helleborus argutifolius ◆	Corsican Christmas rose	7	ro	m	Bright green bold-textured foliage. Yellow-green flowers in early spring.
Helleborus foetidus ◆	bearsfoot hellebore	6	ro	m	Tolerant of alkaline soil. Foliage evergreen.
Helleborus lividus ◆	green hellebore	7	ro	m	Attractive, bold leathery foliage with creamy green flowers tinged purple in late winter.
Helleborus niger ◆	Christmas rose	4	ro	m	Needs a sheltered place. Flowers white, very early.
Helleborus orientalis ◆	Lenten rose	6	ro	m	Charming woodland plant. Easily grown, evergreen.
Hemerocallis lilio-asphodelus ✿	lemon daylily	3	ro	m	Fragrant lemon-yellow flowers in early summer.
Hepatica acutiloba ◆	liverleaf	5	rz	s	Three-lobed leaves persist through winter. Forms with blue, pink and white flowers are available.
Hosta fortunei ✿	Fortune's plantain lily	4	ro	m	Many cultivars available of this superb moisture-loving plant with attractive foliage.
Hosta fortunei var. *hyacinthina* ✿	Fortune's plantain lily	4	ro	m	Fragrant lilac-colored flowers.
Hosta lancifolia	narrow-leaved p. lily	4	ro	m	More sun tolerant than the wider-leaved kinds.
Hosta plantaginea var. *grandiflora* ✿	fragrant plantain lily	4	ro	m	Floriferous and fragrant.
Hosta sieboldiana	plantain lily	4	ro	t	Bold foliage. Needs ample space in semishade. Many cultivars offered.
Hosta undulata	wavy-leaved p. lily	4	ro	m	Leaves curiously twisted. A variegated form is available.
Hyacinthus sp. ✿	hyacinth	4	b	s	Bulbous plant with strongly scented flowers in spring.
Incarvillea delavayi	hardy gloxinia	6	ro	m	Spectacular pink flowers. Nice foliage.
Ipheion uniflorum	spring starflower	8	b	d	For sunny clearings. Foliage emits an onion smell.
Iris douglasiana	Douglas' iris	8	rz	m	West Coast iris. Needs to be kept dry after flowering.
Iris ensata	Japanese iris	5	rz	m	Moist place beside water is the best location for this plant. Many cultivars offered.
Iris laevigata	Japanese iris	4	rz	m	Same conditions as above.
Iris pumila	dwarf bearded iris	4	rz	d	Many cultivars are available. Wants a warm, sunny location.
Iris reticulata	netted iris	5	rz	d	Plant in pockets amid rocks in gritty soil. Many hybrids.
Iris sibirica ◆	Siberian iris	3	rz	t	Flowering season short but spectacular.
Iris versicolor	blue flag	3	rz	m	Easily grown species. For moist soil.
Ixiolirion tataricum	Siberian lily	7	b	m	Intense blue flowers and narrow leaves.
Jeffersonia diphylla	twinleaf	5	ro	d	Attractive foliage. Delicate white flowers with yellow stamens.

▷

BOTANICAL NAME	COMMON NAME	ZONE	PT	HT	NOTES ON CHARACTER
Jeffersonia dubia	twinleaf	5	ro	d	Choice plant with solitary blue flowers. Spreads slowly.
Kirengeshoma palmata		6	ro	t	Large maple-like leaves and creamy white flowers in late summer. A choice plant.
Lamium maculatum	spotted dead nettle	4	rz	d	Attractive fast-growing ground cover with white-striped leaves. Many cultivated forms.
Leucojum aestivum ❀	summer snowflake	4	b	m	Pure white pendulous flowers with green petal tips are borne in early summer.
Leucojum autumnale	autumn snowflake	5	b	d	Fall blooming. White flowers tinged pink at base. Shade tolerant.
Leucojum vernum ❀	spring snowflake	4	b	d	Fragrant early-blooming bulb. Good for massing among shrubs.
Ligularia przewalskii	Shavalski's ligularia	6	ro	t	Bold serrated foliage and tall yellow flower spikes. For sun.
Lilium 'Black Beauty'	hybrid lily	5	b	t	Robust oriental hybrid. Pest resistant.
Lilium 'Black Dragon'	hybrid lily	5	b	t	Strong growing. Impressive color and form. For full sun.
Lilium 'Golden Splendor' ❀	hybrid lily	5	b	m	Rich golden color. Trumpet-shaped flowers.
Lilium 'Green Magic'	hybrid lily	5	b	m	Like other trumpet lilies, needs sun.
Lilium (Oriental Hybrids)	hybrid oriental lily	6	b	t	All oriental lilies are best isolated from other kinds to limit the spread of disease. Many named strains.
Lilium 'Pink Perfection'	hybrid lily	5	b	t	Robust trumpet lily. Easily grown.
Lilium 'Thunderbolt'	hybrid lily	5	b	t	Very tall; orange flowers.
Lilium canadense	Canada lily	3	b	m	Rare and beautiful lily with yellow flowers. Needs good drainage.
Lilium candidum ❀	Madonna lily	5	b	m	Popular white lily. The floral emblem of Quebec province. Protect crowns with airy mulch in winter.
Lilium hansonii	Hanson lily	5	b	m	Vigorous lily for semishade. Flowers deep orange-yellow.
Lilium henryi ◆	Henry lily	5	b	t	Reliable, disease-resistant tall lily. Orange or yellow flowers in early summer.
Lilium martagon ◆	martagon lily	3	b	m	Beautiful spire-like flower spikes. Hardy.
Lilium monadelphum	Caucasian lily	5	b	m	Attractive yellow flowers with semireflexed petals.
Lilium philadelphicum	wood lily	4	b	m	Hardy prairie lily. Provincial emblem of Saskatchewan. Flowers orange-red.
Lilium regale ❀	regal lily	4	b	m	Finest of the hardy lilies. Easy to grow and fragrant. Flowers white.
Lilium speciosum var. *rubrum* ❀		5	b	m	Various shades of pink in each flower. Fragrant.
Lilium superbum	Turk's-cap lily	3	b	t	North American native with orange-crimson flowers.
Limnanthes douglasii	meadow foam	7	ro	d	For a sunny, moist location. Yellow to white flowers.

▷

ABOVE, L TO R: *Begonia grandis* ssp. *evansiana*, Regal lily (*Lilium regale*), Turkscap lily (*Lilium superbum*)

◁ *Plants for the Woodland Floor*

BOTANICAL NAME	COMMON NAME	ZONE	PT	HT	NOTES ON CHARACTER
Lobelia cardinalis	cardinal flower	3	ro	t	Prefers a moist location. Spectacular scarlet flowers.
Luetkea pectinata	partridge foot	3	ro	d	Prostrate plant with small white flowers. Likes sun.
Lysichiton americanum	skunk cabbage	6	ro	m	Bold foliage and yellow spathes. Needs a swampy location. *L. camtschatensis* has white flowers.
Matteuccia struthiopteris	ostrich fern	3	ro	t	Impressive form. Shade tolerant.
Meconopsis betonicifolia	Himalayan blue poppy	6	ro	m	Spectacular intense blue flowers. Needs a woodsy, moist location in semishade.
Meconopsis grandis		6	ro	m	Similar to the above but more persistent.
Meconopsis napaulensis	satin poppy	7	ro	t	Bold plants arise from fuzzy rosettes. Flowers red, blue or white. Biennial.
Meconopsis paniculata		7	ro	t	Similar to the above but with yellow flowers. Dies after flowering.
Meconopsis × *sheldonii*		6	ro	m	Hybrid, similar to *M. grandis*.
Meconopsis villosa		7	ro	d	Reliably perennial. Rounded leaves and yellow flowers.
Mertensia virginica	Virginia bluebell	4	ro	m	Borage-like plants with purple-blue flowers. Spreads fast.
Mimulus guttatus	common monkey-flower	5	ro	d	Seeds itself readily in moist soil. Yellow tubular flowers.
Mimulus lewisii	western monkey-flower	7	ro	m	Sticky foliage and red to white flowers. Likes damp soil in full sun.
Muscari armeniacum ✿	grape hyacinth	4	b	s	Deep blue spikes in early spring. Good low-growing species for the woodland floor.
Myosotis scorpioides	forget-me-not	5	rz	d	Soft hairy stems and clear blue flowers with yellow, pink or white centers, in May. Delightful as a ground cover.
Narcissus asturiensis	Asturian daffodil	4	b	d	Miniature daffodil for full sun.

▷

BOTANICAL NAME	COMMON NAME	ZONE	PT	HT	NOTES ON CHARACTER
Narcissus bulbocodium var. *conspicuus*	petticoat daffodil	6	b	d	Beautiful miniature daffodil. Plant in sheltered location.
Narcissus cyclamineus ✺	cyclamen narcissus	6	b	d	Dwarf daffodils such as these need a protective winter mulch.
Narcissus tazetta ✺	polyanthes narcissus	8	b	m	The narcissus of choice for warmer zones. Very fragrant flowers.
Narcissus triandrus ✺	angel's-tears	4	b	d	Exquisite small flowers.
Narcissus triandus var. *albus* ✺	white angel's-tears	4	b	d	Dwarf narcissus need well-drained, gritty soil.
Oenothera macrocarpa ◆ ✺	Ozark sundrops	5	ro	m	For the sunny woodland edge. Scented yellow flowers open at dawn or dusk.
Omphalodes cappadocica ◆	navelwort	6	rz	d	An agressively spreading ground cover. Blue flowers in summer. Easy to grow.
Ophiopogon japonicus	dwarf lilyturf	7	ro	d	Neat, fine-textured evergreen ground cover.
Ophiopogon planiscapus 'Nigrescens'	black lilyturf	7	ro	d	Similar to *O. japonicus* but with purplish-black foliage.
Osmunda regalis	royal fern	7	ro	t	Elegant, large fern with twice-cut fronds. Fronds die back in winter.
Oxalis oregana	redwood sorrel	7	rz	d	Bright green, nearly evergreen. Suitable for dense shade.
Pachysandra terminalis	Japanese spurge	5	ro	d	Common, but ever-useful ground cover. Best in shade, as it suffers foliar burn in hot sun.
Pachysandra terminalis 'Variegata'	variegated spurge	5	ro	d	Variegated version of the Japanese spurge.
Paris quadrifolia		7	rz	d	Curious plants with green flowers and whorled leaves.
Penstemon davidsonii ✳	Davidson's penstemon	6	ro	s	Suitable for dry, sunny locations.
Penstemon fruticosus ✳	Scouler's penstemon	4	ro	s	Good among rocks in full sun. Purple flowers. This and other penstemons are often short lived. Evergreen.
Penstemon procerus ✳	small-flowered penstemon	3	ro	s	Flowers blue-purple. Withstands wetter locations but needs full sun. Evergreen foliage.
Phlox tenuifolia ✳	desert phlox	8	ro	s	Resilient perennial. Thrives with little water.
Pleione formosana	pleione orchid	8	b	d	Tender terrestrial orchid with pink or white flowers. Mulch in winter to protect from extreme frost.
Podophyllum emodi	Asian mayapple	6	ro	m	Bold peltate leaves. Prefers moist, peaty soil in shade.
Podophyllum peltatum	common mayapple	4	ro	m	Large leaves and white flowers followed by edible berries that ripen in July.
Polygonum vaccinifolium		7	rz	d	Compact deciduous ground cover with showy pink blooms all summer and into fall.

▷

BOTANICAL NAME	COMMON NAME	ZONE	PT	HT	NOTES ON CHARACTER
Polypodium vulgare	common polypody fern	3	rz	d	Easily grown dwarf fern. Evergreen.
Polystichum andersonii	Anderson's holly fern	5	rz	m	Attractive shiny foliage. For shade.
Polystichum munitum	sword fern	4	ro	m	Tolerant of dense shade and summer drought. Attractive fiddleheads in spring. Can get large.
Polystichum setiferum	soft shield fern	7	ro	m	Robust fern of fine texture. For shade. Many cultivars.
Primula alpicola 'Alba'	Asian primrose	6	ro	m	Primrose of exquisite refinement.
Primula alpicola 'Violacea'	Asian primrose	6	ro	m	Beautiful violet-flowered form.
Primula beesiana	Bee's primrose	6	ro	m	Pleasant pastel-colored candelabra-type flowers.
Primula bulleyana	Bulley's primrose	6	ro	m	With *P. beesiana*, parent of many good hybrid strains.
Primula × bulleesiana	candelabra primrose	6	ro	m	Multicolored pastel flowers. Candelabra-type. Spreads rapidly in moist, sunny place.
Primula burmanica	Burma primrose	6	ro	m	Elegant candelabra type. Flowers reddish-purple.
Primula capitata	purplehead primrose	6	ro	d	Unusual dense, farinose violet flowers.
Primula chungensis ✿	primrose	6	ro	m	Yellow-orange candelabra flowers.
Primula cockburniana	primrose	6	ro	m	Fine-textured candelabra type. Flowers dark orange-red.
Primula denticulata	Himalayan primrose	6	ro	d	Robust plant with large purple flowers. Spreads rapidly.
Primula farinosa	bird's-eye primula	6	ro	d	Small, dainty species. Flowers lilac or purple.
Primula florindae	Tibetan primrose	5	ro	m	Robust plant with sulphur yellow flowers. Very distinct and easily grown. Likes wet conditions.
Primula japonica 'Miller's Crimson'	Japanese primrose	5	ro	m	Good color form, vigorous growth in moist soil. 'Potsford White' has white flowers with a yellow eye.
Primula marginata	silveredge primrose	7	ro	d	Leaves delicately silver marginated. Flowers blue-lilac.
Primula polyneura	Veitch primrose	6	ro	d	Attractive triangular leaves. Flowers pale pink to purple.
Primula pulverulenta	silverdust primrose	6	ro	m	Deep red flowers with a purple center. Candelabra type.
Primula secundiflora	sideflower primrose	6	ro	m	Reddish purple flowers, needs good drainage.
Primula sieboldii	siebold primrose	5	ro	m	Broad attractive foliage and variously colored flowers.
Primula sikkimensis	sikkim primrose	6	ro	m	Pendent yellow flowers with long pedicels. Very showy.
Primula veris ✿	cowslip primrose	5	ro	d	Flowers yellow, fragrant.
Primula vialii	red hot poker primula	7	ro	m	Long conical flower spikes crowded with violet-red flowers.
Primula vulgaris ✿	English primrose	5	ro	d	Flowers sulphur yellow. Single and double forms in a wide range of colors are available.
Primula waltonii	primrose	7	ro	d	Violet-blue flowers.

▷

BOTANICAL NAME	COMMON NAME	ZONE	PT	HT	NOTES ON CHARACTER
Pulmonaria saccharata ◆	lungwort	3	ro	s	Good under deciduous shade trees. Leaves attractively spotted or variegated. Flowers white to dark violet, depending on cultivar.
Puschkinia scilloides	striped squill	4	b	d	Flowers white with distinct blue stripe on each petal.
Pyrola asarifolia	wintergreen	4	ro	d	Attractive dwarf plant with glossy kidney-shaped leaves.
Ramonda myconi	ramonda	7	ro	d	Rosette of deeply toothed leaves with reddish hairs. Purple flowers.
Ranunculus gramineus	grassy buttercup	6	ro	d	Narrow foliage and bright yellow flowers. For a moist place.
Rheum palmatum	ornamental rhubarb	7	ro	t	Bold, deeply lobed leaves. Flowers deep red in a large panicle above the foliage.
Rodgersia aesculifolia	fingerleaf rodgersia	6	ro	t	Bold-textured pinnate foliage. White flowers in arching panicles. For a moist place.
Rodgersia pinnata 'Superba'	featherleaf rodgersia	6	ro	m	Divided leaves and feathery flower clusters up to 2 ft (0.6 m) long.
Rodgersia sambucifolia		6	ro	m	Long-stalked pinnate leaves and white flowers.
Romanzoffia sitchensis	Sitka mistmaiden	4	rz	d	Western North American native plant for a damp, shady spot. White flowers.
Romneya coulteri ✳ ◆	matilija poppy	7	rz	t	Bears large white flowers with central boss of yellow stamens from July to October. Blue-green dissected leaves. Can become invasive once established.
Sanguinaria canadensis	bloodroot	4	ro	d	American woodlander with scalloped, heart-shaped leaves. White flowers in April. 'Multiplex' is a good double-flowered cultivar.
Sanguisorba canadensis	American burnet	3	ro	t	A bold plant for moist locations. White flowers in summer.
Sanguisorba obtusa	Japanese burnet	5	ro	m	Like *S. canadensis* but with rose-purple flowers.
Scilla bifolia 'Rosea'	twinleaf squill	5	b	d	Multiplies rapidly, forming an attractive ground cover. Pink blooms in March.
Scilla sibirica ❁	Siberian squill	2	b	s	Forms carpets of deep blue flowers in early spring. Good bulb for naturalizing in moist soils.
Smilacina racemosa ❁	false Solomon's-seal	3	ro	t	Bold foliage and white flowers in May.
Solidago nemoralis ◆	goldenrod	3	ro	m	Attractive in a meadow or woodland clearing. Golden yellow flowers in summer/fall.
Sphaeralcea ambigua ✳	desert mallow	4	ro	m	Orange flowers borne in summer. Best in full sun.
Stylophorum diphyllum ◆	celandine poppy	6	ro	m	Shade tolerant. Yellowish flowers in terminal clusters.
Symplocarpus foetidus	skunk cabbage	3	ro	m	For a boggy place. Bold leaves and early purple-spotted spathes.
Synthyris missurica	mountain kittentail	4	ro	d	Blue flowers appear before the leaves. For semishade.
Thalictrum aquilegifolium	columbine meadow rue	5	ro	m	Fine-textured foliage and greenish white flowers. Graceful and ornamental.

▷

ABOVE, L TO R: *Rodgersia pinnata* 'Superba', *Trillium grandiflorum* and ostrich fern, Zephyr or Atamasco lily (*Zephyranthes atamasca*)

◁ *Plants for the Woodland Floor*

BOTANICAL NAME	COMMON NAME	ZONE	PT	HT	NOTES ON CHARACTER
Thalictrum delavayi	Yunnan meadow rue	6	ro	m	Like *T. aquilegifolium* but with mauve flowers.
Thalictrum flavum	yellow meadow rue	6	ro	m	Bright yellow flowers in compact panicles.
Tradescantia virginiana	spiderwort	5	ro	m	Clusters of violet-blue flowers are carried above arching grasslike foliage all summer. White, pink and rosy red varieties are available.
Trillium chloropetalum ✿	trillium	5	t	m	Bold foliage. White or yellow flowers in spring.
Trillium erectum ✿	stinking Benjamin	4	t	m	Red flowers. For a moist location.
Trillium grandiflorum ✿	wake robin	4	t	m	White flowers, rather variable. Shade tolerant.
Trillium ovatum ✿	Pacific trillium	7	t	d	Flowers white, fading to deep rose.
Trillium sessile ✿	toad lily	6	t	d	Marbled foliage and purple-red flowers.
Tulipa pulchella 'Violacea'	dwarf Taurus tulip	5	b	d	A dwarf species best planted in a well-drained sunny spot. Very early flowering.
Tulipa sylvestris ✿	Florentine tulip	5	b	s	Bright yellow fragrant blossoms in late spring. Best in sunny place that will dry out in summer.
Tulipa tarda	Kuenlen tulip	5	b	d	Dwarf species for full sun. Yellow flowers open in May.
Tulipa turkestanica		5	b	d	Vigorous dwarf species with multiflowered scapes. Flowers white with an orange base.
Veratrum viride	false hellebore	6	ro	t	Interesting bold foliage and greenish yellow flowers in July.
Veronica incana ◆	silver speedwell	3	ro	s	Attractive gray foliage. Flowers violet-blue, in summer.
Viola canadensis ◆	Canada violet	3	rz	d	Shade-tolerant with large pale flowers.
Waldsteinia fragarioides ◆	barren strawberry	3	ro	s	Shade-tolerant ground cover. Strawberry-like foliage and yellow flowers in late spring.
Zephyranthes atamasca	zephyr lily	8	b	d	Crocus-like white flowers in spring. Good for a moist place in open woods in warm climates.

Climbing Plants

CHAPTER SIX

*I*T IS MORE difficult to grow climbers in shaded woodland conditions than in sunny locations. This is because flowering vines move toward the sun even though their roots may be in the shade. This applies to both deciduous and evergreen climbers, though the latter tend to be more tolerant of shade. In nature, climbers are more successful on disturbed sites where they benefit from the shelter and support of adjacent woodland, increased light levels and nutrients released by the disturbance. It follows that climbers grow better in new gardens, in sunny clearings or at the edges of established woodland.

Climbing plants have a special place in the woodland environment. They fill a niche created by trees and shrubs that provide support and protection, enabling the climbers to find their own place in the sun. In conventional gardens, climbing plants are usually trained on artificial supports such as trellises or pergolas. In the woodland garden, they must appear to be a natural part of the plant community.

Although there are many climbing plants in the northern woods, they are most abundant in the tropical and warm-temperate latitudes, where they form a prominent part of the forest flora. Most of the climbers described here are native in the forests of the Sino-Himalayan area. On wooded hillsides where the trees are not too dense, great tangles of *Clematis montana* and *Actinidia* grow, and the bright pink new leaves of *Actinidia kolomikta* can be seen from a great distance. The forests grow at high elevations, so many choice species are hardy in North America. A lesser number of species come from North America and Europe.

The emphasis on climbers in the woodland garden is limited only by the availability of suitable supports on which to grow them. The stump of a felled tree can be attractively hidden with climbing plants, or the large, upended root mass of a fallen tree can be clothed with a vigorous climber. Trees and shrubs of open, multi-branched habit are also good supports, particularly those that have little intrinsic interest of their own.

PRECEDING PAGE: Tellman honeysuckle (*Lonicera* × *tellmanniana*), one of the most spectacular honeysuckles.

Planting Climbers

To start a climbing plant in an established woodland, dig a large planting hole several feet (1 m) in diameter and as much as 2 feet (0.6 m) deep. Provide a root-barrier of plastic or sheet metal to prevent the invasion of roots. A half-barrel with the bottom broken out also works quite well. It is only necessary to exclude the tree roots for a few years until the climber is established. Climbers can sometimes be planted at the base of a tree where there are few feeder roots. Dig the planting hole between the anchor roots and fill it with nutritive soil. Such sites are apt to be dry, so pay special attention to watering (although not to the detriment of the host tree). Work a rich compost, including rotted manure and a long-lasting balanced fertilizer, into the planting soil to encourage rapid growth. Mound the earth in a circle around the climber; this will form a basin that directs water toward the root system. Place a 4- to 6-inch (10- to 15-cm) mulch of organic matter over the planting site to help maintain soil moisture and suppress weed growth. Do not plant the climber any deeper than it was in the container (with the exception of *Clematis*, which should always be planted an inch or two [3–5 cm] deeper), and keep the mulch away from the area immediately adjacent to the base of the plant.

Climbers need only an annual top-dressing of rich compost, rotted manure or leaves. Many woodland soils are acid, so roses and clematis may need an occasional liming to maintain vigor. All species will benefit from a handful of slow-acting fertilizer scattered around their roots once a year.

If you are growing climbing plants into a tree, they will need support until they reach the branches. Tie a few twiggy stems — discarded prunings — to the trunk to guide the climber to the lower branches of the tree. This is particularly important for plants that climb by means of leaf tendrils, such as clematis. The vigor of the climber must be matched to the support. Strong-growing genera, such as *Actinidia*, *Wisteria* and *Celastrus*, will quickly overcome a small tree and can even kill it. Robust trees such as oak, elm and locust can support all but the strongest climbers, but even these must be watched carefully. It may not affect an old tree that has ceased active growth, but a young tree can be harmed by the girdling effect of some vines. Large old trees with open canopies, such as black locust (*Robinia pseudoacacia*), make excellent supports. The rough, fissured bark provides a foothold, and the light canopy allows the vines to receive sunlight.

Conifers can be used for support, but the planting method is different. Instead of planting the climber near the trunk, where shade and competition

Clematis tangutica, vigorous and hardy, has nodding flowers and silky seed heads.

are greatest, plant it just outside the canopy. Drive a stout, twiggy limb into the ground and attach its top to one of the lower branches. This "ladder" leads the climber to the outside branches of the tree. Vigorous climbers such as *Clematis montana* are suited to this method, and the effect can be quite spectacular on the facade of a large conifer.

In the mild climate of Zone 8 or warmer, the beautiful evergreen *Clematis armandii* has an ornamental effect throughout the winter. Deciduous species, such as *C. tangutica* and *C. orientalis*, are best planted in locations where their bedraggled winter appearance is less obvious.

Climbers that enjoy summer heat, such as sweet jessamine (*Gelsemium sempervirens*) or trumpet creeper (*Campsis radicans*), look spectacular scrambling over large rocks. In landscapes that have been cleared, large stumps can be surrounded with rocks to form grotto-like promontories on which clematis and species roses can be attached. The imaginative gardener will devise other rustic supports with natural materials.

Choosing Climbing Plants

In a woodland primarily composed of conifers, there should be an emphasis on deciduous climbers. The flowers of clematis are superb when viewed against an evergreen background. In a deciduous woodland, place more emphasis on evergreen climbers, such as the star jasmine (*Trachelospermum jasminoides*) or *T. asiaticum*, hardy into central Virginia; the Japanese Staunton vine (*Stauntonia hexaphylla*); *Pileostegia viburnoides*, an evergreen relation of the climbing hydrangea; or the evergreen honeysuckle (*Lonicera sempervirens*) are good choices. *Lonicera alseusmoides* is another attractive yet little-known evergreen honeysuckle with yellowish flowers followed by purplish-black fruit. Regrettably, none of these evergreen climbers is hardy much below Zone 7.

The selection of climbers available from nurseries is very limited since demand is small. Botanical gardens may be the best source for the less common species. Fortunately, most climbers are propagated easily by seeds or cuttings. Among the most vigorous are the trumpet vine (*Campsis radicans*), evergreen sausage vine (*Holboellia latifolia*), climbing hydrangeas (*Hydrangea anomala* and *H. petiolaris*), silver lace vine (*Fallopia baldschuanica*) and crimson glory vine (*Vitis coignetiae*). The latter is magnificent in autumn color. The various species and varieties of wisteria are also important, but they need a strong support and plenty of sunshine to succeed.

The less vigorous climbers can be grown on small trees or large shrubs such as laburnums, mock oranges and the shrubby honeysuckles. The chocolate vine, *Akebia quinata*, is hardy and adaptable, as are the various climbing honeysuckles. *Lonicera* 'Dropmore Scarlet' is excellent. In the mildest areas, the climbing nightshades, such as *Solanum crispum* and *S. jasminoides*, are good woodland plants. Easily propagated from summer softwood cuttings, they can be wintered indoors in areas where they are at risk from winter cold.

The jasmines are a group of climbing and scrambling plants that are best suited to the subtropical conditions of the southern United States. In the north, *Jasminum nudiflorum* is widely grown and is seen to best advantage cascading over a rock wall in a sunny, sheltered location.

No discussion of climbers is complete without mention of roses. The large-flowered climbing roses are not appropriate to the naturalism of the woodland garden, and most of them would not thrive in its shaded, humid conditions. However, some of the vigorous small-flowered species and the hybrids derived from them can be planted in woodland clearings where there is sunshine and good air circulation. In the south, the Banksian rose (*Rosa banksiae*) is worth seeking out, as it has few equals. *Rosa bracteata* and its hybrid 'Mermaid' are very beautiful and resistant to disease. Unfortunately, these roses from China and those from the Himalaya, such as *R. brunonii* and *R. longicuspis*, are not hardy in the north. This is also true of the beautiful Cherokee rose (*R. laevigata*), which is grown in the southern United States. In large gardens that contain tall trees suitable for support, the vigorous climber *R. filipes* may be allowed unrestricted growth through open crowns of old trees. The cultivar known as 'Kiftsgate' bears large masses of fragrant white flowers on stems that may reach as high as 40 feet (12.2 m). *Rosa chinensis* 'Mutabilis' is a bush rose of lax growth that may reach 8 feet (2.4 m) high if planted near the support of other shrubs. It is among the most exquisite of all roses. The single fragrant flowers are red in bud, changing through yellow to a distinct coppery tone as the flower ages. This rose gives a welcome splash of color in open woodland glades all summer and autumn until the buds are destroyed by frost. Hardy in Zone 8, this and other China roses seem well suited to sheltered woodland conditions that probably resemble their native habitat in western China.

Climbers to Avoid

Some gardens can accommodate only a small number of climbers, and planting of coarse, vigorous species may be regretted later. English ivy (*Hedera helix*), Boston ivy (*Parthenocissus tricuspidata*) and Virginia creeper (*Parthenocissus quinquefolia*) are best avoided. Japanese honeysuckle (*Lonicera japonica*), Kudzu vine (*Pueraria lobata*) and bittersweet (*Celastrus scandens*) may also cause problems because of their aggressive growth. Oriental bittersweet (*Celastrus orbiculatus*), Japanese honeysuckle and common ivy are the worst offenders, capable not only of the destruction of the woodland floor plants but also of the canopy trees themselves. None of these has much floral interest and their overpowering character may create a somber, melancholy effect in the woodland. (Not all vigorous climbers should be avoided: *Clematis montana*, particularly when represented by a beautiful cultivar such as 'Tetrarose', gives a joyous effect with cascading masses of exquisite pink flowers).

ABOVE, L TO R: Sweet autumn clematis (*Clematis terniflora*), *Schisandra grandiflora* var. *rubrifolia*

LEFT: *Schizophragma hydrangeoides*, a vigorous and self-clinging vine, with *Holboellia coriacea* behind.

Climbers for the Woodland

❀ = scented flowers   ✳ = suitable for dry places   ◆ = suitable for alkaline soils

PLANT HEIGHT CODE (HT): m = medium (to 8 ft [2.4 m])   t = tall (more than 20 ft [6 m])

BOTANICAL NAME	COMMON NAME	HT	ZONE	NOTES ON CHARACTER
Deciduous Climbers				
Actinidia arguta	hardy kiwi vine	t	4	Fast growing, with edible berries. From eastern Asia.
Actinidia deliciosa ❀	kiwi fruit vine	t	7	Rampant grower can cover large tree in time. Plant both sexes if fruit desired.
Actinidia kolomikta		m	5	Very ornamental foliage plant with multicolored variegated leaves. More colorful if planted in sun.
Akebia quinata ❀	chocolate vine	m	5	Semi-evergreen with palmate leaves. Bears edible fleshy fruit.
Aristolochia macrophylla ◆	Dutchman's pipe	t	6	Interesting climber with curious spotted tubular flowers.
Bignonia capreolata ◆	cross vine	t	7	Orange-red tubular flowers in late spring. Climbs by tendrils. Evergreen in warmer zones. Not for deep shade. Purple pods in warm summers.
Campsis radicans ◆	trumpet vine	t	4	Orange to scarlet tubular flowers in midsummer. Pinnate leaves. Needs strong support. *C. grandiflora* (Zone 7) is similar but less hardy.
Campsis × *tagliabuana* ◆	hybrid trumpet vine	t	5	Similar to *C. radicans* but with larger flowers.

▷

BOTANICAL NAME	COMMON NAME	HT	ZONE	NOTES ON CHARACTER
Celastrus orbiculatus ◆	oriental bittersweet	t	4	Twining vine with attractive orange-red berries and good fall color. Can overpower weak trees.
Celastrus scandens ◆	american bittersweet	t	2	Like C. *orbiculatus*, with yellow to red fruit. Male vines will not produce fruit.
Clematis columbiana ◆	Columbia clematis	t	3	Solitary blue to purple flowers and ternate leaves. Very hardy western American species.
Clematis integrifolia ◆	solitary clematis	m	3	Pale bluebell-shaped flowers in summer.
Clematis macropetala ◆	big-petal clematis	m	5	Azure blue flowers in May–June. Prune after flowering. 'Blue Bird' is a superb cultivar.
Clematis montana 'Alba' ❀ ◆	anemone clematis	t	6	Covered with white flowers in spring. A vigorous and elegant climber.
Clematis montana 'Pink Perfection' ❀ ◆	anemone clematis	t	6	Lovely pink-flowered cultivar.
Clematis montana 'Tetrarose' ❀ ◆	anemone clematis	t	6	Large purplish-pink flowers and bronzy foliage.
Clematis montana var. *rubens* ❀ ◆	anemone clematis	t	6	Free-flowering type with rosy sepals and purplish young stems.
Clematis orientalis		t	4	Yellow flowers with thick reflexed petals. Blooms in late summer.
Clematis tangutica ◆	golden clematis	m	5	Bright yellow flowers appear from late summer until frost. Can be cut back to base annually.
Clematis terniflora ❀ ◆	sweet autumn clematis	m	6	Autumn-flowering clematis covered with small, fragrant white flowers. Formerly known as C. *maximowicziana*.
Clematis texensis ◆	scarlet clematis	m	5	Brilliant scarlet, urn-shaped flowers late summer. 'Duchess of Albany' a good cultivar.
Clematis viticella ◆	Italian clematis	m	5	Blue or rosy purple flowers during summer. Cut back fairly hard in early spring.
Eccremocarpus scaber	Chilean gloryflower	m	9	Orange-scarlet flowers borne all summer. Dies to ground in colder areas.
Hydrangea petiolaris ◆	climbing hydrangea	t	5	Clings by aerial roots. White flat-topped flower clusters in June. Attractive peeling bark. H. *anomala* is similar.
Lonicera 'Dropmore Scarlet'		l	5	Vigorous climber with showy scarlet tubular flowers produced from July to October.
Lonicera etrusca ❀ ◆	Etruscan honeysuckle	m	7	Semi-evergreen European honeysuckle with red-tinted flower buds and fragrant yellow flowers.
Lonicera periclymenum ❀ ◆	woodbine honeysuckle	m	5	Twining climber with deliciously fragrant red and yellow-white flowers in summer. 'Belgica' and 'Serotina' are well-known forms.

▷

BOTANICAL NAME	COMMON NAME	HT	ZONE	NOTES ON CHARACTER
Lonicera × tellmanniana ✿	Tellmann honeysuckle	m	6	Beautiful yellow blossoms borne in terminal clusters of 6–12 flowers. Flowers best with roots in shade and top in sun.
Parthenocissus quinquefolia	Virginia creeper	t	3	One of the finest climbers for its red fall color. Able to climb trees without support due to its self-clinging habit. Can become invasive.
Parthenocissus tricuspidata	Boston ivy	t	4	Rapid grower with three-lobed leaves that turn brilliant scarlet in fall. Self-clinging. Native to Japan.
Polygonum baldschuanica (*Fallopia*)	silver lace vine	t	4	Rampant twiner useful for covering unsightly objects in a hurry. Creamy flowers during August.
Rosa banksiae ✿	Lady Banks' rose	t	7	Vigorous climber. White or yellow fragrant flowers. Almost without prickles.
Rosa bracteata ✿	Macartney rose	t	8	Vigorous, rambling rose with large, lemon-scented yellow single flowers. The cultivar 'Mermaid' has sulphur yellow flowers with showy brown stamens.
Rosa brunonii ✿	Himalayan musk rose	t	8	A rampant climbing species with large fragrant clusters of white flowers.
Rosa filipes 'Kiftsgate' ✿		t	6	Small, fragrant white flowers cover the plant in June, followed by showy red fruit. Climbs by hooked spines, needs plenty of room.
Schisandra grandiflora var. *rubrifolia*	schisandra	t	8	A rare climber from China found on the Buddhist mountain of Omei Shan. Attractive red flowers and fruit.
Schizophragma hydrangeoides ◆		m	5	Similar to climbing hydrangea with showier white flowers. Good for growing on a large tree. Slow to become established.
Sinofranchetia chinensis		m	6	Large, vigorous twining climber with trifoliate leaves and attractive blue-purple grape-like fruit.
Vitis coignetiae ◆	Japanese gloryvine	t	5	Handsome lobed grapevine leaves turn brilliant scarlet in fall. Climbs by tendrils.
Vitis vinifera 'Purpurea' ◆	dyer's grape	m	6	Intriguing whitish new foliage turning to deep purple.
Wisteria floribunda ✿ ◆	Japanese wisteria	t	5	Very vigorous climber. Long drooping racemes of fragrant flowers in early summer. Violet, pink, red or white flowers, depending on cultivar. Can overwhelm small trees.
Wisteria sinensis ✿ ◆	Chinese wisteria	t	5	Similar to *W. floribunda*, with shorter, less fragrant racemes. Some cultivars such as 'Black Dragon' (purple) are double flowered.

Evergreen Climbers

BOTANICAL NAME	COMMON NAME	HT	ZONE	NOTES ON CHARACTER
Clematis armandii ✿ ◆	evergreen clematis	m	8	Evergreen lance-shaped leaves and fragrant white blossoms in April. A choice plant.
Euonymus fortunei var. *radicans* ◆	wintercreeper	m	5	Evergreen self-clinging scandent shrub useful in colder areas where few evergreen climbers survive. Grows well in sun or deep shade. Variegated cultivars offered.

▷

BOTANICAL NAME	COMMON NAME	HT	ZONE	NOTES ON CHARACTER
Gelsemium sempervirens ✿	Carolina jessamine	m	7	Fragrant funnel-shaped yellow flowers in spring. Not suited to cool summer climates.
Hedera canariensis 'Variegata' ✴	Algerian ivy	t	8	Bold leathery evergreen leaves with silvery white margins and reddish petioles.
Hedera colchica 'Dentata Variegata'	variegated Persian ivy	t	6	Large heart-shaped evergreen leaves with creamy blotches useful for dry sites in full sun.
Holboellia coriacea	China blue vine	t	7	Vigorous twiner with dark green, glossy leaflets in groups of three. Flowers white, flushed purple. In warm summers curious fleshy purple pods are produced.
Jasminum officinale ✿	white jasmine	m	9	Semi-evergreen scandent shrub with heavily scented white flowers during summer.
Lonicera alseuosmoides	evergreen honeysuckle	m	7	Unusual evergreen species with lustrous leaves. Flowers not showy, followed by black berries.
Lonicera ciliosa ✿		m	5	Fine American species with yellow to orange tubular flowers followed by red berries.
Passiflora caerulea	passion flower	m	9	Whitish blue flowers of remarkable structure. Climbs by tendrils.
Pileostegia viburnoides		t	8	Self-clinging vine with narrow leathery evergreen leaves and white flower corymbs in late summer. An excellent evergreen vine.
Rosa laevigata ✿ ◆	Cherokee rose	t	9	Beautiful glossy semi-evergreen leaves and white, fragrant flowers in May, followed by large bristly fruits.
Rosa longicuspis ✿		t	8	Semi-evergreen with handsome dark foliage and white, banana-scented flowers followed by orange-red fruits.
Solanum crispum ✿ ◆	Chilean potato vine	t	8	Vigorous semi-evergreen climber with rich purple-blue flowers with yellow stamens from July–September. 'Glasnevin' has a longer flowering season.
Stauntonia hexaphylla	Japanese Staunton vine	t	8	Large long-stalked palmate leaves give this twining vine an exotic appearance. Fruit is edible and sweet.
Trachelospermum asiaticum ✿	star jasmine	m	9	Twining vine with deliciously fragrant cream to yellow pinwheel-shaped flowers in late spring.
Trachelospermum jasminioides ✿	star jasmine	m	9	Similar to the above but with larger leaves and white flowers fading to cream.

▷

Planting, Pruning and Maintenance

ONE OF THE MOST appealing features of the woodland garden is that it is modelled on a natural plant community in which each plant has its own niche in the woodland mosaic. The main controlling factor is the amount of shade cast by the canopy. In nature, when a woodland tree or group of trees is lost, the balance is changed and sun-loving meadow plants may gain a temporary foothold. Inexorably, the natural forest succession begins anew, and trees and shrubs ultimately win the battle for space.

In a woodland garden, the overall impression should be of tranquil stability, as in a mature forest. The art of the gardener is to maintain this idealized woodland picture: part reality, part illusion.

Planting

The best time to plant the woodland garden is in spring, when the moisture content of the soil is greatest because of winter rain or snow and also when environmental stress is lessened. Those in moderate climates, where the earth remains relatively warm until the end of the year, can also plant in fall. In very cold climates where frost penetrates deeply into the ground, fall planting may be unwise.

Planting holes for most trees and shrubs should be dug at least 1 foot (30.5 cm) deep and 5 feet (1.5 m) wide for most shrubs — wide enough for the root system in 5 to 10 years. Rotted leaves or peat moss are the preferred soil amendments because they are closest to the natural process of decay and renewal. Avoid raw organic matter such as sawdust or bark, which rob the soil of nitrogen as they decompose. Before any planting is done, the soil may be treated with a phosphatic fertilizer such as bone meal or superphosphate. Mound the soil slightly to allow for settling.

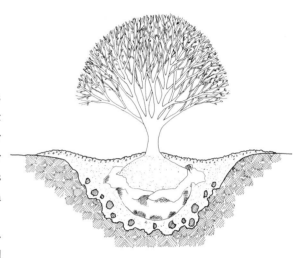

Figure 12

Planting a **balled and burlapped** tree or shrub:

1) Dig a hole twice the diameter of the root ball.

2) Break up subsoil, but then firm it well beneath the root ball.

3) Place plant in hole, making sure to match the soil line on the stem with the level grade of surrounding soil. Do not plant deep.

4) Cut and peel back burlap.

5) Backfill with rich soil of similar texture to existing soil, then firm well.

6) Leave a dish-shaped depression around the plant to catch water.

7) Mulch surface with loose organic material such as partially decayed leaves or pine needles.

PRECEDING PAGE: A young evolving woodland, showing the removal of surplus sapling trees as the canopy develops.

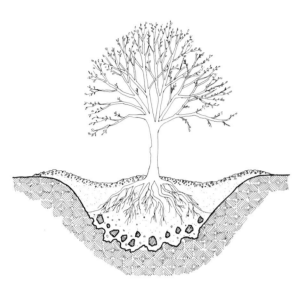

Figure 13

Planting a **bare-root** tree or shrub:

1) Dig a hole twice the diameter of the rootball.

2) Break up the subsoil, then firm it well before planting.

3) Construct a cone-shaped mound over which roots are spread.

4) Position the plant, gently spreading the roots over the mound. Make sure to match the soil line on the stem with the level grade of surrounding soil.

5) Backfill with enriched soil similar to existing soil on site.

6) Firm well, and leave a dish-shaped depression to collect water.

7) Mulch surface with organic material.

Amend the natural soil enough to promote optimum growth but not so much that an interface is formed between two unrelated soil masses. Adding a reasonable amount of decayed organic matter — 5 to 10 percent — is important on new raw sites, particularly where the natural soil is mostly clay. The soil into which trees and shrubs are planted may settle considerably over a period of several years, particularly when large amounts of organic matter have been added to the soil. Consequently, the root system of a plant may eventually be positioned considerably below the surrounding grade. This may become a problem on wet soils, particularly with plants like rhododendrons, whose roots should be near the surface. The use of heavy annual mulches can aggravate the problem. Settling may have some advantages on very dry sites where the cavity collects water, but in most cases it is deleterious to the health of the plant. The solution is to mound up the planting site 3 in (7.5 cm) above grade at the time of planting to allow for subsequent settling.

On new sites, the natural tendency is to plant too many trees. After a few years, it will become clear which trees are hardy enough to remain as permanent components of the woodland. At this time, you can reassess the position of the trees and transplant if necessary before the trees are too large to move. Surplus trees should be removed or relocated before they impair the growth of other, more permanent specimens.

It is seldom possible to think of all the factors when positioning trees. Gardeners do make mistakes, and young trees will usually transplant without much shock during the first few years.

New plantings should always be thoroughly watered. The first watering is an integral part of the planting process since it reestablishes physical contact between roots and soil. Only after the first heavy watering should mulch be placed on the soil.

Pruning

Maintaining the woodland garden requires sustained observation and an eye for keeping the various components in balance. The more aggressive plants are restrained by pruning (or removal) before they impair the growth of species slower to become established.

In a mature woodland, the trees that form the canopy may be old specimens that require pruning of dead and awkwardly placed branches. Examine every tree and make an inventory that lists the species, age, size and condition of each one. Note injuries, diseases and other extraordinary features. Assessing each tree individually assures the health of the whole woodland. If in doubt, have a qualified arborist give an opinion.

Trees are wonderfully complex organisms, possessing many natural defenses against disease. Once disease symptoms are noticed, the damage may already be far advanced. For example, when the fruiting bodies of fungi such as bracket fungus are noticed in a tree, damage may already be widespread beneath the bark. Proper pruning cuts and prompt attention to wounds of all kinds will limit or prevent the penetration of these parasites in the first instance.

Early shaping of young trees and moderate pruning are the best defenses against disease that can enter later through breakage points caused by weak limbs and neglected pruning. In broad terms, there are two main seasons for pruning: first, from mid- to late summer when most woody plants have largely ceased growth; second, in late winter when the risk of damage from extreme cold is over. Avoid pruning when leaves are emerging in spring or during the leaf fall period in the autumn. Woody plants are most vulnerable to wounding during these times. Never remove the top of a healthy tree. Topping is detrimental to the long-term health of a tree and will not make it more wind-resistant. In fact, topping encourages the growth of multiple, weakly attached leaders that increase the mass at the top of the tree, making it more susceptible to wind damage.

Prune dead, dying or diseased limbs in summer, when the defoliated limbs are conspicuous and signs of disease are readily apparent. Trunk sprouts are most effectively pruned in summer, when they are less likely to recur. Heavy limbs dropped on the understory won't do as much damage as in winter, when plant tissue is brittle. Wounds heal faster in the warm months, but parasites are also more active.

Thin the canopy when trees are in leaf. The process may be done slowly, limb by limb, until the correct amount of light is admitted. Generally, most remedial tree work is better accomplished during the warm months, yet it is often postponed until the winter for reasons of economy or tradition. Winter pruning is often performed under difficult conditions caused by frost and snow, and it is more difficult to determine the health of the trees.

It may be necessary to do extensive felling and clearing during the cold

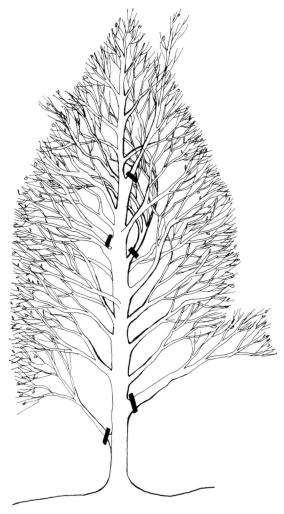

Figure 14

A young tree, densely branched, showing the early thinning process of pruning away congested and crossing branches. Note that the shoot near the top should be removed. This is competing with the leading shoot for dominance and may lead to a weak fork in later years, causing breakage, which allows the entry of fungal diseases. Low branches may be pruned, but avoid removing all of these, as they are important for shading the young trunk and to help build stem girth. As the tree matures, these low branches may be removed gradually to expose more trunk.

months. However, opening up the woodland interior to more sunshine may sunburn the trunks of thin-barked trees. Dogwoods, beeches and maples are particularly susceptible. Rapid heating and cooling of the bark in winter can be quite debilitating. Temporarily wrapping or covering the trunks with evergreen boughs may help.

If it is necessary to remove a large limb from a tree, take it off in several pieces to avoid damage to the tree and the plants beneath. To promote quick closure of wounds, make pruning cuts slightly beyond the swollen portion where they attach to the main stem or subsidiary branch. This swollen area secretes protective chemicals that compartmentalize healthy tissue. Flush cuts create a larger wound that bypasses this protective zone; these cuts heal much more slowly and increase the plant's susceptibility to disease. Don't leave a long stub, which can decay back into the main trunk.

Young trees may require some training to develop the natural form inherent in the species. For example, a single-trunked, pyramidal form is characteristic of the tulip tree (*Liriodendron*), and the common white dogwood (*Cornus florida*) has a spreading form. Relatively minor corrections at a young stage will save major work and possible trauma to the tree later on. The aim should be to encourage the growth of a strong central leader or several sturdy, well-spaced limbs. The natural form of well-shaped, mature trees of the species is the best guide.

As a young tree grows, don't be in too much of a hurry to remove the twiggy lower branches, except those that are crowded, badly spaced or structurally weak. If twiggy growth is allowed to remain on the main stem, it sustains, protects and helps thicken the growing trunk, resulting in a sturdier tree. Premature removal of lower limbs on young trees results in a weak, spindly stem that may be unable to support a strong canopy. Staking a young tree is only a temporary expedient lasting a few months after planting. The stakes should be removed as soon as possible so that the tree can develop naturally. In most cases, staking is not necessary, since the surrounding plants offer protection.

Pests and Diseases

In the mixed mosaic of the woodland, there should seldom be any serious concern with common pests or diseases that tend to be a problem where many plants of the same kind are grouped together, such as in an orchard.

Trees of ancient lineage such as the maidenhair tree (*Ginkgo*), dawn redwood (*Metasequoia*) and tulip tree (*Liriodendron*) have an extraordinary resistance to plant pests, as do most of the members of the genus *Magnolia*. If spraying for plant pests should ever become necessary, do it strictly on a spot-treatment basis. Indiscriminate, overall spraying may disturb the balance of the whole woodland by destroying beneficial organisms.

Plants under stress for one reason or another — drought, excessive shade or sun, competition, poor nutrition — are more susceptible to pests. Vigilance and a timely response will forestall many problems associated with stress.

Attacks of insect pests such as aphids, mites and caterpillars can sometimes be lessened if not eliminated by forceful sprays of water repeated several times. This simply knocks off the offending pests. They cannot easily return to the host and will probably be eaten by predators. Insecticidal soaps are a useful and environmentally benign treatment for many pests; timely pruning of infested branches helps prevent the spread of others. Hand removal of larger pests such as caterpillars or snails may be practical. Nighttime is often best for hunting these and other nocturnal pests. Use chemical treatments only as a last resort. Complex chemicals developed for the agriculture industry can have long-lasting and undesirable side effects, killing bees and other beneficial insects. Some of the natural insecticides derived from plants, such as nicotine (tobacco) or pyrethrum (chrysanthemum), can be used with less fear of accumulative residues.

Fungicides such as lime-sulphur, when used as a dormant-season spray on deciduous trees and shrubs, help control diseases such as powdery mildew, scab and rust. The use of special highly refined oils in summer is also effective in smothering the insects and eggs of many pests, including scale insects. Dormant-season oil sprays are also effective in controlling insects that over-winter on deciduous trees and shrubs. Biological controls, such as *Bacillus thuringiensis* (B.T. for short) and parasitic nematodes, are examples of specific and safe methods of insect control. Healthy coexistence of all the woodland organisms is possible, but a severe outbreak of pests or diseases should be dealt with promptly, preferably with organic controls that are specific to the particular problem. Seek expert advice before taking any action and be aware of the recommendations of your local horticulture/agriculture expert.

Weeds

This principle applies also to the use of herbicides. The use of these chemicals is never a pleasant thought, but in the early years of landscape development, chemical thinning of overly aggressive plants is a useful, labor-saving practice. Anyone contemplating the use of herbicides should seek the advice of professionals. Herbicides should be used only after a careful analysis of the benefits is weighed against traditional methods of weed control, as little is known about the long-term cumulative effects on the environment.

Once a reasonable balance of all the woodland plants has been obtained, manual methods of weed control are most appropriate. A mechanical tool such as a rotary weed cutter is useful to control brush and weeds in open areas between plantings or to mow small meadows or walking trails. This is an effective and fast method if the operator is skilled enough to avoid damaging young plants and the bark of trees. Young trees can be protected with expandable plastic tubes, wire or bamboo stakes.

Weeds, the bane of all gardens, are no less a problem in the woodland, particularly in a new garden where the soil has been disturbed. While a limited weed population is permissible in the woodland — an adjunct of its rustic character — aggressive perennial weeds must be rigidly excluded. A black plastic membrane covered with a heavy leaf mulch up to 6 inches (15 cm) will suppress and eventually eliminate difficult weeds such as quack grass, mare's tail and sorrel. Most of the common weeds of pasture and cultivated land are not competitive in the shade of a well-managed woodland and will eventually disappear. Mulching discourages re-invasion by weeds. The best technique is to leave an area fallow for a few months or a year before planting. As weeds emerge they can be removed.

Although herbicides are sometimes used, weeds in small gardens are easily controlled by traditional manual methods. This brings the gardener into close contact with the plants and encourages a sensitivity to the needs of each plant and its complex relationship with the other vegetation that makes up the community.

The natural appearance of a woodland garden benefits from a moderate amount of studied neglect. Don't strive for too neat an appearance. However, surplus organic debris, such as rotting logs, stumps and dead roots, should be removed to prevent the spread of fungal diseases such as shoestring, or honey fungus (*Armillaria mellea*), if this is known to be present.

The picturesque effect of mosses, algae, lichen and ferns growing on the trunks of trees enhances the woodland atmosphere. If the humidity is adequate, growth can be encouraged by inserting small pieces of moss and ferns into bark crevices. Moss on the ground often indicates soil compaction, wet ground and low fertility, problems that can be corrected by tilling and mulching with leaf mold or applying lime if the soil is very acid. But before removing moss, consider its potential as a ground cover. Some of the most beautiful woodland gardens take advantage of the enchanting effect of shady, mossy glades.

Watering and Mulching

In areas where rainfall does not keep up with evaporation, woodland plants may come under more severe drought stress than their open-planted counterparts. This is because of the enormous volume of water absorbed and transpired by large trees. Summer rains in most areas are not adequate to replenish this loss, and the woodland floor may become very dry. Plants native to these conditions often have wide, mat-like roots or deep root systems that seek moisture below. In addition, they often go dormant or semi-dormant by late summer. Exotic plants, which are frequently native to areas of ample rainfall, are at a disadvantage.

Thorough watering is important during the active growth period of rhododendrons and other moisture-loving plants. Once the current year's growth has ceased, most plants are semi-dormant and better able to tolerate drought. Some woodland plants, particularly broad-leaved evergreens, should not enter the winter with dry roots. Water plants before applying winter mulches, as surface mulches are absorbent and may prevent deep penetration of irrigation water or winter rains.

It is increasingly important to conserve water and design irrigation systems that limit waste. Ideally, woodland gardens should be designed using plants that do not require regular watering, if at all. This may, of course, not always be practical.

An underground irrigation system laid beneath a planned system of pathways, as discussed in Chapter 2, limits the amount of damage done to the roots of existing trees, provided the paths are made well clear of the trunks and major roots. The paths identify the location of water pipes and maintenance is easier.

LEFT: Chiascuro, the interplay of light and shadow in a lush forest of the Pacific Northwest.

There is also less potential for damage from digging equipment.

It is difficult to design an irrigation system that provides even coverage under a tree canopy because of the many plants in the woodland. Drip irrigation beneath the shrubs may work reasonably well, but the pipes and nozzles may interfere with maintenance. One good solution is a grid of sprinklers attached to the top of vertical pipes set firmly into the ground and raised above the level of the highest understory plants. These may be extended in height as the woodland matures in size. If the pipes are painted dark green, they are barely noticeable. Overhead irrigation of this type to some degree simulates rain forest conditions, cleansing the foliage of dirt and freshening the woodland atmosphere. Irrigation systems can be the basic hose and sprinkler method or can be fabricated from available component systems; more elaborate setups can be designed by a professional irrigation specialist. The system should have drain plugs so it can be emptied in the fall for frost protection.

In those parts of North America with prolonged hot summer weather, soil-borne diseases such as *Phytophthora* root rot and verticillium wilt may strike without warning, often causing the collapse of entire plants. Rhododendrons and the small maples are particularly susceptible. There appears to be a connection between watering and these diseases. Water drawn from stagnant ponds may be contaminated; splashing of soil particles by coarse irrigation nozzles can also spread disease. Irrigation should simulate gentle rain, and the soil should be protected by an absorbent, organic mulch. If possible, avoid watering during the hottest part of the day.

The key to the successful maintenance of the woodland garden in all climates is the intelligent use of mulches. Not only does mulch reduce the cost of maintenance by suppressing weeds and conserving moisture, but it is the greatest single factor in maintaining good, healthy growth in all woodland plants. The steady decay of forest litter provides just the right amount of nutrients in the correct proportions for optimum growth.

The mature woodland will probably produce enough natural mulch, but young woodland gardens will require large amounts of additional leaf mulch. Mulch has the effect of simulating cool, moist forest conditions. Three or four inches (8–10 cm) of mulch is not too much — it will largely disappear into the soil within a year. Municipal park authorities often have surplus leaves that they may be pleased to dispose of. Compost them for a year before use for a more attractive and easily handled product. Adding some animal manure to the leaves enriches the mulch and speeds breakdown. If this is not available, a high-nitrogen fertilizer will work well. Lime also assists in breaking down the cellulose content of leaves, but it should not be applied simultaneously with nitrogen. In small gardens, where a degree of neatness is desirable (the larger the garden the more rustic it can be), the leaves can be shredded, immediately producing an attractive mulch that will not blow away as do whole dry leaves.

If you are composting leaves, turn the pile at least twice a year. This admits air and water, which are vital to decomposition. Where leaves are not available, use chopped hay, wood chips, wood shavings (not sawdust) and rotted manure. Industrial byproducts such as cocoa bean shells, spent hops and bark mulch are better than nothing, but they all have drawbacks due to their raw nature. Most of them inhibit bacterial and fungal activity, often leading to diminished availability of nutrients. All these materials are improved by mixing them with manure and composting for six months to a year.

The use of chemical fertilizers is by no means necessary in the woodland garden, particularly when a rich source of organic matter is available. If you do use chemical fertilizers, apply them when the soil moisture is greatest, in late winter or early spring. Fertilizers accelerate the growth of woodland plants and may be useful to establish plants in a garden, but as the garden matures, fertilizer can be dispensed with altogether.

Rhododendrons and their relatives are somewhat sensitive to fertilizer root burn, particularly at the upper range of pH. On soils tending toward alkalinity, fertilizers with a sulphate base, such as ammonium sulphate or potassium sulphate, are preferable since they have an acidifying effect. On acid soils, pelleted slow-acting formulations should be used to lessen the possibility of an accidental overdose.

Propagation

Although a woodland garden can be made using plants chosen entirely from the standard kinds available from nurseries, a little further searching will uncover a far greater range of fine plants from specialist nurseries. One of the great joys of gardening is experimenting with unfamiliar or rare plants and observing their progress in new surroundings. In this way, new plant compositions are added to the landscape repertoire, and our gardens are enriched. Native plant and special plant societies, as well as botanical gardens in your area, are potential sources of

Rhododendron 'Rosebud,' a fine double azalea suitable for massing. Also shown is *Viburnum davidii*.

good plants. These organizations frequently have plant sales as fund-raisers. To buy from them is to support their good work. The gardening enthusiast, however, will not wish to stop there.

Except for a few nurseries that happen to be enthusiastic about rare plants, the trial of new material is limited to botanical gardens and private plant collectors. There is no reason why this should be so, as anyone willing to learn a few basic principles of plant propagation and possessing a garden in which to plant the offspring may make a real contribution to extending the number of species grown in gardens. It is important to know, however, that there is never any justification for digging up wild plants. This may put threatened plants at risk, and in any case, wild-collected plants seldom adapt to average garden conditions.

Most gardeners, regardless of the size of their plant collections, are happy to share cuttings or seeds with anyone having a genuine interest in plants. Seeds offer the easiest method. They can be transported over great distances without spoilage, and most seeds retain their viability for long periods of time. Unlike cuttings, which produce a clone of the parent plant, seeds may not produce a plant identical to the parents because of the possibility of hybridization or normal genetic variability.

Much time is invested in growing woody plants from seed. The progeny are unlikely to be more ornamental than the parent, and the effort is seldom worthwhile with plants of mixed ancestry, such as rhododendron hybrids. On the other hand, seed may be the preferred method to propagate unusual species of trees and shrubs. The feeling of anticipation in nursing seedlings to maturity is very pleasant, particularly when the seeds have come from a wild source or if they are species new to gardens. Do remember, however, that seeds from the wild must come from a known reputable source.

Growing from Seed

Seed propagation is the most efficient method of reproduction to have evolved in the plant kingdom. Most seeds will germinate with little difficulty but, like most natural processes, it is not always as simple as it might appear. Seeds of many trees and shrubs have various kinds of built-in dormancy factors that prevent them from all germinating at the same time — a survival advantage. These dormancy factors must be overcome before germination can occur. In some cases the embryo of the seed is dormant, and the seed must be chilled at 32–40°F (0–4°C) for about three months before germinating. Sometimes two such periods are required with a warm spell in between (double dormancy). Other seeds have a thick coat that must be eroded before moisture can penetrate to initiate germination. A simple expedient is to rub them on sandpaper until a spot of the inner seed is exposed.

In practice, one simple method works for most types of seed. All seed should be clean and fresh, and it is better to sow it immediately after it is received. Basic equipment consists of a refrigerator, plastic containers with tight-fitting lids, and a well-lit window ledge or greenhouse where the temperature is between 60 and 70°F (15–21°C).

The plastic containers (recycled food containers are ideal) should have drainage holes at the bottom. Fill them to within 1 inch (2.5 cm) of the top with a good seed-starting mixture consisting of equal parts clean pasteurized soil, peat moss and perlite (or sand). Sow the seeds thinly and cover them lightly. Place the container in a tray of water until the moisture rises to the surface and then let it drain away. Close the lids tightly, and refrigerate the containers at a temperature of 32–40°F (0–4°C). No further watering is required.

Check the containers each week for activity; if germination occurs, remove the containers from the fridge and uncover them. Normally the containers will remain in the refrigerator for three months. After this period, even if germination is not evident, put them in a warm place, about 60–70°F (15–21°C), and check them daily. As soon as the seedlings emerge, remove the container lid. A well-lit window ledge is a suitable growing place. If no germination occurs in a month to six weeks, this usually indicates a double dormancy factor. Replace the lids and put the containers back in the refrigerator for another three months.

The whole procedure of stratification (cool, moist storage) and germination is best done during the winter so that the young plants can be transplanted and set outdoors after the danger of frost is past (mid-May in most areas). When you're ready to repot the seedling, use soil mixtures with a slow-release, balanced fertilizer. Peat pots are excellent for the first transplant, as these may be transplanted again directly outdoors. Cold frames are ideal for this purpose, since the young plants may need protection for the first year or so, not only from severe weather, but also from rodents or even deer in rural areas. Once the young plants are established, keep the cold frame open as much as possible during the day to avoid overheating.

Keep records of such things as the source of the seed, treatment, date of sowing and germination. Use some form of permanent label so that each plant can be readily identified.

The foregoing description of seed propagation applies to the more difficult subjects — mostly trees, shrubs and some woody ground covers. Many species germinate without stratification. Most of the ericaceous plants, including rhododendrons, are in this category; these can be germinated in moist, finely granulated sphagnum moss. Some of the well-known trees and shrubs of southern hemisphere origin, such as southern beech (*Nothofagus*) and *Eucalyptus*, with the exception of alpine species such as snow gum (*E. pauciflora* ssp. *niphophila*), do not need stratification. If you think stratification is unnecessary, try a normal warm germination treatment first. If this fails, try stratifying the seeds as described above.

Herbaceous plants do not, as a rule, require stratification. *Helleborus* and the European lilies, such as *Lilium martagon*, are an exception. These plants have double dormancy, and two years may elapse before seedlings are obtained. Never be in undue haste to throw away seed flats. Much valuable seed has been wasted when a little patience might have been rewarded with a good crop of seedlings.

LAYERING

Propagation by layering is well suited to the woodland garden because the desired conditions are usually present — protection, shade, humidity and a moist, well-aerated rooting medium. This method is a leisurely process, often taking a year or two. Gardeners who enjoy pottering about and who do not want a large number of new plants will find the method to their liking. Layering is the ideal process for increasing shrubs and climbers that are difficult to root from cuttings.

Layering in its simplest form consists simply of bending down a suitably placed branch, partially breaking or cutting it through, and pinning it down securely beneath a few inches of moist, well-aerated woodland soil. A few refinements will secure faster, better results. Choose young, vigorous stems that are generally no thicker than 1/2 inch (1.3 cm). Make the cut on the underside, as this permits the branch to be bent vertically, or as near vertical as possible, without breaking it. The vertical position makes a better-formed plant. Make a few additional surface cuts on the upper side of the bend and dust the whole

Figure 15

Layering of rhododendrons is often the easiest way to propagate difficult species:

1) Select a low limb.
2) Partially cut stem beneath to facilitate bending.
3) Treat cut with a rooting hormone suitable for semi-hardwood cuttings.
4) Pin branch down with a wire hoop or large rock.
5) Cover with a 50/50 sand-peat mixture and keep moist. The layered branch can be separated and transplanted once it is sufficiently rooted, usually within one or two years.

Resembling a cyclamen in form, the dainty *Narcissus cyclamineus* is easily propagated by splitting the bulbs.

wounded area with a hormone rooting powder. Some propagators of the old school insert a chip of willow wood or a grain or two of wheat to hold open the split in the well-founded belief that these materials contain root-promoting substances. The cut portion of the stem is then pegged down and covered with 3–4 inches (8–10 cm) of rich organic earth. A flat stone placed on the stem helps prevent it from springing out and keeps the earth moist. Detach the layer from the mother plant when a well-developed mass of roots has formed, usually in 18 months to 2 years. Layering may be done any time between May and September and will work on a wide variety of shrubs. Check to see that the selected shoots are not arising from the rootstock of a grafted plant, as is sometimes the case with some rhododendrons and witch hazels.

Dividing Plants

Division is the preferred method of propagating many ground covers and herbaceous plants because it offers an easy way of increasing these plants relatively quickly. Primulas, lilies, hostas and a host of perennials are easily divided. For example, the perennial species of *Meconopsis*, such as *M. grandis*, should be divided every third year or so; this has an invigorating effect on the stock. This holds true for most perennials, particularly those that grow in a clump. The best time for division is early spring, just as the new growth is visible. Then it is easy to see which parts of the plant are the most vigorous and the weaker parts can be discarded. The clumps should be teased or torn apart if possible, as this helps to retain the roots. For tough clumps, use a sharp knife rather than chopping with a spade.

Taking Cuttings

Many woodland shrubs can be increased by semi-hardwood cuttings in summer or hardwood cuttings in fall. Both these methods can be practiced outdoors. Take semi-hardwood cuttings of deciduous and evergreen plants during the summer; hardwood cuttings of deciduous woody plants in the fall. The traditional cold frame is still a useful device for growing cuttings. The glazed (or plastic) surface of the frame must be shielded from direct sun at all times, yet the frame should be placed where it can be warmed by the sun. Warmth is critical to the development of roots. Maintain the necessary humidity by keeping the frame tightly closed until the cuttings are rooted. The medium should be 50 percent peat and 50 percent perlite or coarse sand. Dip the base of the cuttings into a medium-strength rooting hormone to promote rooting. As with layering, the process is slower than indoor methods, and the cuttings may need to remain in the cold frame for up to two years before they are adequately rooted. In cold climates, the frame should have insulated walls and heavy blankets of insulation placed over the glass or plastic during long periods of sub-zero weather.

Working Indoors

An effective propagation frame can be made in a greenhouse or even in the basement of a home. For the latter it is necessary to install grow lamps above the cutting bed. These fluorescent lamps give light with a spectrum close to natural light. The cutting bed, which can be a simple wooden box about 6 inches (15 cm) deep, should have some kind of bottom heat, such as electrical heating cables controlled by a thermostat to maintain the rooting medium at a constant temperature of 75°F (24°C). This temperature is also suitable for the germination of seeds. The air temperature can be considerably lower. Provide a very fine wire mesh bottom for drainage of the propagation box, and keep the rooting medium moist at all times. The box must have a transparent plastic cover, held above the cuttings or seedlings with a simple frame, to provide humidity.

An advantage of using lights is that they can be connected to a timer and the day length extended. This is very useful, as seedlings and cuttings that would normally become dormant in the autumn may be kept growing through the following winter. Seedlings and cuttings grown with this method grow more quickly and have a higher survival rate.

Planting Out Seedlings

Don't be tempted to plant out seedlings and rooted cuttings in the woodland before they are strong enough to survive. Much effort is wasted when immature plants are lost to pests or drought, or are smothered by more aggressive plants. Grow plants to at least a 1-gallon (4-litre) container size before planting them out.

Be sure to label your plants with legible, durable tags. All plastic-type labels are short-lived when used outdoors; wooden labels eventually discolor or rot. The solution is to use a weatherproof metal, such as thick aluminum foil. A low-cost, permanent label can be made from aluminum foil folded to form a thick layer, with the name written on the foil with a nail or other sharp object. The foil can be pierced and attached to plants with plastic-coated wire. An embossing machine is available that makes embossed aluminum strip labels.

Plant labels are frequently lost, and memory is short. As a fallback, draw up a planting plan of plant locations.

Preventing Winter Damage

The woodland garden, a protected environment that buffers the extremes of severe winter cold and summer heat, is the ideal place to try new plants. One or the other of these factors has to be reckoned with in many parts of North America.

One of the most important factors in winter hardiness is to ensure the soil is well drained. Excess moisture late in the season delays ripening of the plant tissue, which is essential to winter hardiness.

In the northern states and most of Canada, the soil may freeze to a considerable depth. This is one of the major limiting factors in trying to grow plants new to these areas, particularly broad-leaved evergreens such as rhododendrons and camellias. These plants continue to transpire moisture from the leaves even when the roots are unable to supply water because of frozen soil. The plants may die from desiccation. If the natural leaf-fall of the woodland is supplemented by a thick bed of loose leaves over the roots, the deep freezing of the soil may be lessened or overcome. Timing is important: mulching must be done after the plants are thoroughly dormant and hardened to cold. This may be as early as October in the north or as late as December in milder areas. Oak leaves are ideal, since they do not pack down like the flat leaves of maples. Surplus leaves can be removed in spring and scattered through the woodland.

Anti-desiccant sprays are of some value in reducing water loss from evergreen plants in winter. They work by coating the leaf surface with a thin film of degradable wax or plastic. The spray is applied on a dry day when the temperature is well above freezing. It can also help plants withstand transplant shock, but it will not protect from sun scald. In fact, it works best on shaded plants.

Another factor contributing to winter injury of sensitive plants is sunshine. The winter sun can be particularly bright over inland areas, and it has a rapid warming effect on broad-leaved evergreens. Rapid warming or freezing of leaves and bark can damage or kill plants. Even the trunks of deciduous trees are not immune. Site tender broad-leaved evergreen plants where they will be shaded for a few hours when the sun is at its zenith. If this is not possible, build a temporary canopy of cut evergreen boughs to shield them from the sun.

The most important cold hardiness factor is the intensity and duration of winter cold. The USDA plant hardiness zone map for North America (see pages iv–v) provides an indication as to which woody plants will survive in a given area based on the expected minimum winter temperatures. Hardiness ratings based on this map are given in many books, but these ratings can only be used as a general guide because local conditions create microclimates of warmer and colder pockets within the hardiness zones. Warm microclimates are more likely to occur on the hillsides of sheltered mountains, near large urban centers, and near large bodies of water, such as coastal areas or large inland lakes that do not freeze over in winter. On a smaller scale, warmer pockets exist adjacent to the south or west side of buildings. Colder microclimates are found at valley bottoms with poor air circulation, at high elevations, and in exposed areas open to prevailing cold winds.

Protection from wind is important to the survival of plants at the borderline of hardiness. At subfreezing temperatures the windchill factor is severe, and the desiccation of plant tissues is accelerated. Hardy conifers at the fringes of woodland gardens soften the tendency for wind to be funneled under the canopy.

There is a relationship between nutrition and winter hardiness. Strong, vigorous plants that have been given well-balanced nutrition are more likely to survive extreme weather conditions. Lush leafy growth and no flowers may be a sign of too much nitrogen, while short growth, pale green leaves and profuse flowering may indicate nitrogen starvation. Both conditions make a plant more susceptible to winter injury. While the scientific basis for adequate nutrition is soil or tissue analysis, in practice, the use of a balanced fertilizer formulated for ericaceous plants serves most plants quite well. A light fertilizer application coinciding with fall rains will sustain woodland plants through the winter when root growth continues, and it helps to get them off to a good start in spring. When plants have reached the desired size, fertilizer may be largely discontinued.

In areas where fall rains are not reliable, broad-leaved evergreens should be thoroughly watered after the fall feeding and before the first hard frost. This helps prevent winter drought and the resulting injury from desiccation. Anti-desiccant sprays can also help.

The plant collector will wish to experiment with new plants of unknown hardiness or with plants known to be on the borderline of hardiness. These plants are usually obtained as small specimens, often little more than rooted cuttings or seedlings. In cases where a species is at the limit of its distribution, the limiting factor is the killing of very young plants during an occasional severe winter. As an example, the madrone (*Arbutus menziesii*) is at the limit of its natural range in southwestern British Columbia. Large specimens are common on warm, dry sites. The wider distribution of this species is limited by winterkill of young plants — both in the wild and in cultivation. In colder winters many plants with trunks of 2 inches (5 cm) or less in diameter in coastal British Columbia are killed. Older plants, of 2 inches (5 cm) or more, survive unscathed. The lesson here is that young plants should be protected from winter cold for as long as possible before being fully exposed to winter conditions. Plant older specimens in the spring, and use cold frames, heavy mulching, windbreaks and temporary canopies of evergreen boughs for winter protection.

Authors' Favorite Plants

WE ARE OFTEN ASKED what plants we would choose to include in the design of a small woodland garden. The following pages describe a limited number of favorite plants in all the major categories for the woodland landscape. Although some of them are rare and difficult to find, a large proportion can be found by a little diligent searching in seed catalogues and among specialist nurseries. Or consult a botanical garden or specific plant societies in your area.

The information offered here is based on personal experience, mostly gained in the Pacific Northwest and in the Great Lakes region. No attempt is made to repeat detailed botanical or horticultural information that is readily available in other, more comprehensive works. Some of these are listed in the bibliography.

Unless otherwise noted, the plants discussed will succeed in well-drained woodland soil that is neither strongly acid nor alkaline.

Plants that are discussed at some length in the text, such as rhododendrons and camellias, are not included here. Comments on these and other plants groups can be found in the lists in Chapters 3 to 6.

Scientific Names

Scientific names conform to those used in *The New Royal Horticultural Society Dictionary of Gardening*, published in 1992 by the Royal Horticultural Society, London, England, and amended by *The Royal Horticultural Society Plant Finder*, 2002-2003 edition.

PRECEDING PAGE: Massed rhododendrons beneath a canopy of pines. A *Trachycarpus* palm gives an exotic touch.

Common Names

Common names for plants are noted next to the accepted scientific name. Common names of plants are often a source of confusion and controversy. This fact prompted the development of internationally accepted botanical nomenclature with its use of accepted scientific names to identify distinct types of plants. Common plant names vary from country to country, even within nations, often resulting in one type of plant being known by several names. For this reason we have sometimes omitted them. Using the scientific name for plants greatly reduces the possibility of confusion. Common names do allow us to give plants an easily remembered descriptive name and are used in the plant lists to this end. Any ambiguities should be resolved by referring to the scientific name.

Plant Height

Measurements cited in the lists refer to the expected mature or fully developed height attainable in ordinary cultivated settings. Herbaceous materials may reach this height in one growing season; woody trees and shrubs will, of course, take longer. Exceptional growing conditions affect the eventual size of plants, and the sizes should be adjusted accordingly.

Hardiness Zone Ratings

Hardiness zone ratings indicate cold tolerance on a scale of one to 11, one being subarctic and 11 being subtropical and frost-free. These zones are illustrated in the Plant Hardiness Zone Maps on pages iv–v. Factors other than tolerance of low temperatures affect hardiness. These include nutrition, summer temperatures, rainfall and autumn weather patterns. All these affect the conditioning of the plant tissues. Good soil drainage is also an important factor in winter hardiness. For example, many plants that are well adapted to a continental type of climate (cold winters, hot summers and a dry fall) may not be successful in a coastal oceanic climate because this type of climate favors continued growth in the fall. This may result in severe frost damage to non-adapted species at temperatures considerably higher than the same species might tolerate with ease in its native habitat. In short, the natural ripening and dormancy that occur in a warm, dry autumn season is favorable to the development of frost hardiness. Mild, moist autumn weather may induce late growth susceptible to frost damage. This accounts for the fact that a shrub that is hardy in Boston, Massachusetts (Zone 5), may not be successful in the Pacific Northwest (Zone 7 or 8). Such problems can be partially overcome by selecting planting sites that simulate and accentuate the environmental factors of the natural habitat. For example, the flowering dogwood (*Cornus florida*), a woodland plant in eastern North America, is more successfully cultivated in the Pacific Northwest when planted in the open, exposed to the sun, with good air circulation.

The hardiness zone given for each plant indicates the coldest zone in which it could be expected to be hardy. In most cases (though not all) the plant would succeed in the warmer zones. For example, the bald cypress (*Taxodium distichum*) is rated for Zone 4, but it is found growing naturally in the warmer Zone 10. Obviously, this plant has a very wide tolerance to climate, which suggests a much greater geographical range in prehistoric times. On the other hand, a plant of the North such as lady slipper orchid (*Cypripedium calceolus*), is intolerant of heat and would not succeed in a warm southerly latitude.

Some parts of North America have local microclimates that provide favorable planting sites, allowing the cultivation of plants not normally considered hardy in these areas.

Because of these factors, the hardiness zone ratings may not be accurate for all areas. Experimentation may yield some useful results by extending the territorial range of cultivated plants.

L TO R: *Aucuba japonica*, Siberian alder (*Alnus hirsuta* var. *sibirica*)

The Authors' Selections

Abelia × grandiflora
GLOSSY ABELIA
3 ft (0.9 m)   Zone 6   ◆

The abelias are rather formless, twiggy shrubs that benefit from selective spring pruning to improve their shape. A sheltered, semishaded location is best — growing against a wall or natural rockwork, for instance. The lustrous dark green leaves are attractive. The fragrant flowers are white tinged with pink and are borne late in the summer on the current year's growth. It is a hybrid between two Chinese species.

Abeliophyllum distichum
WHITE FORSYTHIA
3 ft (0.9 m)   Zone 5   ✿

This small deciduous shrub is one of the loveliest early bloomers. A sunny clearing or the woodland fringe is the best location for this shrub, and its flowers are displayed to the best advantage with an evergreen background of conifers. As with forsythia, some old wood should be pruned out each year to restore vigor. Native to Korea.

Acer buergerianum
TRIDENT MAPLE
10–30 ft (3–9 m)   Zone 6

Originally known as *A. trifidum* for its three-lobed leaves, this small tree has an open form in mild climates, and is more densely branched in colder ones. In the coastal Northwest it is prone to weak watersprout growth, probably due to excessive moisture. It is more successful in a continental climate, similar to its original home in China.

Acer griseum
PAPERBARK MAPLE
10–40 ft (3–12 m)   Zone 5   ◆

One of the best and most robust of the small maples. We cannot recall having lost a tree to disease in 20 years of gardening. Other small maples seem susceptible to wilt diseases such as *Verticillium*. Beautiful orange-colored bark and purple-red autumn color enhance the woodland. The small trifoliate leaves are fine-textured. The tree, which is of Chinese origin, is difficult to raise from seed because of low germination rate.

Adiantum pedatum
MAIDENHAIR FERN
12–18 in (30–45 cm)   Zone 4

An exquisitely textured deciduous fern for semishade and moist soil, it is a perfect companion for woodland flowers. The variety *aleuticum* is native in the Pacific Northwest.

Aesculus pavia
RED BUCKEYE
10–15 ft (3–4.6 m)   Zone 5

Found in the woodlands of the southeastern United States, sometimes associated with a native azalea, *Rhododendron canescens*, and the climber *Gelsemium sempervirens*, this large shrub bears red flowers in May, followed by interesting fruits.

Alnus hirsuta var. sibirica
SIBERIAN ALDER
10–15 ft (3–4.6 m)   Zone 4

This is one of the best of the alders, making a wide-spreading shrub or tree suitable for wet locations or normal soil. The leaves are a lustrous, dark green. The large, attractive seed cones are persistent, giving the plant an interesting appearance in winter.

Akebia quinata
CHOCOLATE VINE
10–15 ft (3–4.6 m)   Zone 5   ✿

This Chinese climber with digitate leaves belongs to the Lardizabalaceae, an interesting family of plants that includes the evergreen climber *Stauntonia hexaphylla* and the shrubby *Decaisnea fargesii*. Small in scale when grown on a robust shrub or trellis, it bears inconspicuous but charming chocolate-colored flowers in June, followed by large, fleshy purple berries in warm summers. It bears watching, as it can become so vigorous it smothers less aggressive plants.

Amelanchier canadensis
SHADBLOW
30–40 ft (9–12 m)   Zone 4   ◆

A very hardy native tree or shrub for the understory or woodland edge, it produces masses of showy white flowers that, although rather ephemeral, are nonetheless one of the most welcome sights of spring. A tree of neat growth and interesting texture, it also provides spectacular autumn color.

Aquilegia canadensis
COLUMBINE
12 in (30 cm)   Zone 4

One of the loveliest of the columbines, it is a true woodland plant. The scarlet and yellow flowers are the most intensely colored in the genus but are rather short-lived. The species *A. alpina* is a fine, robust plant with blue flowers. The Himalayan *A. fragrans* should be tried in milder areas. All the columbines are easily raised from seed. Drifts of columbine make a fine ground cover in woodland that is not densely shaded.

Astilbe chinensis 'Pumila'
DWARF ASTILBE
10–12 in (25–30 cm)   Zone 6

This is a good dwarf plant with no hint of coarseness. All astilbes are good woodland plants that bear pink to red and white flowering plumes. They succeed best in partial shade and moist earth. Plant them beside ponds or streams, massed in wet woodland clearings or on seepage slopes.

Aucuba japonica
SPOTTED LAUREL
6–8 ft (1.8–2.4 m)   Zone 7

The evergreen aucubas need shade, and their lustrous green or variegated foliage brightens the woodland path. Cultivars 'Picturata' and 'Serratifolia' are bold in foliage and bear bright red berries through the winter. Plants of both sexes are required for reliable berry production. These plants of Japanese origin are among the best shrubs that tolerate deep shade. They also have a reputation for being tolerant of air pollution.

Betula albosinensis
CHINESE PAPER BIRCH
25–40 ft (7.6–12 m)   Zone 5

A beautiful birch with burnished, coppery-colored bark. In the Pacific Northwest the tree has a tendency to grow too quickly, causing weak growth. A drier, sunnier climate is more to its liking. Growing it on poor, sandy soil with limited water, conditions that most birches tolerate, will produce the best growth.

Betula utilis var. jacquemontii
HIMALAYAN BIRCH
25–50 ft (7.6–15 m)   Zone 6

The finest of the white birches; in open woodland the stark white bark is spectacular. This tree is fast-growing but suffers less from structural weakness and disease than the American and European birches.

Bletilla striata
CHINESE GROUND ORCHID
10–12 in (25–30 cm)   Zone 8

A hardy and adaptable terrestrial orchid, it grows best in moist yet well-drained organic soil in semishade. In cold areas, mulch the roots to protect them from hard frost. Flowers are rose pink, but white forms exist. Very beautiful when planted in drifts.

Cardiocrinum giganteum
GIANT HIMALAYAN LILY
6–8 ft (1.8–2.4 m)   Zone 6   ✿

This magnificent species epitomizes the deep woodland valleys of the Himalayas and is an important part of any collection of Asian woodland plants. The long, narrow, trumpet-shaped white flowers are borne atop tall stems in late spring. As with all lilies, perfect drainage is necessary, and a deep woodland soil is preferred. The bulbs are very close to the surface and should be protected with organic mulches where winters are cold. The succulent new leaves are attractive to slugs.

Cercis canadensis
REDBUD
20–40 ft (6–12 m)   Zone 5

All four commonly cultivated species of *Cercis* are grown in various parts of North America. They are members of the pea family (Fabaceae) and have a wide tolerance of different soils, even succeeding in poor, alkaline conditions. In the Northeast, *C. canadensis* and its beautiful white form, 'Alba', is the best choice. The variety *texensis* is heat tolerant and best for southern gardens. In the South and Northwest, the Mediterranean species *C. siliquastrum*, or Judas tree, seems better adapted. The western redbud (*C. occidentalis*) is less often seen in gardens. The habit of producing flowers on the bark of old branches, even on the trunk, is intriguing. The Chinese redbud (*C. chinensis*) has not been in cultivation long enough throughout North America to fully judge its merits. All the redbuds need adequate sunshine to properly ripen their growth.

Chimonanthus praecox
WINTERSWEET
6–8 ft (1.8–2.4 m)   Zone 6   ✿

This Chinese plant was introduced to gardens in 1766 yet remains uncommon in gardens. Leaf and form have little merit, but this is forgiven because of the richly fragrant flowers that open in midwinter. It may be grown as a free-standing shrub or spread against a south- or west-facing wall or rock face.

Chionanthus virginicus
FRINGE TREE
6–12 ft (1.8–3.7 m)   Zone 5   ✿

The fringe tree is a slow-growing tree of strong character in old specimens. In common with deciduous trees and shrubs of the eastern part of North America, it is late to leaf out in the spring. The tassel-like white flowers are interesting and are followed by blue-black olive-like fruits. It prefers a sunny location but will also succeed in semishade.

Clematis armandii
EVERGREEN CLEMATIS
15–20 ft (4.6–6.1 m)   Zone 8   ◆ ✿

A native of China, this beautiful species is distinguished by its fine, lustrous, dark green foliage and elegant habit. A profusion of fragrant white flowers is borne in April or earlier in mild areas. A rampant grower once established, it is able to recover from the base if winter-killed. It should not be pruned unless absolutely necessary.

Clematis montana var. rubens
15–30 ft (4.6–10 m)   Zone 6   ◆ ✿

This Chinese variety is a strong-growing climber. It produces abundant, small, shell-pink flowers in May. An old fir or pine tree makes a good support. No pruning is necessary, but old straggly plants may be cut back severely to rejuvenate them. Prune after flowering.

Clematis tangutica
10–12 ft (3–3.7 m)   Zone 5   ◆

A hardy species from Asia with pendent yellow flowers, it looks best when allowed to scramble over vigorous shrubs such as viburnums, particularly the evergreen kinds. Attractive silky seedpods are produced in late summer, and these remain on the bare stems through the winter.

Clematis viticella
10–12 ft (3–3.7 m)   Zone 5   ◆

A vigorous species useful for covering other shrubs in a sunny location, it flowers abundantly on new growth in midsummer. It can be cut down to the ground before growth begins in the spring. Most forms are purple, but there are red and white cultivars available. The species is native in southern Europe.

Colchicum autumnale
AUTUMN CROCUS
8–10 in (20–25 cm)   Zone 5

This European plant seems perfectly designed for the annual cycle of the woodland. Its flowers appear as the leaves of the canopy are falling, and the large leaves, which are such a welcome feature of spring, begin to shrivel and decay before the canopy is fully dressed with leaves in summer. *Colchicum* flowers are vulnerable to autumn rains; the protection of woodland and a soft, absorbent mulch will prolong their flowering season. There are striped and double cultivars in both pink and white. 'Water Lily' is particularly good.

Cornus canadensis
DWARF CORNEL
3 in (7.5 cm)   Zone 3

Widely distributed in North America, this is among the finest of dwarf plants for the woodland floor. The white blossoms produced in May are perfect miniature dogwood flowers. It spreads quickly to form a woodland mat if the soil is spongy and rich in organic matter.

Cornus
'Eddies White Wonder'
15–20 ft (4.6–6 m)   Zone 6

Not for deep shade or beneath the drip line of other trees, this and other flowering dogwoods require a sunny woodland glade and good air circulation. Correct siting is the only effective way to avoid the disfiguring fungal leaf spot disease. *Cornus florida* and *C. nuttallii*, the parents of this spectacular hybrid, share the same needs. The latter is probably too vigorous for all but the largest of woodland gardens. The pink forms of *C. florida* are delightful small trees of picturesque form.

Cornus kousa var. chinensis
CHINESE DOGWOOD
15–30 ft (4.6–10 m)   Zone 6   ◆

This species is the best of the dogwoods for woodland gardens. Flowering in June, a full month later than the North American species, it produces attractive long-stalked red fruits in the fall. This species is generally hardier and more disease resistant than the other dogwood species.

Corylopsis pauciflora
WINTER HAZEL
4–6 ft (1.2–1.8 m)   Zone 6   ✿

Native of Japan, this charming low shrub is grown for its pretty yellow flowers, which appear before the leaves in late winter. Winter hazels such as *C. spicata* and *C. wilsonii* are of similar character but are much larger.

Corylus colurna
TURKISH HAZELNUT
50–60 ft (15–18 m)   Zone 4

The finest and largest of the hazelnut trees, its rugged form and long catkins borne in February are superb for winter effect, and the tiny red female flowers are like jewels on the winter twigs.

L TO R: Giant Himalayan lily
(*Cardiocrinum giganteum*), Redbud
(*Cercis canadensis* var. *texensis*)

Crocus tommasinianus
3–4 in (7.5–10 cm)   Zone 5

This is one of the smallest species, with flowers that are purple to lavender. Crocuses are ideal for massing under deciduous trees in the woodland garden. There is a wide choice of species and large-flowered hybrids, but species seem more appropriate in the wild garden. Crocuses are native to a wide area of Europe and the Middle East. They adapt well to most parts of North America.

Cyclamen coum
3–4 in (7.5–10 cm)   Zone 7   ◆

A dainty plant, often in flower before the snowdrops, it enjoys the protection of planting beneath rhododendrons and other shrubs in peaty, well-drained soil. Pink and white forms exist. The autumn-flowering *C. hederifolium* needs the same conditions. Both are natives of southern Europe.

Cypripedium calceolus
LADY SLIPPER ORCHID
6–12 in (15–30 cm)   Zone 4   ◆

This species is a bog plant in its native North America. *Cypripedium californicum*, *C. montanum* and *C. reginae* are also occasionally cultivated. These orchids are best planted in tussocks of sphagnum moss and peat above the waterline beside streams or ponds. Most terrestrial orchids prefer a moist, mossy habitat. It is a challenge to grow wild terrestria orchids in woodland gardens. The behavior of terrestrial orchids in cultivation is often unpredictable because their needs are not always well understood. Most require symbiotic association with soil fungi, which if not present may cause the orchids to fail. For example, the exquisite and rare *Calypso bulbosa* of the Pacific northern woods has been successfully grown in a limited way and then only by specialists. They must not be dug up unless threatened with immediate destruction of their habitat. When orchids or, for that matter, any native plants are purchased, buyers should check that they are not wild-collected plants. If so, they should be refused.

Daphne mezereum
FEBRUARY DAPHNE or **MEZEREON**
3–4 ft (0.9–1.2 m)   Zone 5   ◆   ❀

This deciduous winter-flowering daphne is available in pink and white forms, although the latter seems to have a weaker constitution. The flowers are very fragrant, and its red berries are ornamental but poisonous. The European daphnes seem to benefit from an occasional dressing of dolomite lime.

Daphne odora
WINTER DAPHNE
3–4 ft (0.9–1.2 m)   Zone 7   ❀

A beautiful, fragrant flowering shrub for the woodland path, this Asian evergreen is rather tender and needs protection. The cultivar 'Aureo-Marginata', a plant of moderate size and great refinement, seems to be hardier than the species.

Darmera peltata
UMBRELLA PLANT
24 in (60 cm)   Zone 6

This vigorous herbaceous plant has large, handsome leaves that turn attractive colors in autumn. The pink flowers are produced before the leaves in early spring. An excellent plant for the waterside, it will grow almost submerged.

Davidia involucrata
DOVE TREE
20–40 ft (6–12 m)   Zone 6   ◆

The dove tree should be grown in all woodlands in those regions where it is hardy. Native to southwestern China, it is fast-growing in deep, rich soil. The white flower bracts are carried in great profusion on older trees and never fail to attract attention. The variety *vilmoriniana* has darker green, glabrous leaves and is probably more common in cultivation.

L TO R: Dove tree (*Davidia involucrata*), Burning bush (*Euonymus alata*)

Dicentra formosa
WESTERN BLEEDING HEART
16 in (40 cm)   Zone 5

This rapidly spreading, herbaceous plant is for semishaded, moist locations. The more showy cultivated species, *D. spectabilis*, is taller, to 24 in (61 cm), with rosy red flowers. It requires more sunshine than *D. formosa*.

Enkianthus campanulatus
6–12 ft (1.8–3.7 m)   Zone 5

An elegant deciduous twiggy shrub of layered habit with attractive, bell-shaped flowers in May, it is a good companion for evergreen rhododendrons and azaleas. It provides good autumn color. After many years this Japanese species may grow to small tree size.

Epigaea repens
TRAILING ARBUTUS
4–6 in (10–15 cm)   Zone 2

The trailing arbutus is a neat evergreen ground cover for shade and is the official flower of the Canadian province of Nova Scotia. It needs an acid, peaty soil with good drainage.

Erica carnea
HEATH
6–12 in (15–30 cm)   Zone 5   ◆

outstanding selections.

The true heaths comprise a group of about 500 species, most of which are not hardy in the colder temperate areas. All succeed best in the open, away from trees, but in colder areas they can be massed in open deciduous woodland where the protection may be an advantage. *Erica carnea* is the hardiest, most adaptable species, with numerous cultivars. 'Vivellii' is an excellent cultivar with dark green foliage and deep red flowers. The variegated 'Aurea' and the white-flowered 'Springwood White' are other

Erythronium americanum
DOGTOOTH VIOLET
4–6 in (10–15 cm)   Zone 4   ◆

This native of eastern North America is the hardiest of the genus. It is most successful planted in woodsy soil under deciduous trees such as oak. The white *E. albidum* is very beautiful and equally hardy. The western species such as *E. tuolumnense* and *E. revolutum* and their hybrids are good for massing on semishaded banks. The Eurasian *E. dens-canis* is at home in moist, peaty soil in the rock garden or beside a sunny woodland path. This species, with its beautifully marked leaves and rosy lilac flowers, deserves to be planted more often.

Euonymus alatus
WINGED SPINDLE BUSH
6–8 ft (1.8–2.4 m)   Zone 3

A picturesque deciduous shrub with curiously winged stems, it is best known for its brilliant scarlet autumn color. The cultivar 'Compactus' is a smaller version of the species with improved fall coloring. Other *Euonymus* species are interesting and trouble-free. The evergreen *E. fortunei* has many dwarf and variegated cultivars that are useful in colder areas as ground covers. *Euonymus sachalinensis* from Japan becomes a large shrub with striking purple-red flowers, excellent as a specimen in light shade.

Eucryphia × intermedia
BRUSH BUSH
10–20 ft (3–6 m)   Zone 8

A vigorous hybrid originating in Ireland between a Chilean and Tasmanian species, it is distinguished for its white four-petalled flowers bearing a central boss of stamens that resemble a shaving brush. Valuable for its late-summer flowering habit, when few other large shrubs are in flower, and its hardiness when compared to other eucryphias. This small tree is best suited to a sunny clearing in sheltered woodland where cold winter winds will not scorch its evergreen leaves. Another choice selection, although less hardy, is *E. × nymansensis*, a slender evergreen tree with large, pure white flowers.

Fatsia japonica
JAPANESE ARALIA
6–8 ft (1.8–2.4 m)   Zone 7

This impressive evergreen with large palmate leaves gives a tropical effect in the exotic woodland but may look out of place in some situations. It is best combined with other evergreen shrubs. The large panicles of creamy white flowers are interesting in the late fall. It needs shade from hot sun and shelter from the wind. It is susceptible to infestation by aphids and mealybugs, which are disfiguring unless treated promptly.

Franklinia alatamaha
FRANKLIN TREE
10–15 ft (3–4.6 m)   Zone 5 ✿

Extinct in the wild and possessing a romantic history of being found then lost, this lovely relative of the camellia needs a warm, fairly sunny location if it is to produce its white flowers regularly. The autumn color is magnificent, and the striated bark provides winter interest. In the Pacific Northwest it needs a sunny, heat-retentive position to flower well.

Galanthus elwesii
GIANT SNOWDROP
6–10 in (15–25 cm)   Zone 5

This slightly larger version of the common European snowdrop is an ideal plant for lining the woodland path. Tending to form slowly expanding clumps, its spread may be accelerated by splitting and transplanting. There is no more welcome harbinger of spring than snowdrops in the woodland.

Garrya elliptica
SILK TASSEL BUSH
8–10 ft (2.4–3 m)   Zone 8 ✳

This evergreen shrub of the warm California woods adorns the winter woodland with its beautiful catkins. Hardy only in the milder areas, even there it requires semishade and protection from cold winds. We have had some success planting it near the base of old locust trees. No doubt other deciduous trees, such as oaks, would offer an equally benign habitat. This is probably related to the need for some dryness at the root in late summer to accelerate ripening of the new growth.

Gaultheria procumbens
WINTERGREEN
6 in (15 cm)   Zone 3

Planted in a semishaded peat bed, it will spread quite rapidly. The dark evergreen leaves and red berries make a pleasing contrast. *Gaultheria miqueliana* is an Asian plant with similar needs, but it is less hardy (Zone 6).

Gelsemium sempervirens
CAROLINA JESSAMINE
10–15 ft (3–4.6 m)   Zone 7 ✿

This choice evergreen climber requires a warm, semi-shaded place at the woodland fringe. It has not succeeded in the Pacific Northwest because the autumn is not warm enough to ripen its wood. The yellow flowers appear in April and are very fragrant.

Gentiana asclepiadea
WILLOW GENTIAN
12 in (30 cm)   Zone 6

This easily grown gentian may be divided and naturalized in open woodland. Most gentians are best grown in a rock garden, but the Asian species such as *G. septemfida*, *G. tibetica* and *G. sino-ornata* can be attempted in open woods.

Halesia carolina
SILVER-BELL TREE
10–20 ft (3–6 m)   Zone 5

A delightful small tree of great charm, producing white bell-shaped flowers in May. In the woodland it makes an open-branched tree under which other shrubs can be massed. *Halesia monticola*, the mountain silver-bell tree, is similar in most respects but becomes much larger.

Hamamelis mollis
CHINESE WITCH HAZEL
10–20 ft (3–6 m)   Zone 5

The Chinese witch hazel (*H. mollis*) is more widely grown than any other species. 'Pallida', one of the most popular cultivars, bears soft yellow, fragrant flowers. There are many good hybrids developed from crosses between *H. mollis* and *H. japonica*. One of the best of these is the coppery orange-flowered *H. × intermedia* 'Jelena'. Of the American species, the Ozark witch hazel (*H. vernalis*) is rather rare in gardens. This species is spring-flowering with short, often dull red petals. The Virginia or common witch hazel (*H. virginiana*) is unique in being fall-flowering. This tree has an attractive horizontal branching form. The large wide leaves turn butter yellow in the fall, partially concealing the bloom. This species is sometimes used by nursery owners as a rootstock for grafting the other witch hazels. Unfortunately, there is a tendency for it to produce suckers, which may overtake the desired cultivar unless vigorously removed. Because of this, when buying a witch hazel, avoid grafted plants if possible. All the witch hazels have attractive autumn color. If they can be sited in front of large conifers or broad-leaved evergreens, the flowers will be displayed more effectively, especially if they are backlit by the winter sun.

Hedera canariensis 'Variegata'
ALGERIAN IVY
12 ft (3.7 m)   Zone 8 ✳

This variegated ivy and the related *H. colchica* 'Dentata Variegata' can be quite beautiful if allowed to climb over an old tree or scramble over old walls and rock outcroppings in semishade. The common ivy (*H. helix*) should be used with restraint because if left to spread unchecked, it can totally overcome native species and less aggressive plants.

Helleborus niger
CHRISTMAS ROSE
8–12 in (20–30 cm)   Zone 4 ◆

This European species and the Lenten rose (*H. orientalis*) succeed in ordinary garden soil in front of shrubs or in semishade beside the woodland path. The bold, cup-shaped flowers and the evergreen palmate leaves give them a strong visual appeal. They are winter-flowering and should be lightly mulched with compost or pine needles to lessen damage by winter rains and frost. They respond quite well to feeding, and an annual dressing of aged manure is beneficial. On acid soils, a light application of dolomitic lime will help to retain vigor.

Hepatica acutiloba
LIVERLEAF
4–6 in (10–15 cm)   Zone 5 ◆

These early-flowering anemone-like plants retain their attractive leaves during the winter. They are found in rock crevices in calcareous woodland in the Carolinean zone of the United States and Canada. There are blue, pink and white forms. See *Helleborus* for growing information. They are easily propagated by division after flowering.

Hosta spp.
PLANTAIN LILY
various heights   Zone 4 ❀

This genus of superb Asian foliage plants is supremely adapted for shady locations. Hostas enjoy deep, rich soil and abundant moisture. They will succeed in quite deep shade but flower more freely in dappled sunlight. The hostas vary in height from *H. lancifolia*, about 12 in (30 cm) high, to the bold blue foliage of *H. sieboldiana*, 2 ft (0.6 m) or more. *Hosta undulata* has wavy variegated leaves and lavender flowers, while *H. plantaginea* bears white scented flowers.

Hydrangea anomala
and **H. anomala var. petiolaris**
CLIMBING HYDRANGEAS
15 ft (4.6 m)   Zone 5 ◆

These species are the hardiest of the Asian hydrangeas. They are useful for covering old stumps or clothing a fence or wall, even on the north side. All hydrangeas should be pruned selectively, not severely, as hard pruning removes flowering wood and causes declining vigor.

Ilex verticillata
WINTERBERRY
6–8 ft (1.8–2.4 m)   Zone 3

This beautiful deciduous holly from eastern North America is good for massing in moist, open woodland. The red berries brighten the winter landscape and are a favorite food for birds. Some of the finest hollies are difficult to find in nurseries but can be found through the Holly Society.

Incarvillea delavayi
CHINESE GLOXINIA
12–15 in (30–38 cm)   Zone 6

A choice herbaceous perennial requiring a rich, well-drained soil in semishade, its large, rose-pink, trumpet-shaped flowers resemble *Gloxinia*. The roots are fleshy and need the protection of a winter mulch to prevent deep frost penetration. Lack of mulching is probably the cause of limited success in all but the mildest areas.

Iris ensata
JAPANESE IRIS
18 in (45 cm)   Zone 5

This beautiful iris has many forms and cultivars. It is superb when planted in rich soil near the water's edge in a sunny location. It should be divided every four or five years to retain vigor (discarding the old center pieces), and an annual mulch of rotted manure is beneficial. Most iris species require more sun than the woodland can provide. However, the early-flowering bulbous irises such as *I. histrioides* and *I. reticulata* may succeed in open woodland, associated with crocus species.

Jasminum nudiflorum
WINTER JASMINE
6 ft (1.8 m)   Zone 5 ◆

An indispensable plant for the winter garden, it is very effective when cascading over a rock face or wall, or grown as a spreading shrub, adjacent to dark green conifers such as yews. These are a fine contrast to the bright yellow flowers. The other jasmines are scarcely hardy enough for northern gardens.

Jeffersonia diphylla
TWIN-LEAF
10–12 in (25–30 cm)   Zone 5

This American herbaceous species is a charming woodland plant with interesting leaves and delicate white flowers. The blue-flowered Asian counterpart, *J. dubia*, is equally ornamental but may not be as hardy.

Kalmia latifolia
MOUNTAIN LAUREL
6–8 ft (1.8–2.4 m)   Zone 4

These evergreen shrubs fit naturally into the woodland, preferring quite acid soil. *K. latifolia* has glossy leaves and pink and white, or red flowers in June. There are some fine cultivars such as 'Ostbo Red' and 'Pink Frost'. The smaller bog laurel (*K. polifolia*) is a very hardy plant for moist locations. It has narrow shiny leaves, silvery below, and rose-colored flowers in May.

L TO R: Chinese witchhazel
(*Hamamellis mollis* 'Pallida'),
Mountain laurel (*Kalmia latifolia*
'Ostbo Red')

Kirengeshoma palmata
3 ft (0.9 m)   Zone 6

An unusual-looking herbaceous perennial from Japan and Korea, it has large, maple-like leaves and creamy yellow flowers in late summer. Propagate by division. A very striking effect can be created by planting groups in sunny woodland clearings.

Lamium maculatum
DEAD-NETTLE
6–8 in (15–20 cm)   Zone 6

A useful herbaceous ground cover for shady areas that are apt to be dry, the leaves are attractively blotched silvery white and may persist through the winter in mild areas.

Leucojum vernum
SPRING SNOWFLAKE
8 in (20 cm)   Zone 6

A bulbous plant, it has pendent, fragrant white flowers in spring. This species and the taller, summer-blooming *L. aestivum* are suitable for planting with other bulbs between shrubs. A third species, *L. autumnale*, blooming in late summer, completes this charming trio.

Lilium   See Chapter 5   ✿

Liquidambar styraciflua
SWEET GUM
50 ft (15 m)   Zone 5

This beautiful tree tolerates fairly wet (but not stagnant) soil, a characteristic it shares with the bald cypress (*Taxodium distichum*), with which it is sometimes associated in the wild in the southeastern United States. In common with that species it is equally at home in ordinary garden soil. The winged, corky stems, pendent fruits and lustrous maple-like leaves make this tree a universal favorite. Its autumn color is brilliant, particularly in those parts of its range that enjoy a warm fall.

Lonicera × tellmanniana
HONEYSUCKLE
15–20 ft (4.6–6 m)   Zone 6   ✿

This beautiful deciduous climber is rare in gardens. Like all climbing honeysuckles, it needs a place where its roots are shaded but its twining stems can grow toward the sun. The flowers are yellow flushed with red.

Lysichiton americanum
SKUNK CABBAGE
18–24 in (45–60 cm)   Zone 6

A common bog plant in the Pacific Northwest, this plant is among the most spectacular of the aroids, with bright yellow spathes and bold leaves that may exceed 3 ft (1 m) in length. A muddy stream bank is the best location. *Lysichiton camtschatcense* is a related species from Japan that flowers later, with white spathes. Do not be tempted to bring the flowers of these and other aroids indoors. The odor can be quite offensive!

Magnolia denudata
YULAN MAGNOLIA
to 50 ft (15 m)   Zone 5   ◆

This is one of the hardiest and most satisfactory magnolias. All the species have similar cultural needs, and all of them need the shelter of nearby trees or an open deciduous canopy that will protect the flowers from the wind during rough spring weather. There is little to be gained by planting magnolias in the open, only to have the flowers stripped off by high winds or lashing rain. The large-flowered kinds, such as *M. sargentiana*, *M. dawsoniana* or *M. sprengeri*, are particularly vulnerable. The ideal habitat for these species is open pine or oak woods that allow sufficient light to penetrate but provide the necessary shelter. Under these conditions they will grow almost as high as the sheltering canopy. The flowers are particularly effective when seen against

L TO R: Spring snowflake (*Leucojum vernum*), Virginia bluebells (*Mertensia virginica*)

an evergreen background. The larger Chinese and Himalayan species, which include those mentioned above and the spectacular *M. campbellii*, may grow vigorously for a decade or two before flowering, particularly when grown from seed. Grafted plants start to bloom at a much earlier age. These species are limited to the mild, high-rainfall areas of the Pacific Coast (Zone 8) and a few favored areas of the Southeast. Other Asian species, such as *M. kobus*, *M. denudata* and hybrids like *M.* × *soulangiana*, are better adapted to the Great Lakes areas and the Northeast (Zones 5–6). With the exception of *M. grandiflora*, the evergreen sweet bay of the American South (Zone 7), which is among the finest of all evergreen trees, the American magnolias are less spectacular than the Asian species. They are, however, trees of strong character that find a place in large gardens and botanical collections. All magnolias require deep, well-drained, loamy or sandy soil.

Mahonia × wagneri 'Moseri'
OREGON GRAPE
4–6 ft (1.2–1.8 m)   Zone 6   ◆

This interesting variant was developed in France and has leaves tinted pink and red. The striking coloration is enhanced by sun and cold weather. The mahonias are among the easiest and most adaptable shrubs, equally at home in sun or shade except for the Asian species *M. japonica* and *M. lomariifolia*, which demand shade. Hybrids of these two species, such as *M.* × *media* 'Arthur Menzies' and 'Charity', are particularly fine, bearing showy spikes of yellow flowers during late autumn and winter.

Matteuccia struthiopteris
OSTRICH FERN
3 ft (0.9 m)   Zone 3

A superbly ornamental fern for associating with large rhododendrons or in any reasonably moist shady place, it is a deciduous species that may be interplanted with evergreen ferns such as polystichums to relieve the monotony of a fern carpet on the woodland floor. The fiddleheads of the new spring growth give a fine effect, and the russet brown leaves of autumn blend well with the brighter autumn colors.

Meconopsis spp.
ASIATIC POPPY
12–30 in (30–75 cm)

No hardiness rating is given for *Meconopsis*, as success with this choice group of herbaceous plants depends almost as much on skillful siting and cultivation as on actual cold hardiness. In the Devonian Botanic Garden in Edmonton, Alberta, which is in Zone 3, several species are grown successfully, including *M. betonicifolia*, *M. horridula* and *M. napaulensis*. The overwintering rosettes of foliage must be protected from extreme dampness and freezing where snow cover is not reliable. In cold areas, continuous snow cover is the best protection, and this may be enhanced by placing brush over the plant crowns. Loose organic mulches offer an alternative means of protection.

Mertensia virginica
VIRGINIA BLUEBELLS
12–24 in (30–60 cm)   Zone 4

This species is capable of carpeting the woodland floor with nodding clusters of fine blue flowers in April and May. It is found in moist leafy soil, even succeeding on the flood benches of woodland streams. Propagation is by seed, which should be sown immediately when ripe.

Metasequoia glyptostroboides
DAWN REDWOOD
to 100 ft (30 m)   Zone 5

A place should be found in the larger woodland garden for this deciduous tree, if for no other reason than its interesting history and the exciting discovery in the wild of a tree once thought to be extinct. This tree is fast-growing, but there is no coarseness in its makeup. The foliage is elegant and forms an attractive reddish-brown carpet when it falls. A grove of several or more trees is a good habitat for other Chinese plants that will tolerate light to moderate shade. As the trees grow, the lower limbs may be selectively removed to accommodate plants of the woodland floor. The dawn redwood is tolerant of soils where the water table is occasionally high, but not to the extent of the bald cypress (*Taxodium*).

Mitchella repens
PARTRIDGE BERRY
3–4 in (7.6–10 cm)   Zone 4

This North American, fine-textured, evergreen ground cover is suitable where fine detail is required; for example, use it in rock crevices or for filling in between the anchor roots of large trees. It requires partial shade and moist, peaty soil.

Myosotis spp.
FORGET-ME-NOT
6–12 in (15–30 cm)   All zones

The familiar blue forget-me-not is a useful ground cover for damp spots in the woodland. These are annual or biennial plants but will seed themselves in profusion and help choke out more weedy plants.

Nandina domestica
HEAVENLY BAMBOO
4–6 ft (1.2–1.8 m)   Zone 7

Nandina is interesting throughout the year, and never outgrows its allocated space. The evergreen compound leaves have attractive autumn tints. Fall color develops best in a site that receives several hours of sunshine a day. Panicles of white flowers in spring are followed by red berries, which contrast nicely with the tinted foliage. In common with many Japanese plants, it likes a warm situation and will even withstand a reasonable amount of drought if sited out of direct sun. A dwarf form, *N. domestica* 'Nana Purpurea', is in most respects a miniature version of the type but does not seem to flower, at least not regularly.

Narcissus spp.
DAFFODIL
10–18 in (25–45 cm)   Zone 5   ✿

Most narcissus, except perhaps the very large showy kinds, are perfectly in tune with woodland gardens. The common daffodil (*N. pseudonarcissus*) can be massed in meadow-like clearings between trees, while the dwarf kinds, such as *N. cyclamineus* and *N. bulbocodium*, are best in sheltered places near the woodland path. They are not fastidious as to soil type but must have good drainage. Some dryness of the soil in late summer assists in the ripening of the bulbs.

Nyssa sylvatica
TUPELO or SOUR GUM
60 ft (18 m)   Zone 5

N. sylvatica has few equals for its brilliant red autumn foliage. In its native habitat, it is often found in swamps, and an appropriate garden setting is on a stream bank or beside a pool. A promising Chinese species, *N. sinensis*, is seen in some collections in milder areas, but little is known of its performance in North America.

Omphalodes cappadocica
NAVELWORT
6–8 in (15–20 cm)   Zone 6   ◆

This aggressive herbaceous ground cover for semishade has flowers similar to those of *Myosotis*. *Omphalodes verna* flowers earlier. In common with *Myosotis*, they prefer moist, organic soil.

Ophiopogon japonicus
LILYTURF
8–10 in (20–25 cm)   Zone 7

The ophiopogons are neat, tufted, grass-like plants belonging to the lily family. Appropriate to the semi-formality of Japanese and Chinese gardens, they are also charming between rocks or beside shaded woodland walks. They spread rather slowly and always present a groomed appearance, since the foliage is evergreen. *Ophiopogon planiscapus* 'Nigrescens' is a novel form with dark purple, almost black, leaves.

Osmanthus × burkwoodii
6–10 ft (1.8–3 m)   Zone 7   ◆

A vigorous evergreen with a dense-textured habit of growth, it is good for screening and background planting. The white flowers are early to appear and very fragrant. Other *Osmanthus* species are chiefly of value for the fragrance of their inconspicuous flowers. *Osmanthus fragrans* is hardy outdoors in the mild areas of Zones 8 and 9.

Oxalis oregana
REDWOOD SORREL
8–10 in (20–25 cm)   Zone 7

A rapidly spreading ground cover for deep shade, even under conifers such as *Sequoia*, with which it is associated in its native habitat, *O. oregana* is attractive planted with ferns. *Oxalis tetraphylla* is a sun-loving species with attractively marked leaves and pink flowers. It produces underground tubers.

Osmunda regalis
ROYAL FERN
4–6 ft (1.2–1.8 m)   Zone 7

This elegant deciduous fern is suitable for interplanting with *Meconopsis* and other woodland flowers. The American species *O. cinnamonea* is similar.

Oxydendrum arboreum
SORREL TREE
60 ft (18 m)   Zone 5

One of the finest trees and widely adaptable in North America, its white flowers resemble those of *Pieris* and are attractive late into the fall. It is also one of the best trees for fiery autumn tints. Rather slow-growing in most garden situations, it responds to moist, leafy or peaty soil.

Paeonia lutea var. ludlowii
SHRUB PEONY
6 ft (1.8 m)   Zone 7   ◆

The peonies as a group must have full sun, but this yellow-flowered Chinese species and the red *P. delavayi* are popular with collectors of Asian plants and have a place in sunny woodland clearings associated with Asian rhododendrons and *Meconopsis*. They are bold, woody plants with stout stems and handsome deciduous leaves. The leaves have a tendency to lodge in the branches and mar the appearance of the plant in winter unless removed to reveal the interesting branching pattern and prominent winter buds.

Parrotia persica
PERSIAN PARROTIA
15–20 ft (4.6–6 m)   Zone 7

A strong-growing tree with a horizontal branching habit, it is resistant to drought and plant pests when established. Related to the witch hazels, this small tree may require some pruning to achieve a good form, since it has a tendency to produce long, rangy branches. The bark, peeling off in platelike sections, is interesting on older specimens, and the small, intense red flowers are quite attractive when viewed at close range.

Paulownia tomentosa
PRINCESS TREE
to 60 ft (18 m)   Zone 6

When well grown, standing above other Asian plants of smaller stature, this tree has a noble form unique among flowering trees. The blue foxglove-like flowers are produced in abundance in spring if the previous summer has been warm. Unfortunately, the large, vulnerable flower buds are sometimes frozen in cold winters. It requires shelter from strong cold winds and a sunny location to fully ripen its late growth.

Photinia serratifolia
8–12 ft (2.4–3.7 m)   Zone 8   ◆

An evergreen shrub or small tree of exceptional quality, it has a vertical habit of growth when young. The glossy foliage is a fine burnished red when new in spring. Mainly of value as a foliage plant, it also bears flat-topped panicles of creamy white flowers.

Picea breweriana
BREWER'S SPRUCE
to 60 ft (18 m)   Zone 7

This is perhaps the only spruce suitable for woodland gardens, as most spruces are intolerant of shade. It is native to the high sheltered valleys of the Siskiyou Mountains of southern Oregon. Somewhat shade tolerant if the leading shoot can grow toward the open sky, it enjoys the presence of nearby trees and protection from wind. The graceful drape of the branchlets is equaled only by the Himalayan *P. smithiana*, which is not so elegant a tree when young. All spruces must be watched carefully for infestations of spider mites and spruce aphid, which can be debilitating if allowed to spread.

Pieris formosa var. forrestii
HIMALAYAN PIERIS
6–12 ft (1.8–3.7 m)   Zone 8

A splendid Chinese evergreen shrub of attractive form and foliage, it bears abundant drooping panicles of white flowers in April. It is most noted for its spectacular, brilliant red young growth, which from a distance looks like exotic flowers. This variety resents severe winter cold and young growth can be damaged by late spring frosts. Hardier, and almost as impressive, is *Pieris* 'Forest flame', a hybrid between *P. formosa* and the much hardier (to Zone 5) *P. japonica*. This and many *P. japonica* cultivars have red-to-bronze-colored new growth and pendent clusters of white, pink or rosy-red flowers. The mountain pieris, *Pieris floribunda*, native to the southeastern United States, is also an excellent shrub and is the hardiest species (to Zone 4). It is easily distinguished from other species by its upright clusters of white flowers and smaller stature. The flower buds of this species develop in fall and remain conspicuously attractive through winter. *Pieris* species are excellent companions for rhododendrons, as both share a preference for moist, acid soil and partial shade.

Pinus wallichiana
HIMALAYAN PINE
to 60 ft (18 m)   Zone 7

A graceful tree for Asian plant collections, this pine does not cast too dense a shade. Very fast-growing on sheltered sites with protection from wind, it is less susceptible to white pine blister rust disease than its North American relative, the eastern white pine (*P. strobus*), which is not recommended where this disease is prevalent.

Pleione formosana
GROUND ORCHID
6–8 in (15–20 cm)   Zone 8

An exotic terrestrial orchid for milder areas, this is a rather tender species not tolerant of extreme cold or heat. Pink and white flower forms are available. Plant it in moist sphagnum in rock crevices or between the rotted roots of old stumps. It can be overwintered by mulching with fern fronds, which are removed in spring.

Podophyllum peltatum
MAYAPPLE
2 ft (0.6 m)   Zone 4

The mayapples are superb foliage plants for shade, spreading quite rapidly in moist, organic soil. The Asian species *P. emodi* and *P. hexandrum* may be less hardy than the American species.

L TO R: Sorrel tree (*Oxydendrum arboreum*), *Polystichum setiferum*

Polygonum vaccinifolium
3–4 in (7.6–10 cm)   Zone 8

A ground-hugging, deciduous, drought-resistant dwarf ground cover for sun or semishade, it bears small pink flowers all summer and into the fall. *Polygonum affine*, a herbaceous species, grows about 8 in (20 cm) high. Its dense heads of pink flowers are ornamental in summer and fall, even after they have faded. The foliage is tinted red.

Polystichum munitum
SWORD FERN
2–5 ft (0.6–1.5 m)   Zone 7

This aggressively spreading evergreen fern covers vast areas of deep woodland in the coastal forest zone of the Pacific Northwest. Its vigor may be controlled by removing most of the older fronds before new growth begins in spring. The deer fern (*Blechnum spicant*) is a similar but smaller evergreen species better suited for small gardens. It is very ornamental lining the woodland walk.

Polystichum setiferum
HEDGE FERN
12–15 in (30–38 cm)   Zone 6

Many interesting forms of this European evergreen fern exist and are worth seeking out from collectors. They are suitable for shaded walks beside streams, among rocks and in other places where they can be seen in winter.

Primula japonica
JAPANESE PRIMULA
15–20 in (38–50 cm)   Zone 5

This is the best known and perhaps the hardiest species for general garden planting. There are red and white forms. Most species of primula grow best in moist, aerobic soil, but not where the water table rises to the surface, causing stagnant conditions. Given a constant supply of moisture, they will be most successful in quite sunny locations, in woodland clearings and around pond margins. *Primula helodoxa* and *P. sieboldii* are shade tolerant. The candelabra primulas, such as the *P. × bulleesiana* hybrids, are spectacular when planted in large drifts beneath deciduous trees. All the species likely to succeed in woodland gardens are fairly coarse and respond to annual mulching with rotted manure. After flowering, the seeds can sift down into this favorable medium for germination and regeneration of the plantings. Older plants sometimes fall prey to white grubs and leatherjacket larvae, which chew the roots.

Robinia pseudoacacia
BLACK LOCUST
100 ft (30 m)   Zone 3 ✹ ✳ ◆

Attractive trees useful for pioneering a future woodland site, they are tolerant of dry, barren soils. *Robinias* have a pleasant feathery canopy casting light shade; woodland plants thrive beneath them. Two good cultivars are 'Frisia', with golden foliage, and 'Tortuosa', with picturesque contorted branches. Both are smaller than the species.

Rodgersia aesculifolia
18–24 in (45–60 cm)   Zone 6

This and other *Rodgersia* species have bold foliage and attractive plume-like flowers. They succeed best on wet seepage slopes and associate well with primulas and other moisture-preferring plants.

Sanguinaria canadensis
BLOODROOT
3–6 in (7.6–15 cm)   Zone 4

A worthy associate of erythroniums, trilliums and other American plants of the woodland floor, its flowers are white and rather ephemeral. However, those of the double form 'Multiplex' last longer. The leaves wither early in the summer, leaving a rather bald appearance unless evergreen plants are interspersed with it.

L TO R: Bloodroot (*Sanquinaria canadensis* 'Multiplex'), *Stachyurus praecox*

Sarcococca humilis
SWEET BOX
12–24 in (30–60 cm)   Zone 6 ✿

These neat little evergreen shrubs have lustrous, dark green, shiny leaves and an engaging, spreading habit. The flowers are deliciously fragrant, and the large anthers, the most prominent part of the flower, are pink. An ideal plant for planting beside a woodland walk or adjacent to a bench where the fragrance can be enjoyed in early spring. *S. confusa* is a taller shrub with fragrant white flowers in late winter, followed by black berries. *S. hookeriana* and *S. ruscifolia* are similar.

Skimmia japonica
2–4 ft (0.6–1.2 m)   Zone 7 ✿

The skimmias are nicely rounded, low shrubs that are good companion plants for the deciduous woodland, where their evergreen form and attractive red berries relieve the stark winter landscape. They are dioecious, so it is necessary to interplant male plants if berries are desired. *Skimmia japonica* 'Fructo-alba' is an attractive white-fruited form. *S. reevesiana* has bisexual flowers, producing bright red fruits, but it is rare and hard to find.

Sorbus alnifolia
KOREAN MOUNTAIN ASH
30–40 ft (9–12 m)   Zone 5 ◆

This attractive deciduous tree has simple leaves, unlike most *Sorbus* species, which have compound leaves. All members of the genus produce fruit that is a great favorite with birds. In *S. hupehensis*, the fruit is white or pinkish. *Sorbus* 'Joseph Rock' bears yellow fruit. A grove of various *Sorbus* species on a hillside or knoll makes an attractive feature. The canopy does not cast too dense a shade, and plantings of dwarf rhododendrons or even heather may be made beneath them.

Stachyurus praecox
6–8 ft (1.8–2.4 m)   Zone 6

This rather sprawling deciduous shrub, though quite hardy, is best planted under the protection of a canopy of larger shrubs. The yellow flowers hang in graceful drooping racemes on the reddish leafless branches in February. *S. chinensis* has longer racemes and blooms later.

Stewartia pseudocamellia
JAPANESE STEWARTIA
15–30 ft (4.6–9 m)   Zone 7

A tree of pleasing form, its smooth branches and flaking bark give an interesting pattern on the trunk and its main limbs. As the name suggests, the flowers are like those of *Camellia*, a genus to which it is related. *Stewartia* is one of many interesting genera in the *Camellia* family, Theaceae, that have representatives in Asia and the eastern part of North America. Although the American species of *Stewartia* are very beautiful, they have not been widely cultivated.

Taxodium distichum
BALD CYPRESS
50 ft (15 m)   Zone 4

A hardy and adaptable tree in many parts of North America, though mainly a tree of swamps in the south, it grows well in normally drained soil in the north. Very ornamental planted on little islands in ponds or on the banks of lakes. The tree is late to leaf out in the spring, providing an opportunity to grow a wide variety of American wildflowers beneath its limbs. The cultivar 'Pendens' is sometimes seen in collections; its slightly pendulous branchlets are distinctive. The autumn color of *T. distichum* is a pleasant russet brown.

Taxus baccata 'Dovastoniana'
ENGLISH YEW

8–12 ft (2.4–3.7 m)   Zone 7   ◆

A distinctly beautiful yew, this is a cultivar of wide-spreading form with pendulous branchlets. A golden form of this cultivar, 'Dovastonii Aurea', is also beautiful. All the yews are useful as understory trees in high deciduous woodland, which is their native habitat. *Taxus baccata* 'Repandens' is a dwarf cultivar, excellent as a ground cover. *T. brevifolia*, native to the Northwest, is scarcely different from *T. baccata*. In the Northeast, *T. canadensis* may be grown where the English yew is not hardy. The Japanese yew (*T. cuspidata*) is the hardiest (Zone 6), most adaptable species. *T. cuspidata* 'Aurescens' is a fine, low-spreading cultivar with yellow foliage that will measure 8 ft (2.4 m) wide and 3 ft (0.9 m) high after 15 years.

Thamnocalamus spathaceus
UMBRELLA BAMBOO

6–10 ft (1.8–3 m)   Zone 7

A clumping bamboo with no aggressive tendencies, its slender stems and narrow leaves give an impression of refinement. *Sinarundinaria nitida* is similar, but has purple stems.

Tradescantia virginiana
SPIDERWORT

30 in (75 cm)   Zone 5

This herbaceous perennial was one of the first American plants to be introduced into European cultivation. Species and hybrids under the name of *T. × andersoniana* are plants of interesting form. The predominant flower color is blue, but red, pink and white forms also exist. A moist but sunny location is best.

Trillium grandiflorum
WAKE-ROBIN

10–20 in (25–50 cm)   Zone 4   ✿

The trilliums are perfectly adapted to woodland conditions; their broad, flat leaves reach maximum size before the canopy trees are fully leafed out. The western North American species, *T. ovatum*, is similar. Most of the species have white flowers, often tinted pink as the petals age. *Trillium erectum* and *T. chloropetalum* have red flowers, although the flowers of the latter species may also be yellowish white. This variable and beautiful western species often has mottled leaves, a characteristic it shares with the evocatively named toad trillium (*T. sessile*) of eastern North America. All the trilliums thrive in well-drained sandy loam or leafy soil, but *T. erectum* is tolerant of wetter conditions.

Trochodendron aralioides
WHEEL TREE

15–30 ft (4.6–9 m)   Zone 7

A surprisingly hardy small evergreen tree in view of its exotic, subtropical appearance, it bears clean, wavy-toothed, apple green leaves along smooth green stems and has attractive pointed buds in winter. A sheltered, semishaded woodland dell is the preferred habitat. Some forms have dull green leaves; others have foliage of a more lively green, but this may be related to the amount of exposure at the planting site. Interesting, if inconspicuous, bright green wheel-like flowers are borne in June.

Vaccinium vitis-idaea
COWBERRY

6–8 in (15–20 cm)   Zone 3

A hardy creeping ground cover for moist, well-drained soil, this plant is distinguished by its shiny evergreen leaves and red berries. The western evergreen huckleberry (*V. ovatum*) is limited to mild coastal areas of the Pacific Northwest.

Veratrum viride
FALSE HELLEBORE

24 in (60 cm)   Zone 6

A bold, impressive plant with large corrugated leaves and interesting panicles of greenish yellow flowers, it prefers wet seepage slopes but will thrive in moist woodland soil. A European species, *V. nigrum*, has striking blackish purple flowers.

Viburnum plicatum
'Grandiflorum'
JAPANESE SNOWBALL

6–10 ft (1.8–3 m)   Zone 6   ◆

If forced to choose one plant from all the lovely species of *Viburnum*, this would be our choice. White globular flowers appear in spring. No fruit is produced, as the flowers are sterile. *Viburnum × bodnantense* would be a close second for its fragrant pink winter flowers, so precious in the woodland. The pink cultivar 'Dawn' is widely grown. Many of the viburnums are fine plants for the woodland if sited where shade is not too dense, but the American species, *V. cassinoides* and *V. nudum*, do tolerate shade. They have interesting leaves and black fruit but are not showy. The laurustinus (*V. tinus*) is one of the most ornamental of the evergreen species. It bears its white clusters of flowers mainly in spring but beginning in midwinter whenever the weather is mild. It is hardy to Zone 7. The leather-leaf viburnum (*V. rhytidophyllum*) is the hardiest of the evergreen species (Zone 6). A large plant, it is useful for providing a background for other shrubs. Most of the viburnums grow quite large and dense. This character, and the abundant fruit usually freely produced, places them in the front rank of shrubs valuable for encouraging birds in the garden.

Epilogue

THE MYTH OF NOAH and the ark has new credence as the world's plant resources are overtaken and destroyed by the rising tide of human population.

Gardens, large and small, public or private, may be the ark of the plant world. Very few gardeners can resist the lure of plant collecting. Instead of collecting hybrid plants, which have but a fleeting, fashionable importance, the acquisition, conservation, propagation and distribution of rare or threatened species makes a real contribution to the preservation of the world's flora.

Horticultural societies and garden clubs can show leadership in this conservation activity that supports the work of botanical gardens and arboreta.

In its mild, sheltered glades, the woodland garden comes close to being the ideal sanctuary for the rare jewels of the plant kingdom.

Acknowledgments

THE AUTHORS WISH to thank Mary Stewart, former president of the VanDusen Botanical Gardens Association (VBGA), for her sound advice, encouragement and support. We also wish to express our appreciation to the McLean Foundation for their substantial financial assistance, and Alix Brown, past president, VBGA, for her contribution.

Rena Pita, landscape artist, provided the pen-and-ink drawings.

Finally, we'd like to recognize the gardeners at VanDusen Botanical Garden, past and present, who helped build some of the woodland landscape that inspired this book.

Bibliography

Beckett, Kenneth A. 1981. *The Complete Book of Evergreens*. London, England: Ward Lock.

Brickell, Christopher, ed. 1981. *The Royal Horticultural Society's Concise Encyclopaedia of Gardening Techniques*. London, England: Mitchell Beazley Publishers.

Brown, Claud L. and Katherine Kirkman. 1990. *Trees of Georgia and Adjacent States*. Portland, OR: Timber Press.

Brown, George E. 1972. *The Pruning of Trees, Shrubs and Conifers*. London, England: Faber and Faber.

Callaway, Dorothy J. 1994. *The World of Magnolias*. Portland, OR: Timber Press.

Cobb, James L.S. 1989. *Meconopsis*. Portland, OR: Timber Press.

Coombes, Allen, ed. 1991. *The Hillier Manual of Trees & Shrubs*. Sixth Edition. Ampfield, England: Hillier Nurseries (Winchester) Limited.

Coombes, Allen. 1992. *Trees*, Eyewitness Handbooks. London, England: Dorling Kindersley.

Cotton, Lin. 1980. *All About Landscaping*. San Francisco, CA: Ortho Books.

Courtwright, Gordon. 1988. *Trees and Shrubs for Temperate Climates*. Portland, OR: Timber Press.

Cox, Peter A. 1990. *The Larger Rhododendron Species*. Portland, OR: Timber Press.

Cox, Peter A. 1985. *The Smaller Rhododendrons*. Portland, OR: Timber Press.

Davies, R.J. 1987. *Trees and Weeds, Weed control for successful tree establishment*. Forestry Commission Handbook 2. London, England: HMSO Books.

Dirr, Michael A. and Charles W. Heuser. 1987. *The Reference Manual of Woody Plant Propagation*. Athens, GA: Varsity Press.

Druse, Kenneth. 1992. *The Natural Shade Garden*. New York, NY: Clarkson Potter.

Foote, Leonard E. and Samuel B. Jones, Jr. 1989. *Native Shrubs and Woody Vines of the Southeast*. Portland, OR: Timber Press.

Galle, Fred C. 1987. *Azaleas*. 2nd ed. Portland, OR: Timber Press.

Grant, J., and C. Grant. 1954. *Garden Design Illustrated*. Seattle, WA: University of Washington Press.

Grant, J., and C. Grant. 1990, *Trees and Shrubs for Pacific Northwest Gardens*. Portland, OR: Timber Press.

Halfacre, Gordon R. and Anne R. Shawcroft. 1989. *Landscape Plants of the Southeast*. 5th ed. Raleigh, NC: Sparks Press.

Harper, P., and F. McGourty. 1985. *Perennials*. Tucson, AZ: HPBooks.

Highshoe, Gary L. 1988. *Native Trees, Shrubs, and Vines for Urban and Rural America*. New York, NY: Van Nostrand Reinhold.

Howard, Frances. 1959. *Landscaping with Vines*. New York, NY: Macmillan.

Huxley, Anthony, ed. 1992. *Royal Horticultural Society Dictionary of Gardening*. London: Mitchell Beazley Publishers.

Jefferson, Michael Brown and Harris Howland. 1995. *The Gardener's Guide to Growing Lilies*. Portland, OR: Timber Press.

Johnson, Hugh. 1973. *The International Book of Trees*. New York, NY: Simon and Schuster.

Jones, David L. 1987. *Encyclopedia of Ferns*. Sydney, Australia: Lothian Publishing Company.

Jones, Samuel B. and Leonard E. Foote. 1991. *Gardening with Native Wildflowers*. Portland, OR: Timber Press.

Kaye, Reginald. 1968. *Hardy Ferns*. London, England: Faber and Faber.

Kelly, John. 1988. *Foliage in Your Garden*. London, England: Penguin Books.

Kruckeberg, Arthur R. 1982. *Gardening with Native Plants of the Pacific Northwest*. Vancouver/Toronto, Canada: Douglas & McIntyre.

Krussmann, Gerd. 1984–86. *Manual of Cultivated Broad-leaved Trees and Shrubs*. 3 vols. 2nd ed. Portland, OR: Timber Press.

Lancaster, Roy. 1974. *Shrubs for your Garden*. Calverton, UK: floraprint.

Lancaster, Roy. 1974. *Trees for your Garden*. Calverton, UK: floraprint.

Lord, Tony, ed. 2002. *Royal Horticultural Society Plant Finder*. London: Mitchell Beazley Publishers.

Mickel, John T. 1994. *Ferns for American Gardens*. New York, NY. Macmillan.

Mitchell, Alan. 1993. *The Gardener's Book of Trees*. London, England: J.M Dent.

Morse, Harriet. 1962. *Gardening in the Shade*. Rev. ed. New York, NY: Charles Scribner's.

Paterson, Allen. 1987. *Plants for Shade and Woodland*. Markham, ON: Fitzhenry & Whiteside.

Perry, Bob. 1989. *Trees and Shrubs for Dry California Climates*. Claremont, CA: Land Design Publishing.

Phillips, R., and M. Rix. 1989. *Shrubs*. New York, NY: Random House.

Phillips, Roger. 1978. *Trees in Britain, Europe and North America*. London, England: Pan Books.

Pojar, J. and A. MacKinnon. 1994. *Plants of Coastal British Columbia*. Vancouver, BC: Lone Pine.

Richards, John. 1993. *Primula*. Portland, OR: Timber Press.

Robinson, William. 1994. *The Wild Garden*. Orig.: 1870. Reprint by Sagapress. Portland, OR: Timber Press.

Sally, Homer E. and Greer, Harold E. 1992. *Rhododendron Hybrids*. Portland, OR: Timber Press.

Smith, L. Ken. 1976. *Garden Construction Know-How*. San Francisco, CA: Ortho Books.

Stevenson, Violet. 1985. *The Wild Garden: making natural gardens using wild and native plants*. New York, NY: Penguin Books.

Sunset Books and Sunset Magazine Eds. 1995. *Sunset Western Garden Book*. Menlo Park, CA: Lane Publishing Co.

Thomas, Graham Stuart. 1990. *Perennial Garden Plants*. Portland, OR: Timber Press.

Vertrees, J.D. 1987. *Japanese Maples*. 2nd ed. Portland, OR: Timber Press.

Walters, James E. and Balbir Backhaus. 1992. *Shade and Color with Water-conserving Plants*. Portland, OR: Timber Press.

Wyman, Donald. 1971. *Wyman's Gardening Encyclopedia*. New York, NY: Macmillan.

Young, James A. and Cheryl G. 1986. *Collecting, Processing and Germinating Seeds of Wildland Plants*. Portland, OR: Timber Press.

Index

Page numbers in **bold** refer to diagrams.

For individual plants, please refer also to plant lists.